D1070610

1215: THE YEAR OF MAGNA CARTA

1215:

THE YEAR OF
MAGNA CARTA

DANNY DANZIGER &
JOHN GILLINGHAM

Hodder & Stoughton

Copyright © 2003 by Danny Danziger and John Gillingham

First published in Great Britain in 2003 by Hodder & Stoughton
A division of Hodder Headline
The right of Danny Danziger and John Gillingham to be identified as
the Authors of the Work has been asserted by them in accordance with
the Copyright, Designs and Patents Act 1988.

A Hodder & Stoughton book

1 3 5 7 9 10 8 6 4 2

A CIP catalogue record for this title is available from the British Library

ISBN 0 340 82474 3

Typeset in Bembo by
Palimpsest Book Production Limited,
Polmont Stirlingshire
Printed and bound in Great Britain by
Mackays of Chatham plc, Chatham, Kent

Hodder and Stoughton
A division of Hodder Headline
338 Euston Road
London NW1 3BH

For Caroline, and Toby, Mary and Guy

For Brenda, Emma, Kate, Simon and Tom

Contents

SCOTLAND

KINGDOM OF MAN
(to Norway)

St Andrews

Glasgow •Edinburgh

NORTH SEA

Newcastle

IRELAND
(English conquest in progress)

R. Shannon

Dublin

York

Limerick

Nottingham

R. Trent

Norwich

Waterford

WELSH STATES
(Vassals of Henry II)

R. Severn

ENGLAND

R. Thames

London

Cardiff •Bristol

Winchester

Dover

Southampton

Exeter

FLANDERS

Bouvines ▲
1214

English Channel

ATLANTIC OCEAN

Dieppe

Rouen

Bayeux •Caen

Andely

Paris

NORMANDY

HOLY
ROMAN
EMPIRE

R. Rhine

FRANCE

MAINE

Le Mans

R. Seine

Rennes

BRITTANY

Angers

Tours

ANJOU

Chinon

TOURAINE

1202

Mirebeau

Poitiers

BERRI

POITOU

R. Loire

Bay of Biscay

La Rochelle

LA MARCHE

•Limoges

SAINTONGE

LIMOUSIN

Angoulême

AUVERGNE

PÉRIGORD

Bordeaux

R. Garonne

AGÉNAIS

R. Rhône

▲ Battle

Eastern limit of English possessions in France, 1180

Lost by the English in France by 1200

Frontiers in 1180

GASCONY

TOULOUSE

Bayonne

•Toulouse

LEÓN

CASTILLE

NAVARRE

BÉARN

ARAGON

MEDITERRANEAN
SEA

0   km   200
0   miles   100

Introduction

The Treasures Gallery of the British Library is an extraordinary place. The hum of the humidifiers drowns out the endless roar of traffic along London's Euston Road; it is calm and quiet in the Gallery. The lights are very low; it takes a little time to adjust your eyes to the gloom, but too bright a light would damage the priceless books and manuscripts that lie in cases and displays around the warren of rooms.

Shakespeare's First Folio and Leonardo da Vinci's notebook, with his extraordinary mirror-image right-to-left handwriting, are open to view, as well as dozens of books of such physical beauty as to rival any painting. There is the Lindisfarne Gospels, written and illuminated by the monk Eadfrith in honour of St Cuthbert around AD 698, in the monastery of Lindisfarne, on Holy Island, just off the coast of Northumbria. That was roughly around the time that Bede was writing his history of the English Church and its people. It is wonderfully illuminated, with incredible, vivid colours. At a time when most other books in Europe tended to use only three, this book has virtually every colour you could imagine: rich ruby reds and intense aquamarines along with deep, majestic purples.

Beowulf is in the gallery too, and the Barcelona Hagadah, named after the heraldic shield it bears, an exquisite Hebrew service book from 1350, still read each year in Jewish homes at the Seder meal on the eve of Passover. The Sherborne Missal, the Roman Catholic book of prayers made for Sherborne Abbey in Dorset between 1400 and 1407, is there. It is a masterpiece of book painting, a massive volume of seven hundred pages, with lavishly decorated margins peopled by kings, nobles, bishops, monks, saints and angels in a celestial throng and, most unexpected of all, a choir of the native birds of the British Isles. It is possibly the only service book of stature to have survived the Reformation intact. Continuing around the Treasures Gallery, there are manuscript scores by Mozart, Handel, Chopin and Beethoven, handwritten lyrics of two of the Beatles' most famous songs, 'Ticket to Ride' and 'I Want To Hold Your Hand', and there's a Gutenberg Bible. In the mid-fifteenth century, Johannes Gutenberg invented a way of mechanising the production of type, and the Bible he printed in Mainz, around 1485, was the first major book printed in the West. About 180 copies were made, and significant parts of forty-eight copies still survive. The British Library has two complete copies, and the cover of the one on display is richly illuminated in gold; it is a thing of beauty.

But what we have come to see, laid out under a bullet-proof glass casing, isn't illuminated: it has no drawings or illustrations in the margins, and, to be perfectly frank, is a dull, rather ugly-looking thing. There is, however, a bigger crowd here than at any other exhibit. There are Japanese tour-leaders waving umbrellas, and Americans who breathe reverentially over the glass. Even French schoolchildren are a little less boisterous in front of it. Everyone here, from these nations and many others, has come to see it before they see anything else, and believes it to be an important document.

What we are looking at is a single sheet of parchment. Originally, it would have had a green and black wax seal, attached to a vellum strip at the bottom of the Charter, that would have shown the King, King John, enthroned, and holding his sceptre. But it is rare for the document and the seal to have survived together for such a long time. It is quite densely arranged, lots of long lines in a cursive but quite showy hand, not written in the characteristic Gothic script you see in music and liturgical manuscripts.

The parchment is slightly oblong, almost square. When it was written, in 1215, they were using a gall-based ink. If you look at an oak tree, you will see little pimples, called galls, growing from the bark. They develop when a wasp stings the tree to lay its eggs: the tree prevents the poison spreading by forming a little nut around it. If you tap into that nut, you get a clear liquid, an acid almost; when this is used as an ink on parchment or vellum, it etches itself into the membrane. And when you add something like soot, or most effectively, iron salts, the ink turns a rich dark colour, although over time it will fade to a mid-brown. The ink here has retained its blackness pretty well – those scribes were professionals and knew how to mix their materials. Their pens were quills: they would have taken the flight feather of a goose, possibly a swan, and cut it into shape. If you were right-handed, you took a left wing feather, because the feather curves the other way, and you compensated according to the direction in which you wrote. Every ten lines or so, possibly less, depending on how long the lines were, you'd dip your quill into the ink and re-trim the nib with a penknife – which is where the word comes from.

This document, which we know as Magna Carta, was

at first known as the Charter of Liberties. A few years later it became known as Magna Carta, the 'big charter', to distinguish it from another important, but much shorter, contemporary piece of legislation, the Forest Charter.

We don't know for sure how many copies of the 'big charter' were made in 1215, but only four exist now. One is in Lincoln Cathedral; another is at Salisbury Cathedral. The remaining two are in the British Library, and it is a miracle they both exist, because one of them was badly damaged by a fire. Before the government set up a British Museum and Library, the charter was kept in an outhouse store, roughly on the site where Westminster School is now, close to Westminster Abbey. One night, late in the year of 1731, a fire broke out, and despite the best attempts of the librarian and his father-in-law to save what they could, certain documents, including a copy of Magna Carta, and the Beowulf manuscript, were badly damaged, and has gradually deteriorated over the years.

The other copy of Magna Carta, the one under the bullet-proof glass, lies there intact, nearly eight hundred years old. It is just as famous as any document you can name in any museum or parliament. It holds its own against the American Declaration of Independence, indeed, the authors of that document professed to have read Magna Carta before they put pen to paper. There are sixty-three clauses in Magna Carta, but there are two that reverberate down the centuries, and have come to represent today a ringing expression of freedom for mankind the world over.

Nullus liber homo capiatur, vel imprisonetur, aut disseisiatur, aut utlagetur, aut exuletur, aut aliquo modo destruatur, nec super eum ibimus, nec super eum mittemus, nisi per legal judicium parium suorum vel per legem terre.

Nulli vendemus, nulli negabimus aut differemus rectum aut justiciam.

To translate from the original Latin into English:

No free man shall be taken or imprisoned or deprived or outlawed or exiled or in any way ruined, nor will we go or send against him, except by the lawful judgement of his peers or by the law of the land.

To no one will we sell, to no one will we deny or delay right or justice.

The eloquence of those sentences, the nobility and idealism they express, has elevated this piece of legislation to eternal iconic status. In America, Magna Carta is revered as the foundation stone of modern freedom. It is an important document in Britain too. It has always been regarded as a romantic and formative piece of legislation; the image of the barons curbing the power of an overreaching monarch appeals to the British sense of fair play. Rudyard Kipling was moved to verse:

And still when Mob or Monarch lays
Too rude a hand on English ways,
The whisper wakes, the shudder plays,
Across the reeds at Runnymede.
And Thames that knows the moods of kings,
And crowds and priests and suchlike things,
Rolls deep and dreadful as he brings
Their warning down from Runnymede.

What drew us to write about this particular moment in time was both the familiarity of Magna Carta, and the people around at this time. King John, that charismatic villain, as he is always depicted, his brother, Richard Coeur de Lion – and we should call him that rather than Lionheart because, like all the Plantagenets, he was essentially French. John and Richard's parents were Henry II and Eleanor of Aquitaine – depicted in the film *Lion in Winter* by Peter O'Toole and Katharine Hepburn. 'Who will rid me of this turbulent priest?' Henry exclaimed in a moment of anger, referring to his friend Thomas Becket, archbishop of Canterbury, and the initiative of four knights at court who overheard this and subsequently killed Becket in front of his altar at Canterbury is one of the most poignant stories in British history.

At this time, the Crusades were in full swing, and Jerusalem had been captured by the Muslim leader, Saladin. In fact, the decades on either side of 1200 marked the climax of the conflict, and the bloody struggle for control of Jerusalem, a city that three faiths, Jewish, Christian and Muslim, regarded as sacred. In that city we can see a direct and continuing link with today. Eight hundred years ago, it was our western society which considered it was waging a holy war; from the time of the First Crusade, Jerusalem has had the power to draw men on – as it still does – to fight, kill and die.

In Europe, St Francis of Assisi founded the mendicant order of monks, the Franciscans, and St Dominic founded the Order of Dominican Preachers. By the end of the century, 150 friaries had been established in England alone.

The pope in 1215, Innocent III, was one of the ablest

popes in the Church's history. In 1215 he presided over a great assembly of clergy, the Fourth Lateran Council whose decrees not only gave lasting shape to the teaching and structure of the Catholic Church but also affected the way justice was carried out throughout western Europe.

England was a staunchly Catholic country, but Pope Innocent and King John of England often quarrelled. Innocent placed England under an Interdict, which effectively banned church services throughout the country and, for good measure, excommunicated John, the first English sovereign to suffer such a fate. (Henry VIII and Elizabeth I were to be next.)

Beyond Europe, 1215 saw the fall of Peking to the armies of Genghis Khan, who broke through the Great Wall of China. After that, the Mongols moved on to sack Samarkhand and advance into Persia and Russia. Soon they would terrify Europe – they were the thirteenth-century equivalent of the Vikings – but twice as ruthless.

There remained parts of the world which the thirteenth-century expansion of Europe did not reach, cultures and peoples in Australia and Polynesia of whom even the best educated European knew nothing. Above all, despite the Viking voyages to the north-east coast of America, they knew nothing of the advanced culture of the Maya in Central America, nor of the great mounds being built in the Mississippi region, and the awesome apartment houses in what is now New Mexico. Meanwhile, in England, some 150 new towns sprung up, places like Chelmsford, Leeds, Liverpool and Portsmouth. By 1300, nearly a hundred thousand people lived in London alone; the whole country had a population of around four million.

The beginning of the next millenium saw life lived at

a subsistence level. Two hundred years later, life was more comfortable: important technological advances had been made. Improvements in spinning, weaving and dyeing made cloth manufacture more efficient. Bright colours were available for the first time. The spinning wheel had been invented. Horses were harnessed to create more traction power. Windmills were first erected at this time; clocks appeared, spectacles too. Indeed, it has been argued that spectacles were vital for scientific and scholarly advance, enabling the middle-aged and elderly to continue book and other close work for decades longer than any of their ancestors. The new inventiveness was clearly visible in the technology of war: siege artillery, in the form of trebuchets that hurled huge missiles with great accuracy over long distances, were in their day as deadly as Exocets. New armour and helmets allowed the rich to hammer away at each other in colourful tournaments, which took place across the land.

There was a more effective transport system, better designed and faster carts – and cart parks for parking at crowded market places. Smoother roads were built, and hundreds of old, wooden bridges were replaced with stone ones. New ports, such as Boston and Lynn, later King's Lynn, and Newcastle, were founded, quays were built and cranes constructed to load and unload goods, and a new design was developed for a bulk-carrying cargo ship called the cog, which allowed merchants to transport more goods. Trade with Europe and the rest of the world meant that exotic new foods and clothes became available. Although the technological advances helped men to become more productive, no one found ways of making improvements to the yield of crops until the eighteenth century.

As the population of England continued to grow, the rich grew richer, and life for the poor became harder. Poverty, famine and disease stalked the land. Medical and nutritional knowledge was minimal, and people from all classes suffered terrible physical ailments. Large intestinal worms burrowed into nearly every orifice, although skeletal evidence shows that at least their teeth were sound: sugar and chocolate were not yet part of the English diet.

It was at this period also that the first English university, in Oxford, came into being, at which the greatest scientist of the age, Robert Grosseteste, lectured. Cambridge was established in the 1220s. Elsewhere, vast Romanesque and Gothic buildings were constructed, some of which are still standing – the magnificent Keep at Rochester Castle, Orford Castle in Suffolk, the Tower of London and many great Cathedrals, such as Salisbury, Durham and Lincoln. Architects and builders had a greater understanding of physics, which allowed them to build with a mastery of space and light, the triumph of a revolution in engineering that flooded once gloomy interiors with brightness. Stained glass enhanced their beauty.

The England and Europe of 1215 are much more visible to us today than those of the year 1000. For one thing, relatively few buildings that were standing in 1000 can still be seen. Above ground not even ruins survive. Most churches built before 1000 were wooden, and now in England only one pre-Conquest wooden church is still in use, at Greensted in Essex. During the eleventh and twelfth centuries, masonry became the fashionable building material for major churches, and even for thousands of local churches. The same development in building technology has resulted in many castles, either much altered or ruined, surviving from the same period. We can easily see, visit, explore and touch many thousands of buildings that were standing in 1215, but hardly any from 1000.

We can also read their thoughts. In the England of 1215 writers felt at home in both French and English, and those who were highly educated could express themselves in Latin too. People today often imagine that hardly anyone except monks wrote anything down in the Middle Ages, but that was not the case. Indeed, so much was being written by all sorts of people, women as well as men, that for the first time since the fall of the Roman Empire, we have a real idea of daily life and thought. Fiction becomes important, whether verse or prose, written in French and English. The new vernacular literatures of the twelfth and thirteenth centuries, the Arthurian romances, the stories of Tristan and Isolde, the bawdy tales known as the *fabliaux,* survive in far greater quantities than earlier works. And for all the importance of a poem like *Beowulf,* the only activities on which it sheds much light are feasting and fighting. The new stories represent a revolutionary breakthrough – at any rate from the point of view of the historian trying to understand how men and women felt in the past: it is the literature of the cultural movement often called the twelfth-century Renaissance, the cultural background of the men and women who made history in 1215.

A new genre of lifestyle and etiquette literature sprang up, of which the greatest was *The Book of the Civilised Man*, written by Daniel of Beccles. He instructs the aspiring gentleman on how to behave in an enormous variety of social situations: in church, as a page in a noble household, at the dinner table, as a guest, in the street (don't eat in the street and don't peer into other people's windows), in a

brothel – and many more. He tells you when, where and
how you can urinate, defecate, spit, belch and fart politely.
He offers advice on how to live a long, healthy and happy
life, what to eat and drink, with some recipes thrown in,
discusses exercise, when to take baths, how often to have
sex. Moderation in all things is the guiding principle, season-
ally adjusted: in summer, for example, you should cut back
on hot baths and sex. Cheerful songs will keep you in a
good mood. Cultivate entertaining conversation, avoid
quarrels, and get yourself some new clothes now and again.

In 2003, we wait to see what will unfold in the next
century on the assumption that, whatever the disasters, life
will go on. Many who lived in the year 1000 wondered if
human experience had run its course. The Christian dating
system, the *Anno Domini*, had been devised to mark the
gap between Christ's first appearance on earth and his
second coming: it was not unreasonable to fear – and for
many to hope – that the end of the world was nigh.

By 1215, the average man and woman searched for God
in their great cathedrals, which had taken thousands of
workers decades to finish, and they asked for relief from
their ills. They also gave thanks for their blessings, and they
knew that their world would go on. Nearly eight hundred
years later, we must acknowledge that, by their hard work,
bravery and application, they assured our future, here, now
in the twenty-first century.

On the day we finished this book, we drove out to
Runnymede to get a feel of the place where King John had
met the barons and had been forced to put his seal to the

Magna Carta. It was a cold, dank December day, and although it was only a little after three in the afternoon, the light was beginning to fade. The fields were wet and muddy.

There are two memorials at Runnymede – chosen as a site because of its connection with freedom, justice and human liberty.

The John F. Kennedy Memorial is Britain's tribute to the thirty-sixth president of the United States of America, John Fitzgerald Kennedy, who was assassinated on the 22 November 1963. Following his tragic death, it was decided by the House of Commons that a memorial should be erected in his memory. Under the John F. Kennedy Memorial Act, one acre of land at Runnymede, forming part of the Crown Estate, was transferred to the people of the United States by way of a gift from the Queen and her government.

The memorial is entered from the wet fields of Runnymede through a gate. Once the visitor passes through this gate, he or she sets foot on American soil. The gate gives access to a pathway of fifty individually carved gran-ite steps, each representing an individual state. The me-morial itself is carved in Portland stone. The hawthorn beside the stone is a symbol of Catholicism, reflecting President Kennedy's religion, but equally symbolic is the American scarlet oak which stands guardian behind the stone, and flowers into a vivid red in November, the time of the anniversary of President Kennedy's death. The inscription is from the president's inaugural address of 28 January, 1961. 'Let every nation know, whether it wishes us well or ill, that we shall pay any price, bear any burden, meet any hardship, support any friend, or oppose any foe in order to assure the survival and success of liberty.'

The second memorial is a rotunda, built by the American Bar Association, as 'a tribute to Magna Carta, symbol of freedom under law'. In 1971, the American Bar Association came here again and pledged their adherence to the principles of the Great Charter – and again, in July 1985, returning once more in July 2000 'to celebrate Magna Carta, foundation of the rule of law for ages past and for the new millennium . . .'

It is very moving that a nation, which wasn't founded until nearly six centuries after Magna Carta was first discussed here, should invest such belief in and commitment to this ancient document.

A heavy rain was falling on the muddy, churned fields of Runnymede as we made our way back to the car, both pleased and saddened to have finished a book which was an enormous pleasure to write.

Danny Danziger   John Gillingham

For all mistakes the authors blame each other.

CHAPTER I

The Englishman's Castle

Neither we nor our bailiffs shall take other men's timber for castles or other work of ours, without the agreement of the owner.

Magna Carta, Clause 31

This was a time when a labourer was paid a penny a day, and when an income of ten pounds a year was enough for a country gentleman to maintain a comfortable lifestyle. A wealthy magnate, possessing twenty or thirty manors, had an annual income of several hundred pounds and lived luxuriously in his castles and country houses. It is hard for us to visualise this today. Surviving castle walls tend to make us think of cold, dark, draughty, damp and thoroughly uncomfortable rooms. And so they were by twenty-first century standards. But by the standards of the time, when they compared the way they lived with the way in which their parents and grandparents had lived, the rich families of King John's England felt they were enjoying all mod cons.

When we see ancient, crumbling stone walls, we think of dungeons and sieges. Instead, we should think of chimneys and fireplaces. Until the twelfth century most castles and great houses were built of timber, and usually one storey high. Heat was provided by open fires or braziers in the centre of the floor, the smoke being drawn out through a louvre in the roof. In stone buildings fireplaces and chimneys were encased in the thickness of the walls and one room could be piled on top of another to make a tower. While early fireplaces usually had short flues, by the later twelfth century it was known that an extended flue produced a stronger draught.

Stone walls were not just fireproof and handy for keeping enemies out, they could also be used for plumbing in running water. The lead pipes in the Great Tower, King Henry II's keep, at Dover Castle drew water from a well sunk more than 240 feet into the chalk. Thick walls could contain corridors and private rooms – above all, latrines, usually approached round a sharp bend so that the person using it could have some privacy. You no longer had to go outside to use a lavatory.

In 1215 new fashions were beginning to change the way the houses of the aristocracy were designed. For many centuries before this, the residences of the aristocracy had nearly always consisted of a number of buildings within an enclosure. The principal buildings were a hall, for receiving visitors and dining, a chamber block, where the lord's family had their private space, which it was rude to enter uninvited, a kitchen and at least one privy. These separate units were often linked by covered ways. There would be other buildings too: extra accommodation for visitors or senior servants, stables, a brewhouse, and workshops for jobs such as carding and spinning wool, or retting flax. Poultry and other animals ran freely in the yard.

The hall was at ground level. In his manual of good manners, *The Book of the Civilised Man*, Daniel of Beccles advised keeping pigs and cats out of the hall, but allowed in a 'gentleman's animals': dogs, hawks and even horses. Only those whom the master had expressly allowed to do so could enter the hall on horseback. King Henry II liked to ride into his chancellor Thomas Becket's hall, jump over the table and join the dinner party. The hall was a public space and some behaviour was frowned upon, as Daniel of Beccles makes clear: don't scratch yourself or look for fleas in your breeches or on your chest; don't snap your fingers; don't comb your hair, clean your nails, or take your shoes off there in the presence of lords and ladies. Messengers should take off gloves, arms and cap before they entered – though bald messengers were permitted to keep their caps on. Urinating in the hall was particularly bad manners – unless you were the head of the household; then it was permissible.

By contrast with the hall, the chamber block often had two storeys, a semi-basement cellar with chamber above – the word 'chamber' could mean either a room or a suite. When stone replaced wood, kitchens especially and chamber-blocks were built or re-built in this more durable and less flammable material. Chairs were rare. Often a bed was the only piece of furniture in a room. During the day people sat on beds made up for the purpose – 'day-beds'. A chair was reserved for a person of status – hence the modern term 'chairman' or, nowadays, 'chair'.

The walls of the grandest rooms in important houses were often painted. Henry II commissioned a mural of an eagle and its four chicks for his Painted Chamber in Westminster Palace. In that room the bed was lavishly decorated, a 'state-bed' on which the king received important visitors. Other walls were decorated with embroideries or tapestries. When a household moved from one residence to another, the best of these wall-hangings were packed and taken along, either in carts or on sumpter-horses, as also were costly soft furnishings such as the coverlets with which day-beds were spread.

The king led the way in setting new fashions. Take, for example, the great tower at Orford, a royal castle built on the Suffolk coast in the 1160s. It was architect-designed, based on a precisely calculated geometrical pattern, a 49-foot-diameter circle with three projecting towers. It contained two fine public rooms, one above the other, both circular, each lit by three double windows, the upper room embellished with a dome-effect ceiling. Similarly the great tower at Conisborough in Yorkshire, built for King John's uncle Hamelin, contained two spacious circular rooms one above the other. At Orford, with a kitchen on each of the two main floors and a bakery, it was possible to provide the five private chambers with what was, in effect, night storage heating. One of these chambers had a well-ventilated privy en suite. In addition a cistern provided running water and three separate privies, although if two people were using a double one, it was not polite, Daniel of Beccles explains, for one to stand up before the other. At Orford the doorways were reminiscent of the pedimented entrances of classical antiquity.

These magnificent stone towers were phenomenally expensive when compared with timber buildings. The timber hunting lodge built for Richard I at Kinver in Staffordshire in the 1190s cost £24 18s 9d. For this the king got a hall with a buttery and pantry, a chamber block, a kitchen and a gaol, all enclosed by a 16-foot-high palisade with a fortified gatehouse, plus a newly made fishpond outside the enclosure. By contrast, the luxurious tower at Orford cost nearly £1,000 and Henry II's great tower of Newcastle-upon-Tyne cost £912. At this date few nobles could afford to build even one such prestigious 'power house'.

Another design feature that became increasingly common during King John's lifetime was the window-seat, which allowed the proud owner of a fashionable new house to make better use of the light and enjoy the view. Increasingly the rich had their windows glazed. In 1237, for example, Peter the Painter was paid 5s 6d for making a glass window in Marlborough Castle. At this time, what is now the tiny village of Chiddingfold in the Sussex Weald was the centre of the English glass-making industry. Those who could afford them chose floor tiles in place of beaten earth or stone floors – and fine tiles were meant to be admired, not covered with rushes or rush matting. In *The Romance of Horn* the poet describes a princess's chamber 'paved with intricately worked marble and blue limestone'. Tiled floors were easier to keep clean too. Comfort and fashion were of primary importance rather than defence. When the rebellion against John broke out in 1215 it was more than forty years since the peace of the English countryside had been seriously disturbed. In the borderlands people were vulnerable to Scottish and Welsh raids; elsewhere they preferred to spend their money on luxury and pleasure rather than on preparation for war.

Hundreds of churches from King John's time still survive today, but only a handful of town and country houses.

Buildings in which people prayed have been used for many centuries without the need for fundamental redesign, but the same cannot be said of domestic accommodation. Changing ideas of comfort and fashion have meant that homes have been torn down and reconstructed time and time again. For this reason books about medieval architecture are almost entirely devoted to churches. We know very much less about domestic buildings – although, thanks partly to the spadework of archaeologists, we are no longer quite as much in the dark as we used to be. We can see now that in this period the basic design of the aristocratic residence was changing. Once separate buildings were being brought together to form a single whole. Service rooms, later known as the buttery and the pantry, were added at one end of the hall, often with cellar space below. The early thirteenth-century fashion for attaching the other end of the hall to the principal chamber block led to the establishment of what is thought of as the classic 'English medieval house', a three-part house, all under one roof, with great chamber and parlour at the 'upper' end of the hall. At the 'lower' end there were service doors from the buttery and the pantry, often shielded by screens from the eyes of upper-class diners at the 'top table'. A passage designed to give direct access into the hall from the kitchen – which, for safety reasons, still remained separate – ran between buttery and pantry. For the next three centuries anyone who had any social pretensions lived in this new type of house.

The palace at Woodstock in Oxfordshire was a royal residence on which a great deal was spent from Henry I's time onwards. Nothing remains of it today, and even the landscape in which it stood was drastically altered when

Blenheim Park was laid out in the eighteenth century. In King John's time a spring fed three pools around which gardens and a group of buildings clustered. Henry II kept the most favoured of his mistresses, Rosamund Clifford, 'Fair Rosamund', in this rural retreat. It included the 'king's high chamber by the pool', the queen's chamber, Rosamund's chamber, the kitchen, a wine cellar, and a chapel. Great houses such as Woodstock were set in ornamental landscapes, often with artificial lakes created by dams, which were appreciated for their beauty as well as for their stock of delicacies such as pike, bream and lamprey – a freshwater eel (Henry I is supposed to have died of a surfeit of lampreys). There was also the pleasure of fishing with rod and line. The Paris-educated Anglo-Welsh intellectual, Gerald de Barri – often known as Gerald of Wales – claimed that his family home, Manorbier Castle, on the Pembrokeshire coast, was the most beautiful place in Wales. He picked out the magnificent pool below the castle walls as one of its finest features, together with its orchard and grove of hazel trees. Gerald described the Bishop of Lincoln's palace at Stow as being 'pleasingly surrounded by woods and pools'; it was here that the most saintly bishop of the day, Hugh of Lincoln, liked to feed his pet swan. Deer parks, orchards, vineyards, enclosed gardens and viewing pavilions, known as gloriettes, were all part of the aesthetic of the country house.

Those who lived in such houses had plenty to keep them busy and entertained. For the staff, nearly all of whom were male and lived in, the day was long, and especially so for the chief officer of the household, the steward or marshal: he was often the first to rise and the last to retire. In summer the porters opened the gates at five in the morning and closed them at about ten in the evening. In winter they opened two hours later and closed an hour earlier. The kitchen staff were next on parade. Lunch (*prandium*), the main meal of the day, was taken at what we would now think of as mid-morning, so even if breakfast consisted only of bread, cheese and ale – and some households did without – the staff was kept busy. Not only was there the food to be prepared, there was also the hall to be cleaned, wall-hangings shaken or beaten, tables (boards on trestles), stools and benches had to be put in place or stacked away. Servants who lived outside the household arrived, often women who worked as laundresses or dairymaids.

When the lord and lady got up, servants and maids helped them wash and dress. They used a soft soap made by boiling mutton fat in wood ash and caustic soda, and a twig, probably springy hazel, to clean their teeth. Men's and women's dress was similar. Both wore stockings (*chauces*) made of wool or silk, then a shirt (*chemise*) with long sleeves, which were often detachable and worn so fashionably tight that they had to be stitched on each time the shirt was worn. Detachable sleeves were a favourite gift, especially as a love-token. A tunic or gown (*bliaut*) went over the shirt, secured with a brooch; above a full skirt a lady's gown had a tight-fitting bodice, while both *chemise* and *bliaut* might be slashed and laced above the waist to reveal her bare skin. Then came a coat, or surcoat, and in cold weather a fur-lined *pellice*, often sleeveless, might be worn on top. Out of doors on a cold day a mantle was thrown over everything, fastened at the shoulder with another brooch. The poor wore shorter garments; for the rich the sheer length of their clothes was a way of displaying wealth – although the young Henry II became known as Curtmantle when he reversed the usual trend and set a fashion for short cloaks. Since clothes were made without pockets, coins and valuables were commonly carried in a purse attached to the belt, though they could be tied into a skirt or shirt sleeves. A cap could be worn either in or out of doors. They wore thin-soled leather shoes. It was said that the shoes of an elegantly dressed gentleman would fit so well that no one could see how he had got into them or imagine how he would ever get out of them again.

The one important difference between men's and women's clothes was that men wore underpants (*braies*), while women often went naked under the chemise. When King Henry I's illegitimate daughter Juliana was forced to jump into a castle moat in February, the chronicler who described her misfortune thought in particular of the numbing effect of the freezing water on her bare buttocks. A woman's hair was usually arranged in two plaits, the longer the better. Ivory or bone combs, but more commonly boxwood, survive from this period, as do small compact mirrors with concave glass for a fuller image. The fashionable look was for white skin and rosy cheeks, and make-up was available for those who needed help with this.

After morning prayers the senior members of the household either breakfasted or got straight down to the day's business. The management of a manor of two – or in the case of the great nobles, dozens of manors – with their farms, tenants, gardens, fishponds, barns and buildings generated a great deal of thought, supervision and decision-making for the head of household. Not that every morning was devoted to business. There were plenty of festivals and holy days – and holidays were not for working. None the

less, on most days there was much to be done. Only stupid
lords – of whom, naturally, there were always some – left
top management entirely in the hands of their senior staff.
The estate had to generate a profit, money had to be spent,
investments made if you and your children were to continue
to enjoy an aristocratic lifestyle. Daniel of Beccles quoted
the Roman poet Ovid, 'It's low class to count your flocks',
only to disagree with him. Daniel's advice was: 'Keep a
sharp eye on your property. Aim to improve the yields of
fields and livestock. This way you can afford to be generous.' Sometimes the head of the household was a woman,
a widow or a wife looking after things in the absence of
her husband. Ambitious men were often away from home,
consulting their lawyers in London or following the royal
court. Other husbands were so keen on hunting that even
when they were in residence the lady of the house was
the real manager of the estate.

Whether it was a feast day or not, meals in an aristocratic household were very formal occasions. Even the
washing of hands before and after every meal was cere-
monious. A pitcher of water, or a pottery *aqua manile* in
the shape of a horse or a ram, designed so that the water
came out of the animal's mouth, would be brought round;
one servant poured the water while another held a bowl
under the diner's hands. In a well-run household the
approved arrangement was for a high table and two side
tables to be set out, and covered with cloth, usually linen.
Spoons, salt-cellars (which might be silver-gilt and very
ornamental indeed) and bread would be laid out, and knives
too – though many people brought their own knife. (At
this date pepper was much too expensive to be left on the
table.) The pantler (from the French word *pain*) with the

bread and the butler (from *bouteille*) with a fine drinking cup – perhaps a mazer, a cup made of maplewood, mounted in precious metals – stood side by side in front of the lords while grace was said. The marshal or steward supervised the serving of food and drink, and kept order in the hall – young servants were notoriously rowdy. According to Daniel's book, the servers should be well groomed and neatly dressed, their hands and nails clean, their hair properly combed. They should make sure there were no long hairs growing out of their noses, and that their shoes didn't squeak. Those serving drink should never fill cups more than two-thirds full. Whereas those serving food had to go to the kitchen to collect each course, the drinks waiters would bring wine or ale from another table, the 'cupboard', in the hall, on which precious plates and goblets might also be displayed. When Thomas Becket was chancellor he was famous for the luxurious state he kept. According to Herbert of Bosham, his friend and biographer: 'His table was resplendent with gold and silver plate, and abounded in dainty dishes and expensive wines. Whatever food or drink was a celebrated rarity, no price was so high that it deterred his agents from buying it.'

Wine was not stored in bottles but kept in wooden casks and drunk young. Henry II's dominions included some of the finest wine-growing areas in Europe: the Bordeaux region, the hinterland of La Rochelle in Poitou, and Anjou and Touraine from where the best wines, the *vins pour la mer*, were taken down the Loire valley to be exported from Nantes. According to one twelfth-century author, English wine could be drunk only with eyes closed and teeth clenched. When John came to the throne he fixed the prices at which the wines of Poitou and Anjou were to be sold. In an effort to boost his popularity, he set them low with, in the view of disapproving contemporaries, the inevitable consequence that 'the whole land was filled with drink and drinkers'. The king's wine was transported in tuns, casks containing 252 gallons, and stored in castles and other houses such as Marlborough and Clarendon until the king called for them. Archaeologists have uncovered the great wine cellar known as 'La Roche' built for Henry II at Clarendon. An audit of John's wine revealed that in 1201 he had over 700 tuns of wine (180,000 gallons) at his disposal. Perhaps he went for quantity rather than quality. In 1201 he visited the king of France at Fontainebleau and was given the run of the palace and its wine cellar. 'After he had gone,' a Frenchman wrote, 'the king of France and his people all had a good laugh at the way the people of the English king had drunk all the bad wines and left all the good ones.' Or was King John just being polite?

In the largest households there might have to be two sittings for lunch. Since ceremony and hierarchy required that the head of household would be the first served and the last to leave the table, lunch might take a long time, two or three hours. It is not surprising that some lords and ladies preferred to eat in the relative privacy of their own chambers – though this was frowned upon by traditionalists who thought it was a lord's duty to maintain his own dignity, and that of his household, by dining publicly.

Tableware – plates, bowls, cups, saucers, and platters for trenchers (the slices of thick bread on which food was served and which could be eaten after the juices had been absorbed) – was generally made of wood, earthenware or pewter, though inevitably the richest households liked to display their silver. At lunch two main courses were served, and two light courses, each course including a great variety of dishes. A week's shopping list made for King John's niece Eleanor of Brittany gives a good idea of aristocratic diet.

Saturday: bread, ale, sole, almonds, butter, eggs.
Sunday: mutton, pork, chicken and eggs
Monday: beef, pork, honey, vinegar.
Tuesday: pork, eggs, egret
Wednesday: herring, conger, sole, eels, almonds and eggs
Thursday: pork, eggs, pepper, honey
Friday: conger, sole, eels, herring and almonds

For those who took their religious observances to heart, Fridays, Saturdays and many Wednesdays were fish-days. There were also, in addition to Lent, a number of fast-days when little but bread and ale were consumed. By these standards the poor virtually fasted every day. They ate eggs, cheese, bread, vegetables and legumes; they drank ale – unprocessed water posed a known health risk. Ironically this meant that they suffered less from tooth decay than the rich who could afford sweeteners. However, bread baked from stone-ground flour often contained grit, so teeth tended to get worn down.

Food was served in units, known as messes, which were shared between two, three or four people. You used your thumb and index finger to take a portion of food, a piece of meat, for example, from the dish and place it on your trencher. (Table forks came gradually into fashion from the fourteenth century onwards.) You cut your portion into small pieces to be chewed politely, then wiped your knife on the bread. Sharing messes put a premium on good table

manners, and Daniel of Beccles has much to say on that
subject: don't lick your fingers; don't put them into the
dish at the same time as a companion; above all, don't grab
the best bits. It was not done to use your fingers or a piece
of bread to get the last morsel out of the dish. Sharing a
soup bowl was an especially delicate operation, and there
were lots of don'ts here. Don't fill your spoon too full;
don't share it; don't leave it in the soup plate; don't soak
bits of bread in it. If the soup is too hot don't blow on it,
although you can stir it with a crust or a spoon or put
croutons into it. There were lots of other rules, many familiar today. Don't get food on the table-cloth, or over your
lips. Don't pick your teeth. Wipe your hands discreetly with
a napkin. Don't stare, don't point at people, or make big
gestures with your arms. Don't play with your knife and
spoon. Don't grumble about what you're given. Sit up
straight. Don't put your elbows on the table. Don't talk
with your mouth full. Don't pick your nose at table. Other
rules remind us that notions of politeness change with time
and place. If you feel the need to spit, then turn round and
spit behind you so that you don't offend others at your
table. If you belch, look up at the ceiling.

After lunch was over, and you had washed your hands,
and the left-over food had been distributed as alms for the
poor, there was free time. You might retire to your chamber for a nap, or take part in a throwing-the-javelin or
heaving-the-stone contest in the courtyard. Then you might
expect to receive visitors for drinks. This was a crucial
moment in the fabric of neighbourliness and networking.
By now those who had gone hunting should have returned.
Daniel of Beccles had plenty to say about visits, on how,
for example, to accept or refuse invitations. Accepting all

invitations shows, he insisted, a lamentable lack of discrimination.

After drinks it was time to attend evensong before going
into the hall for supper at what we might call tea-time, four
o'clock or thereabouts, perhaps again in two shifts. In winter
the hall would be lit, chiefly by tallow candles. These would
most probably have been made on the premises, from the
by-product of animals slaughtered for the larder. In the early
fourteenth century the Bishop of Bath's household used six
pounds of tallow candles a day in winter. Supper was always
a lighter meal than lunch, perhaps just one main course, a
dessert and cheese. But by the time it was over, the lord and
his lady might have spent as much as five or six hours eating
and drinking. After supper, the lord's clerks were expected
to go through the accounts for the day, but for everyone
else it was time for recreation: backgammon, usually called
'tables', music, story-telling, dancing and flirting.

Anyone wanting to listen today to music sounding something like that played in King John's time would have to
go to Turkey or to parts of the Balkans where Ottoman
influence used to be strong, and where strident reed pipes
can still be heard. Or listen to the unforgettably colossal
noise made by the bagpipes of Sardinia. In the West, industrial manufacture and nineteenth-century standardisation
has brought about the demise of the old sound world.
Although there were many kinds of bowed instruments in
those days, none of them was held under the chin like a
modern violin. Rather they were held – much as many
folk instruments of the fiddle type still are – further down
the body, or sometimes played on the lap with an under-
hand bow made from a hank of horsehair. A musical instrument coming into fashion at this time was the lute; its

name is derived from an Arabic word meaning 'the wooden thing'. Then there was the zither-like psaltery, the harpsi-chord, and a rich variety of harps; instruments such as the organ, confined to major churches, and those more suit-able for outdoors or ceremonial occasions such as drums and trumpets. On feast days the sound of a trumpet might well have summoned the household to the hall for lunch and supper.

Entertainment of a bawdy kind was popular. Roland le Pettour (the Farter) was rewarded with an estate in Suffolk in return for entertaining the royal court at Christmas by 'leaping, whistling and farting before the king'. Daniel of Beccles would not have approved of this amusement. In his view it was rude to fart noisily for fun. He would have approved even less of the *fabliaux* which were popular in French-speaking aristocratic circles, and which give us, as few other surviving sources do, an idea of what less earnest people liked to laugh about in twelfth- and thirteenth-century England. So liberally are the four-letter French words , *vit* (prick), *coilles* (balls), *con* (cunt), *cul* (arsehole) and *foutre* (fuck) scattered throughout them that since Victorian times many readers of a sensitive nature have found them distressingly crude and have preferred to avert their eyes.

After evening prayers, the lord went to his bedchamber with at least one servant, carrying a light, accompanying him every inch of the way. It was this chamberlain's duty to inspect the privy before his master used it. When his master had finished, he had to hand him bunches of well-pressed hay with which to wipe his bottom. Daniel advised that the servant stand − that is, not kneel − when doing this. By the end of the thirteenth century the king and queen had separate bathrooms at Westminster, but bath-

rooms were not generally fashionable among the aristocracy until the fifteenth century. Before then it was usual
to bathe in a wooden vat brought into a bedchamber for
the purpose. While the master sat comfortably on a large
sponge his chamberlain would wipe him with another
sponge, dipping it into a basin of herb-infused water, then
rinse him with rose water. Once in bed, linen sheets and
a quilt were pulled over him, and his dressing gown placed
to hand in case he wanted to get up during the night, for
people generally slept naked. Just in case he felt hungry or
thirsty, some bread, ale and wine was left in the room.

It was a sign of status to be accompanied almost everywhere, even when in the bath or the privy. Even so, there
were a few things that people preferred to do alone.
According to the historian William of Newburgh, writing
in the 1190s, when the doctors advised a seriously ill archbishop of York that his only hope of recovery lay in having
sex – many doctors believe in the restorative power of the
sexual act. The Archbishop took the young woman they
provided for him into his private room (*secretum*). But when
the doctors examined his urine next morning they discovered that he had not, after all, followed their advice. He
explained to his friends that he could not break his vow
of chastity – not even for medicinal purposes – and that
he had pretended to do so in order not to hurt their
feelings.

Senior staff and guests went to their own lodgings for
the night. The rest slept scattered throughout the buildings
– in corridors, in warmer rooms such as the hall and kitchen
if they were lucky. They slept on pallet-beds, palliasses stuffed
with straw or rushes. The size of palliasses, some as much
as nine feet by seven, shows that often they were expected

to share. The lord's bedchamber was lit throughout the night, and so too the stables, but everywhere else was left in darkness. Some stories suggest that indoors, with the shutters closed, it was very dark indeed. Gerald de Barri tells of a knight whose girlfriend had promised to creep into his bed at night. When he heard her coming he stretched out his hand to pull her to him, and had it bitten by a dog snuffling around in search of scraps of food. The angry knight grabbed his sword and waited for the dog's next approach. The inevitable happened when his girlfriend arrived. Only their own experience of real darkness, a darkness we can hardly imagine, would have made this morality tale remotely plausible to its audience.

The fact that the permanent household staff was overwhelmingly male caused an obvious problem, and prostitutes provided a solution, but one that needed careful supervision. The porter, who had to ensure that no unauthorised people were bedding down when night came, bore a heavy responsibility. For the king's household there was, in effect, a brothel by royal appointment, with twelve licensed 'demoiselles' who were entitled, and expected, to keep other whores away. When on duty in the king's household even aristocrats, who had large estates of their own, were expected to leave their wives and family at home while they concentrated on the royal service which took them so close to the centre of power. At Christmas 1204 Joan, wife of Hugh de Neville, one of King John's most influential household officials and gambling partners, offered the king two hundred chickens, which he accepted, for permission to lie one night with her husband.

CHAPTER 2

The Countryside

So long as the guardian has the wardship of the land, he shall maintain the houses, parks, preserves, fishponds, mills and other things, and keep his land stocked with ploughs and wainage such as the agricultural season demands.

Magna Carta, Clause 5

In 1215 nine-tenths of the population of England lived in the countryside. Most families lived and worked on small farms, as they had since time immemorial. Nearly all kept animals and grew crops, especially the grain for making their daily bread and ale. Regional differences in soil and climate meant that the precise balance between arable and pastoral was infinitely varied. Summers then were on average 1°C warmer than they are now, winters were milder and rainfall lower. The warmer climate meant that vineyards were planted as far north as Ely, and crops were grown higher up hills and mountainsides than is usual today.

If there was such a thing as a typical family farm, it was between ten and thirty acres in size, with husband, wife and three children. Since records show that better-off farmers had on average more children than the poor, birth control of sorts was practised, probably coitus interruptus. The study of excavated bones shows that people grew to a healthy size: the average adult male was five foot seven tall and had good teeth. A farmer with ten acres was able to produce enough to feed his family, pay rent to his lord, taxes to the king, and tithes to the Church and still have a surplus to sell at market to buy pottery, iron tools, ornaments and ale. In every village several women brewed and sold ale. It was those who farmed less than five acres, or who had no land at all, who suffered when the harvest was poor, when grain prices soared and their wages as labourers or craftsmen no longer sufficed. Faced with starvation they turned to acorns, once the poison had been leached out of them, and to weeds as famine foods. Fortunately in John's reign, there was only one year, 1203, when the harvest failed.

The typical family lived in a two-roomed timber-framed house standing within a plot of land, known as a croft, of up to an acre in extent. There was plenty of room for a vegetable and fruit garden as well as outbuildings for poultry and other livestock, all surrounded by a bank and a ditch. The house had a thatched roof, clay floors, and clay or wattle and daub walls, windows with shutters, and an open hearth in the larger room.

By modern standards farm animals were small. Sheep were about the size of the modern-day Welsh-mountain sheep, and cattle weighed only half as much as their modern equivalents. But most male farm animals were castrated so that they put on weight. Castrated bullocks, known as oxen, could pull the heaviest carts; castrated rams, known as wethers, produced the heaviest fleeces; castrated cockerels, capons, were fattened for the table, and so were castrated boars. Cattle and sheep provided meat, milk, leather, wool, tallow for candles and manure for fields, as well as vellum and parchment for writing. Poultry gave meat, eggs, feathers and quills. Preserved foods such as bacon, sausages and cheese were especially useful. Bees were kept for honey, and horses as well as oxen for pulling carts and ploughs. Woodland provided fuel and building materials, as well as acorns and beech mast, the seeds of the beech on the ground, to feed pigs, animals which could convert virtually anything into meat for humans. Even dry leaves were rolled up and made into faggots for the fire at home. In areas where woods were few and far between, peat provided fuel. In Norfolk peat was dug on such a scale that the resulting pits created the inland lakes known as the Norfolk Broads. These far-mers wasted nothing. Even their own excrement was re-cycled as manure.

Arable farming was a methodical process, painfully slow to our eyes. While a modern tractor might take a day to plough twenty acres, in 1215 this would have taken forty days. Farmers sowed by hand, scattering seed as they walked their fields. To frighten off birds, dead crows – scarecrows – were hung over newly sown fields. Modern organic farm-ing has returned to some of the practices of those days – weeding by hand, for instance. Rotation helped to eradi-cate crop-specific weeds, and traditionally farmers followed a three-course rotation:

1. *Winter-sown crops, such as wheat and rye. Cereal crops grew taller than they do today. In the absence of agro-chemicals, the seed was tightly encased in chaff, which protected it against rust, fungi and birds.*
2. *Spring-sown crops such as barley and, oats and legumes such as peas and beans. Human and animal dung recycled soil nitrogen, but legumes added new nitrogen to the soil by converting atmospheric nitrogen, and subsequent cereal crops did better as a result. The science of this was not understood until the late nineteenth century, but experienced farmers were well aware of the importance of legumes in keeping the land 'in good heart'.*
3. *Fallow. This was turned over to grazing animals, so that it had been both rested and manured before it was next cultivated. By keeping sheep in folds overnight, farmers could exercise some control over the manuring process.*

Traditionally harvest started on 1 August, the festival of Lammas, which took its name from the church service of 'loaf mass' when loaves made with the first ripe corn of the year were consecrated. Harvesting was done by hand with a sickle, and usually lasted well into September. But harvesting handful by handful, though desperately slow, had one advantage. It allowed farmers to mix two crops – for example the mixture of wheat and rye known as maslin – on the grounds that even if the weather meant that one cereal did badly, the other might do better. With the advent of mechanised harvesting, this kind of insurance against harvest failure was no longer possible. Once harvested, the stooks were bound up and carted off to the barns, while gleaners moved on to the fields. Some spikelets of grain were set aside for next year's seed; the rest were threshed, winnowed to separate the grain from the chaff, then ground and used to make porridge or bread.

Woods too were farmed in rotation by a system known as coppicing: trees were cut back to produce new growth. By cutting to a number of differently timed cycles, for example, every five, ten or fifteen years, coppicing produced a constant supply of wood of different thicknesses.

These farming practices were age-old, based on the trial and error of countless generations. But it would be wrong to think of the English countryside as an unchanging world in which time stood still. Over much of England and eastern Scotland the landscape itself had been recently transformed. What we tend now to think of as the archetypal English landscape, a countryside of villages and market towns – the England of the Archers, of Ambridge and Borchester – is a recent creation. Throughout Britain and Ireland the truly ancient human landscape was one of hamlets and isolated homesteads, with very few towns, most of those ports, and no villages. By 1215 that had changed. Over large parts of Britain the previous two or three centuries had witnessed farmers abandoning the dispersed settlement pattern in which they and their predecessors had lived for millennia. Instead they now huddled together in villages. In some villages each house stood in a plot identical in size and shape to its neighbours, and all in a neat row along a street or around the village green. Such uniformity betrays the hand of the planner. Someone compelled people to move and that, presumably, was the lord of the manor, for there is no doubt that most of these new group settlements were associated with a manor house and a church, itself paid for by the lord's family. However, some villages reveal a more higgledy-piggledy layout, and here the move to a single centre was probably the outcome of many individual decisions taken over a prolonged period. What forces persuaded these farmers to leave their homesteads in favour of the new-fangled settlement pattern?

The village can be seen as a rational response to population growth. In 1086, when the Domesday survey was made, the population of England was probably about 2.25 million. By 1215 it had risen to somewhere between 3.5 and 5 million. The population continued to grow, reaching 6 million or so by 1300, when England was as densely populated as it would be in the eighteenth century. One response to population growth was to expand cultivation. Large areas of forest, fen, marsh and upland were cleared, drained and farmed. Some of it was potentially good soil, as in the rich silt belt around the Wash. The monks of Glastonbury reclaimed thousands of acres in the Somerset Levels, creating high-quality meadow by building dykes and diverting river courses. But there was a limit to the physical expansion of cultivation. The Domesday Book shows that seven or eight million acres were already under the plough in 1086 – almost as many as in the 1950s. By 1215 some farmers, such as those who made clearings in the Sussex Weald, were struggling to make the best of soil that would always remain poor.

An alternative to expansion was greater efficiency. By living together in a village community, farmers could co-operate more effectively. In conjunction with his neighbours, the farmer who owned only two oxen was able to take advantage of the most up-to-date farm machinery, the heavy plough drawn by eight oxen. Because heavy ploughs were much harder to turn than the old-fashioned scratch plough, it made sense for the land they worked to be divided into long narrow strips so that ploughs were turned as infrequently as possible. Each householder held many strips scattered throughout the two large fields attached to each village. By this method good and bad soil was shared out fairly, and all lived more or less equidistant from their work. Also, in this way the risks were spread.

This co-operative system meant that working the land had to be regulated by rules common to all. Manorial courts undoubtedly helped the lord of the manor to control and take profits from his tenants, but they also settled disputes between villagers and issued by-laws on matters of common concern, such as the use or abuse of grazing rights on common land. A relatively rich farmer, for example, had to be prevented from grazing too many animals on the common. Each year one common field lay fallow, while the other grew winter and spring-sown crops. Any change in the balance between arable and fallow required the village to reach a consensus. Thus, economic rationality created a real village community – though not everywhere in Britain. East Anglia and Kent were two of the most densely settled parts of England, yet in both regions villages remained rare. Here homesteads straggled along the edges of common land, presumably to prevent good arable land from being wasted by being built on. Throughout the west of Britain too, where pastoral farming remained more important than arable, people continued to live and work in the ancient – and more independent – fashion.

The existence of planned villages demonstrates the capacity of lords to assess the economic situation and calculate the levels of investment needed to make radical innovations. In this climate of financial rationality, it was possible to reckon that using slave labour was not cost-effective and should be abandoned. Slavery in Britain had not disappeared with the fall of the Roman Empire in the West. On the contrary it was still flourishing when William I conquered England in 1066. As in Roman times much of the hardest work was done by slaves: ploughing by male slaves, grinding corn with hand mills by slave women. In a slave-owning society, such as Anglo-Saxon England, a master who killed his own slave was guilty of a sin, but not of a crime. Slaves were bought and sold at market – human flexibility meant that one healthy male might cost as much as a plough team of eight oxen. Captured slaves were among the most desirable profits of war. But William I came from Normandy, where slavery was already a thing of the past, and he disapproved. He put an end to the slave trade. Gradually slaves became more expensive to acquire. For centuries an occasional rich lord on his deathbed had been moved to free slaves as an act of Christian piety, but now – at long last – traditional notions of charity went hand in hand with the profit motive. In return for burdensome, often full-time services as ploughmen and shepherds, slaves were freed and given small tenements. By the 1120s Englishmen looked upon slavery as a barbarous custom happily no longer practised in their modern and civilised society. A hundred years before Magna Carta granted rights to freemen, an even more fundamental kind of freedom had been established.

The lords of the Magna Carta generation were able, however, to win a victory in the law courts whose effect was to create serfdom – a condition which many have believed to be just a new kind of slavery. Economic and social circumstance inevitably meant that some people were much less free than others. Those tenants who owed rent in the form of long hours of work on their landlord's estates had little freedom of choice about how they spent their days. A tenant who was not allowed to leave his holding or give his daughter in marriage without his lord's permission – a permission for which he had to pay – felt a frustrating lack of freedom. Such tenant farmers were significantly less free than those who owed cash rents and could earn their money as they chose. Some tenants were prosperous farmers; others were churls or peasants. It had always been part of the morality of kingship that the king and his courts would protect freemen against unjustified oppression – but never to the extent that they would help 'peasants' loosen the ties that bound them to their lords. So, the king's judges formulated a new set of rules whose effect was to disbar half the population of England from access to the public courts. Those tenants who owed the heaviest services to their lords were told that they did not have the right to have their disputes heard in the royal courts as freemen did. In this sense they were unfree, and legally classified as serfs or villeins; and so were their children and their children's children. From now on their disputes, whether with each other or with their lords, could only be heard in the manorial courts – the lords' own courts.

Records kept by these courts, the court rolls, survive from the late thirteenth century onwards. There is no doubt that this arrangement suited the landlords. 'The churl should always be well plucked for he is like a willow that sprouts better the more often it is pollarded.' Even so, in law there were limits to the oppression of serfs by their lords. No lord was legally entitled to kill or mutilate his serf, as owners could their slaves. Although a serf and his family were in effect bought and sold when the land on which he lived, his villein tenancy, was bought and sold, no individual serf was separated from his or her family and taken to market to be sold in the way that slaves – human cattle – had been. Serfs were not slaves. But they felt unfree, and with reason. A long struggle lay ahead, in which the great rebellion of 1381, the Peasants' Revolt, was the principal landmark, before serfdom was at last ended, although it has never been formally abolished.

Meanwhile, the England of 1215 was undergoing a managerial revolution. For many generations past the magnates, those who owned many manors, had lived off the rents and services owed them by their tenants. Their richer tenants, men of gentry status, would take over a whole manor or even several manors. Leases at rents fixed for a term of several lifetimes were common, and tended to turn into hereditary tenures. From the magnate's point of view this had its advantages. It gave him a predictable income and kept administration costs to a minimum. There was no need for anyone to keep detailed records. This absence of records is why it is virtually impossible to write an economic history of the early English countryside.

What would happen to wealthy landlords who spent far more than they could afford and got into debt? The story of Samson, abbot of Bury St Edmunds from 1182 to 1211, as told by one of his monks, Jocelin of Brakelond, is revealing. Samson's predecessor, Abbot Hugh,

> was a good and devout monk but he lacked ability in business matters. For all his financial problems he only had one

remedy: to borrow money, so that he could at least maintain the dignity of his household. Every year during the
last eight years of his life further loans were taken out to
pay the growing interest. Silk copes, gold vessels and other
church vessels were pawned to both Christian and Jewish
money lenders.

This was the situation that faced the new abbot immediately after his election. How could the monks climb out
of the vicious cycle of escalating debt? Was it possible to
run their estates more profitably? Could they re-negotiate
the leases? Was demand for foodstuffs increasing as the
population rose? Jocelin describes a first step in the process,
one in which he himself was involved.

There is an English tradition by which every year on the
day of Our Lord's Circumcision (1 January), the abbot, as
lord, is presented with gifts by a great many people. So I,
Jocelin, thought carefully about what I would give him.
Then I began to write down the names of all the churches
which belong to the abbot, and I added estimates of the
rents at which they could be leased, assuming an average
price for grain.

If prices were increasing, then would they not do better if
they took their manors into their own hands, instead of
leasing them out, appointed bailiffs and reeves to run them,
then sold the surplus on the open market? This, at any rate,
was what Abbot Samson did during the 1180s and 1190s,
and so did a few other of the more enterprising and efficient lords.

Then, early in King John's reign, prices rose sharply,

doubling or even trebling in the first five years of the new century. An ox, which could be bought for forty pence in the early 1190s, now cost eighty pence. The sudden and, to all appearances, unprecedented rise in the cost of living at the beginning of the century meant that great land-owners would have found it impossible to maintain the style to which they were accustomed unless they followed Samson's example and revolutionised the methods by which they managed their estates. And this was what they did. Many lords encountered fierce opposition from their tenants when they re-negotiated leases which fell in, and even fiercer when they tried to cancel them. Jocelin recounts one such case:

> On the death of Robert of Cockfield, his son Adam came to the abbot, and asked that he should have the half hundred of Cosford for an annual payment of £5, saying that his father and grandfather had held it for more than 80 years. Adam came accompanied by his kindred, by Earl Roger Bigod, and by many other important people.

But Abbot Samson resisted this pressure from the local bigwigs, and explained why in a lengthy speech. He was, after all, a famous preacher able to give sermons in Latin, French and English, including Norfolk dialect. The local establishment then offered him a large sum of money to renew the lease of Cosford, but Samson still refused. It required determination (and often forensic skill in the law courts) to resist the pressure and prudent thought for the future to say no to the presents they tried to give him. But gradually, both at Bury St Edmunds and on other estates, the new measures were pushed through.

The rich could now get richer, but the new system was far from being problem free. From now on the lord's expenses and profits were bound to vary from year to year. This made it easy for his officials to cheat him unless a close check was kept on their activities, so on each manor a detailed record of the year was kept, then checked together with similar returns from the other manors by auditors who represented the central administration of a great estate. The earliest such records to survive were drawn up from 1208 on the instructions of the bishop of Winchester, King John's good friend Peter des Roches. As one satirist of the time put it, the bishop was 'slack at scripture, sharp at accounting'. Other estates followed the practice of the businesslike bishop. The survival of masses of these accounts dating from around 1250 to 1400 means that historians know a great deal about the economy of the great estates during that century and a half.

Thirteenth-century auditors had a policy-making as well as a fraud-detecting role. They often noted that those who owed labour services worked without enthusiasm and suggested it might be better to hire wage labourers. In the summer everyone was expected to help with the lord's harvest, but he had to lay on a generous feast to mark the occasion. Was it worth it? the auditors asked. They fixed targets for each manor, and took investment decisions, whether to replace equipment, for instance, or build new barns. The barley barn built at Temple Cressing in Essex around 1230 is still in use today. The landlords' solution to the crisis of inflation meant that to run their estates they now required a whole army of professional treasurers, auditors, bailiffs, receivers and their clerks. Such people needed to learn their trade, and by the early thirteenth century there was a school of business administration at Oxford.

Yet the managerial revolution did little, perhaps nothing, to raise crop yields. By modern standards they remained very low indeed. The earliest surviving manorial accounts show that most lords were content to let a half or a third of their arable land lie fallow, leaving their sheep to manure it, plough the rest with ox teams only once or twice before sowing, and then sow only two to four bushels of seed an acre. By these methods they achieved returns of just three or four times the amount sown – in contrast to modern yields of more than twenty times the amount sown. Since these records relate to the home farms – the demesnes, as they were then called – of the greatest estates in England, it was always assumed that the yields obtained by their tenants or other lesser landholders were even lower, in the belief that the wealthiest would have employed the most advanced agricultural techniques.

But recent research has questioned this assumption. It has discovered that in relatively densely populated regions such as parts of Norfolk more intensive methods were employed, and higher yields achieved. Instead of letting some of the arable land lie fallow, it was all, or virtually all, cultivated. Crops such as peas were grown in great quantity and used not only to add nitrogen to the soil but also as fodder for animals kept in stalls, whose manure was collected and then spread on the soil just before ploughing – much more efficient than relying on grazing animals, whose droppings were often washed away by rain. By ploughing more often, and by speeding it up – using horses instead of oxen to draw the ploughs – and by more frequent weeding, they could achieve over twenty bushels an acre, a yield entirely comparable with that obtained by Norfolk farmers in the eighteenth century.

The secret was evidently in the intensive use of labour: many hands at work weeding, stone-picking and spreading manure. For most wealthy landlords, however, as their auditors could have told them, there was no point in achieving higher yields if it meant higher labour costs. The low yields on their estates made good financial sense. Peasant farmers, however, were their own labour force, and could count on the unstinting help of their wives and children. Since approximately three-quarters of the arable land of England was occupied by tenant farmers of this kind, it looks as though over most of the country average yields were higher than those obtained on the demesnes of the well-recorded great estates.

In other ways, too, the resources of the countryside were exploited more intensively than before. By 1215 England was significantly more mechanised than it had been a hundred years earlier. The windmill was invented in the twelfth century. This bold and brilliant design involved the whole mill building being raised on a post so that it could be turned by means of a long tail-pole to keep the sails facing into the wind. The earliest known windmills were built along the south and east coasts of England. Farmers might choose to grind their own grain by hand at home, but increasingly they had the option of taking it to the mill. In the same century waterpower was used for the first time in the cloth-making process, to drive hammers in fulling mills. (Fulling was the process whereby woven cloth was pounded in troughs filled with water and fuller's earth or alum to thicken and felt it. At the same time more and more watermills were being built or upgraded by use of vertical wheels which required cogs to transfer waterpower to the millstones in the mill. It was much more efficient

than having a horizontal wheel lying in the water channel and turning the millstones directly, but it required investment both in machinery and in building ponds and weirs
to ensure a flow of water sufficient to turn a vertical wheel.
Mill owners now competed with each other for business,
offering better rates or a faster service than their rivals. This
was why Abbot Samson, having invested a tidy sum in
building a windmill for his abbey, 'boiled with fury and
could hardly eat or speak' when he heard that the dean,
too, had built a windmill. The dean said he had built it on
his own freehold property and the wind was free for anyone
to use, but Abbot Samson compelled him to dismantle it.

Improvements in harness and vehicle design meant that
horses became more and more useful. In the Roman world
horses had rarely been used for pulling anything heavier
than a light chariot, but during the twelfth and thirteenth
centuries horses were increasingly used for ploughing and
hauling loaded carts. Horse-drawn carts and ploughs could
go at least half as fast again as those pulled by oxen.
Although horses could not cope with such heavy loads as
oxen, their speed meant that they could be used with more
flexibility. To speed traffic on its way, hundreds of new
bridges were built and old wooden bridges were replaced
with stone. The bridge-building programme was important enough for it to require regulation in Magna Carta
(Clause 23). It also meant that for the first time since
Roman times the road traffic system had been significantly
upgraded.

The old Roman roads had not been maintained for
centuries, but where there were towns and villages to be
served the ten thousand miles of the Roman network
remained in use. Four ancient roads were regarded as the

great highways of Britain: from east to west, the Icknield Way; from south to north, Ermine Street; from south-east (Dover) to north-west (Chester), Watling Street; and the longest of them all, Fosse Way running from Caithness in north Scotland to Totnes in Cornwall. The foundation of new towns such as Bristol, Coventry and Oxford from the late Saxon period onwards meant that many new cross-country roads came into existence.

A medieval road, unlike engineered and metalled Roman and modern roads, hardly existed as a physical object. It was a right of way leading from one town or village to another. If it was much used it became a clearly visible track across the countryside. If the track was obstructed or became impassable in wet weather, travellers still had a right of way. They were entitled to leave the track and move on, even if they trampled down crops in the adjoining fields. Roads like this needed very little maintenance, but most local communities recognised that it was in their own interests at least to ensure that they were passable. If they were dilatory, they might well find the king prodding them, especially if it concerned one of the four great highways for which the Crown had a special responsibility. Icknield Way and Watling Street crossed at Dunstable and in 1285 Edward I forcefully reminded the priory and townspeople of their ancient obligation:

> We have learnt that the high roads going through your town are so damaged and pitted by the heavy traffic of carts that those using them are in constant danger of being badly injured. We therefore command you, each and every one of you according to your station and resources, to ensure that the roads are mended and the holes filled in

as has been done in times past. Otherwise it will be necessary for us to move in and with a heavy hand.

The kings of England, accompanied by their households, a baggage train of ten to twenty carts and dozens of pack-horses, were always on the move around the country, rarely stopping for more than two or three days in any one place. Their government, it as been said, was 'a government of the roads and roadsides'. Unimpressive as they might seem to us, the roads of medieval England met the requirements of government as well as the demands of the market.

CHAPTER 3

Town

We will and grant that all cities, boroughs, towns and ports shall have all their liberties and free customs.

Magna Carta, Clause 13

'The king to all who wish to have burgages in the town of Liverpool, greeting. Know that we have granted to all who take up burgages at Liverpool that they shall have all the liberties and free customs in the town of Liverpool as enjoyed by any other free borough on the seacoast in our land. And so we command that you may travel there safely and in our peace in order to receive your burgages and to live there. In testimony of this we send you our letters patent. Witness Simon de Pateshull, at Winchester, 27 August in the 9th year of our reign.'

With these few words, in a document known as a letter patent drawn up in 1207, King John announced his foundation of Liverpool, a newly planned town alongside a tidal creek known as 'le pool' in the Mersey estuary. Liverpool was to have a remarkable future, but there was nothing at all remarkable about its foundation. Between 1066 and 1230 more than 125 towns were founded in England, with Arundel, Boston, Chelmsford, Devizes, Egremont, Harwich, Kingston-upon-Hull (later called Hull), Lynn (later King's Lynn), Morpeth, Newcastle-upon-Tyne, Okehampton, Portsmouth, Reigate, Salisbury, Truro, Uxbridge, Watford and Yarmouth, on the Isle of Wight, among them. The number had doubled since the Norman Conquest, which represents a faster rate of town foundation than in any other period of comparable length in English history. Looking back from post-industrial Britain we might think that medieval England was an overwhelmingly rural country. That is not how they saw it at the time.

Comparing England with Ireland, the twelfth-century English historian William of Malmesbury wrote: 'Whereas in Ireland the cultivators of the soil are so poor, or rather so unskilful, that the people live in rustic squalor, the English and the French, with their more cultivated way of life, live in towns and carry on trade and commerce.' William's contemporary, Henry of Huntingdon, wrote that England was richer even than Germany and saw its cities, 'glittering on the banks of fruitful and very beautiful rivers', as among the country's greatest assets. This same period saw the beginnings of urbanisation in both Wales and Scotland. The towns that grew up then included, in Wales, Cardiff, Carmarthen, Cardigan, Neath, Pembroke and Swansea; and in Scotland, Berwick, Edinburgh, Glasgow, Stirling, Aberdeen and Perth. In the history of urbanisation in Britain this is the most important period before the Industrial Revolution.

The beginnings of King John's Liverpool are typical of many medieval town foundations. In the short and businesslike letter patent of August 1207 the words 'free' and 'liberties' are prominent. Liverpool was to be a 'free borough'. The king's letter was, in effect, its first borough charter. Its burgesses, those people who took up the king's offer of burgages – plots of land in the new town – were to enjoy certain 'liberties and free customs'. They were to be free to sell, sublet, mortgage or pass on their burgage to heirs. They were to be free from having to pay servile dues or perform labour services, from paying toll at the borough's weekly market, as well as at other markets owned by the same lord. Where, as at Liverpool, the lord was the king this was an extremely valuable privilege since he was lord of most of the oldest and biggest towns in England. Burgesses could have their own oven and handmill: unlike servile tenants they were not compelled to use, and pay for using, their lord's. The law came to recognise the custom that a serf who managed to live in a borough as a burgess for a year and a day was thenceforth to be regarded as a freeman. Hence the medieval saying: 'Town air makes you free.' All this was clearly designed to attract settlers, as was the fact that in new towns burgage rents were set at a low level, typically a shilling (12d) a year.

Liverpool was planned on an empty site. Elsewhere lords issued charters that turned pre-existing villages into boroughs by 'enfranchising' them. In 1196, for example, the bishop of Worcester turned his village of Stratford-upon-Avon into a borough. Within fifty years Stratford had grown into a market town of some seventy acres in extent with a population of about a thousand. Burgage rents alone brought in £12, at least ten times as much as the rents of a seventy-acre rural manor. Even a small borough with just eighty burgage plots paying a shilling each brought in £4 just from rents, more than the property would have been worth as farmland. Adding in market and mill tolls, plus income from the borough court, it could bring in as much as £10.

Founding a town on a new site involved the lord in major capital outlay, in the case of Liverpool the building of a castle and a chapel for the settlers, since it was situated three miles from the parish church of Walton on the Hill. By granting special freedoms to his burgage tenants the lord gave up some profitable rights, but clearly in the expectation that the market would flourish, bringing in a higher rent income from new settlers, more money from the tolls paid at the weekly market by non-burgesses and from fines levied in the borough court. Alternatively once the town was off the ground its lord could guarantee himself a useful sum, known as the 'farm', with virtually no effort on his part, by leasing to the burgesses the right to collect revenues and administer their town. By 1229 Liverpool was paying a farm set at £10. King John's new town was already doing well.

The rate of new foundation was at its height in the fifty years between 1180 and 1230 when no fewer than fifty-seven new towns were founded in England. Before the Norman Conquest the majority of new English boroughs had been royal foundations, but most of those established in the two centuries after 1066 were founded by wealthy landowners, bishops, abbots and, above all, secular nobles. Maurice Paynell, for example, created a new borough at Leeds by the bridge over the river Aire; and Richard de Argentein was responsible for Newmarket in Suffolk. Some boroughs attracted so few settlers that they remained villages – there were to be many of these 'rural boroughs' in Ireland

– but the majority did well. Portsmouth was originally founded by a noble, Jean de Gisors, and was then taken over by Richard I in 1194 and developed as a naval base. Other successful new towns of this period included Honiton, founded by the earl of Devon; Chelmsford, founded by the bishop of London; Salisbury, founded by its bishop; Harwich, founded by the earls of Norfolk. One thing is crystal clear from the story of town foundation in the twelfth and thirteenth centuries. The aristocratic landowners of the age were far from being contemptuous of the profits of trade. The Clare family, for example, as earls of Hertford and Gloucester, came to possess more than twenty boroughs.

Of course the urban boom was very far from being solely the creation of royal and aristocratic enterprise. These lords were riding a wave of rising population and rising production. As settlements grew in number and size more and more people were able to specialise as artisans, craftsmen or shopkeepers, making and selling goods in exchange for the agricultural production of the countryside or raw materials from the forest, quarries and mines. Markets proliferated. There were just two markets in Oxfordshire in 1086, but ten more by the 1220s. Everyone lived close enough to a market to be able to walk there and back in a day. Markets could and did spring up as spontaneously as car-boot sales today, but then, as now, they functioned better with some degree of regulation. Ensuring that markets had to be held on different days in different places, for example, allowed itinerant traders to adopt a circuit that kept them in business throughout the week. Even though a few places, such as Stowmarket, became market towns without ever being granted borough status, chartering a borough

proved the most effective way of regulating – and promoting – a market.

Although a successful urban foundation depended upon
lord and burgesses co-operating as shareholders in a joint
enterprise, their interests were by no means identical, and
as time went by they were increasingly likely to diverge.
Bury St Edmunds was one of the earliest post-1066 urban
developments. Abbot Baldwin (1065–97) laid out five new
streets and a market place to the west of the abbey. The
Domesday Book of 1086 noted that the abbey now had
342 houses on land that had been under the plough in the
time of King Edward 'the Confessor' (1042–66). After a
century of urban growth the monks felt that they were not
making as much profit from St Edmund's town as they
should have been. Early in Richard I's reign they went to
see their formidable abbot, Samson, and complained that
the income they derived from Bury had remained at its
customary level of £40 a year, while 'revenues from all the
better towns and boroughs in England were rising to the
advantage of the lords who possessed them'. These were
monks with an eye on national economic trends. The
burgesses of Bury, however, could not be budged: they
looked to the king to protect what they called their 'liberty'
– which often meant something more like 'privilege'.

The monks of Bury were, however, right about the economy. Trade was booming. One of the principal engines of
the growth of commerce was the increase in the money
supply. At this time the only coin minted in north-west
Europe was the silver penny, so the discovery in the 1160s
of silver bearing ores in the Alps, in Tuscany and, above all,
at Freiberg, near Meissen, in Germany, was of huge importance. In 1180 a new English silver penny was designed,

now known to collectors and numismatists as the Short Cross penny. The cross design on one side of the coin simplified life for those who wanted to cut it into two or four pieces in order to have money of lower denomination, halfpennies or farthings (fourths). Thanks to the influx of new silver, especially German silver, numismatists estimate that after 1180 English mints were striking at least six times as many pennies as in the previous decades. By the 1220s, when surviving mint records allow accurate statistics of coin production to be compiled, over 4 million silver pennies were being minted annually at Canterbury and London, and mint production continued to rise during the thirteenth century. Indeed not until the nineteenth century was the weight of silver minted each year in later thirteenth-century England regularly exceeded.

By 1215 London was the second largest town, after Paris, in north-western Europe. The Londoner William FitzStephen prefaced *The Life of Thomas Becket* which he wrote in the early 1170s with an enthusiastic description of his city:

> Among the celebrated and noble cities of the world, the city of London, the throne of the English kingdom, is more widely famed than any other, and sends its wealth and merchandise further afield. It is blessed in the strength of its defences, the honour of citizens, and the chastity of its wives. The inhabitants of other cities are called citizens, but of London they are called barons. They are known everywhere for the elegance of their manners, dress and cuisine.

Here was a great international market, where goods of all kinds could be bought, both basic commodities such as grain which, in times of harvest failure, could be cheaper here than anywhere else in England, and also a great range of luxury goods. Just thinking of these exotic items so inspired William that he turned from prose to verse:

> *Gold from Arabia, from Sabaea spice*
> *And incense; from the Scythians arms of steel*
> *Well-tempered; oil from the rich groves of palm*
> *That spring from the fat lands of Babylon;*
> *Fine gems from Nile, from China crimson silks;*
> *French wines; and sable, vair and miniver*
> *From the far lands where Russ and Norseman dwell.*

It was not just a poetic flight of fancy: all these items could be bought in the London of his day.

So great was the attraction of the city's market that, by 1215, it had pulled the focal point of national administration into its orbit. Earlier kings of England had looked just as much, if not more, to Winchester, but by the later twelfth century Winchester had been overtaken by Westminster. The palace of Westminster, at its centre the magnificent hall built for William Rufus over a century earlier, became increasingly the heart of government. It was here, even during the prolonged absences of the royal court, that you could find the exchequer and the central law courts. By 1215 the English élite realised they could not do without London and Westminster. Many of them possessed, in addition to their country houses, a residence in London or in one of its two main suburbs, Westminster and Southwark. We have an account, for instance, of how Abbot Walter (1174–1211) of Waltham Abbey took the decision to build a stone house just north of Billingsgate. It was intended to be a place where the canons of Waltham or their servants could stay when they were in London, a warehouse for the goods they bought, and a garage for their carts. London was now England's capital city.

A few important towns, such as Norwich and Bristol, had developed in the course of the tenth and eleventh centuries, but generally speaking the richest towns were the oldest ones, dating back to Roman times, like York, Winchester, Lincoln, Canterbury, Colchester and, of course, London. According to William FitzStephen, however, London was older even than Rome itself, being founded after the fall of Troy by the Trojan exile Brutus, long before Romulus and Remus founded Rome. Indeed, it was Londoners, William explained – in another flight of fancy – who had repulsed Julius Caesar's invasion of Britain. He counted 139 churches, thirteen major ones and 126 parish churches, within the city and its suburbs; seven gates piercing the great wall that enclosed it on the north, linking the king's massive Tower of London in the east with Baynard's Castle and the Tower of Montfichet in the west. Two miles further west, joined to the city by a continuous line of development, lay 'the incomparable royal palace', which was Westminster. It is clear that, just as they are today, London and Westminster were already seen in combination, as the commercial and political capitals of the nation.

William drew attention to three springs famous for their healing waters in the northern suburbs: Holywell, Clerkenwell and St Clement's Well. He described how: 'Beyond the walls to the north lie arable fields, pasture and meadows, with brooks flowing between them and the happy sound of mill wheels turning. Beyond is the forest, where well-wooded copses and the lairs of wild animals can be found: stags and does, wild bulls and boars.' Among the city's amenities of which he was particularly proud was a shop selling ready-cooked meals at all hours of the day and night. Situated on the riverbank, amid the premises of the wine importers, it catered for travellers no matter how early or late they arrived or departed. Besides, William pointed out, if an unexpected guest suddenly turned up on your doorstep, you could pop down to the bankside shop and have a meal before them in no time. Its impressive menu offered a wide range of fish, meat, venison and poultry, either roast, boiled or fried – convenience food to suit all tastes and all pockets. It was this kind of thing, William emphasised, that made city life truly civilised.

He mentioned London Bridge only in passing, which shows that he was writing before the magnificent new stone bridge was built. It was begun in 1176 and took some thirty years to complete. Over a thousand feet long, it remained until 1831. Soon after its completion it survived a disaster that would have destroyed any of its Roman and medieval wooden predecessors. In 1212 a fire broke out on the south bank in Southwark. Crowds crossed the bridge either to view the scene or help put it out but were then surrounded by flames when the fire, driven by a south wind, took hold on the north bank too – presumably via the timber or thatched roofs of houses on the bridge. Boats went to rescue those trapped on the bridge, but so many jumped in them that they sank. Some reports spoke of 3000 dead, others of 3000 badly burned bodies washed up on the banks of the Thames, with an unknown number totally consumed by the flames. Three days after the fire a city ordinance was issued against thatched roofs. From then

on London would be a timber city but one in which roofs
were tiled. An ordinance issued on the same day ordered
that 'scot-ales' (in effect, bring-a-bottle parties) were not
to be held except by licence, which suggests that the fire
started at a party. In William FitzStephen's view, the two
plagues of London were the frequency of fires and the
excessive drinking of fools.

A year or two later, William might have added a third
plague: a rash of muggings and murders were carried out
by gangs of youths, often the sons of rich citizens such
as the Bucuinte family, a thoroughly respectable city
dynasty – despite their name, which means 'greasy mouth'.
As these well-heeled robbers grew in confidence, they
broke into the houses of the wealthy and looted them.
On one occasion they even used crowbars to break into
a stone-built house, but this time a well-armed home
owner was waiting for them. Their leader John Old, reput-
edly one of the city's 'richest and noblest' citizens, was
hanged for his part in this wave of violent street crime.
News stories such as this may well have encouraged a
Winchester author, the monk Richard of Devizes, writing in the 1190s, to adopt a view of London very different from FitzStephen's.

Whatever evil or malicious thing can be found anywhere
in the world can also be found in that city. There are masses
of pimps. Do not associate with them. Do not mingle with
the crowds in the eating-houses. Avoid dice, gambling, the
theatre and the tavern. You will meet more braggarts there
than in the whole of France. The number of parasites is
infinite. Actors, jesters, smooth-skinned lads, Moors, flat-
terers, pretty boys, effeminates, pederasts, singing and

dancing girls, quacks, belly-dancers, sorcerers, extortioners, night-wanderers, magicians, mimes, beggars, buffoons.

After this list, some of it borrowed from the Roman poet Horace, his advice is predictable if prosaic: 'Do not live in London.'

Like nearly all the major towns and cities in England, London 'belonged' to the king. But such was its wealth that at times even he had to bid for its support. By 1200 the Crown had conceded a considerable degree of self-government to the city: from 1191 it was administered by a mayor and aldermen. The first mayor of London, Henry FitzAilwin, remained in office from 1191 until his death in 1212. Where London led, other cities and towns followed. Winchester had a mayor by 1200, Exeter by 1205, Lincoln by 1206, Barnstaple, Oxford, Lynn, York, Northampton, Beverley, Bristol, Grimsby and Newcastle-upon-Tyne by 1216. In 1215, in political trouble, John tried to win the city's support by giving 'his barons of the city of London' a charter confirming their liberties, and adding the right to elect a mayor every year. But only ten days later the city opened its gates to the rebels against him, and then besieged the Tower. It was the loss of his capital city that persuaded the king he must negotiate.

Little of the London and Westminster of 1215 can still be seen today. Westminster Abbey – in which John, like all his predecessors since the last Anglo-Saxon king, Harold, had been crowned – was rebuilt by his son Henry III. None the less, despite all the destruction and rebuilding that has taken place over the centuries there are some amazing survivals, none more so than the great monuments of the first two Norman kings: the White Tower, built by

William the Conqueror, and Westminster Hall, built by his
son, William Rufus. North of the Alps these two were the
most impressive buildings of their kind to be raised since
the fall of the Roman Empire. Unfortunately little of the
rest of the medieval palace of Westminster survived the
great fire of 1834.

Some parts of a few churches remain. Of the priory and
hospital of St Bartholomew's, the choir of the church still
stands. The Temple Church was dedicated in 1185 by the
Patriarch of Jerusalem, come to England to beg King Henry
II to go to the aid of the Holy Land, sore beset by Muslim
forces led by Saladin, one of Islam's greatest champions. It
was in this church that William Marshal, regent of England
after King John's death, was buried in 1219. There is also
the crypt of St Mary-le-Bow, the scene of a controversial
incident in 1196. A London citizen, William FitzOsbert,
known as Longbeard, led a protest movement against the
unfair distribution of taxation. One contemporary described
him as 'the champion of the poor', but according to another,

He plotted great wickedness in the name of justice, a
conspiracy of the poor against the rich. By his fiery
eloquence he inflamed both the poor and the moderately
well-off with a desire for limitless freedom and happiness
and with a hatred for the arrogance of the rich and noble
which he painted in the blackest colours. At public meetings he proclaimed himself the king of the poor, and their
saviour.

Although, said this author, he kept a list of the names of
52,000 supporters, there was no mass rising when the king's
chief minister, the justiciar Hubert Walter, sent officers to

arrest him. Longbeard killed one and then fled for sanctuary to St Mary-le-Bow, accompanied by a number of friends who refused to desert him. Hubert's troops set fire to the church and Longbeard was forced out. After a rapid trial in the Tower of London, he and nine friends were tied to horses' tails, dragged to Tyburn and hanged. The justiciar's disregard of sanctuary shocked some, and all the more since he was archbishop of Canterbury. Soon Longbeard was looked upon as a martyr. The gibbet was secretly removed and venerated as a sacred relic; the earth below it was believed to have healing powers, the place of his death became a shrine. Hubert sent troops to disperse those who watched over it, imprisoned others and set an armed guard there. He also spread scandal: it was alleged that Longbeard had polluted the church of St Mary-le-Bow by having sex there with his concubine and that – even worse – he had invoked the aid of the devil when it became plain that no help could be expected from God. Longbeard's adherents claimed that these reports were lies, but the embryonic martyr's cult withered away – a victory for government news management.

In John's reign London was far from being the only centre of international trade. The king imposed a duty on goods entering and leaving the country, and the records of customs revenue for 1203–4 from the ports of the south and east coasts – all that survive – show that 17 per cent of the total came from London, 16 per cent from Boston, 14 per cent from Southampton, 13 per cent each from Lynn and Lincoln, 7 per cent from Hull, 4 per cent from York and 3 per cent from Newcastle. (The rest came from a number of other ports.) These statistics are intriguing. Although they certainly underestimate London's share of the trade, it is striking none the less to discover just how busy ports such as Boston, Lynn, Hull and Newcastle – all new towns – had become.

The prominence of east-coast ports on this list reflects the rise of another new phenomenon: the international fair. For three or four weeks every year after Easter the little country town of St Ives in Cambridgeshire, for instance, was transformed into a major commercial emporium. Wooden stalls were set up; the front rooms of town houses were rented out as shops; cart parks were full to overflowing. Quite extraordinary quantities of food and drink, oats and hay were brought in to provision the influx of buyers and sellers and their horses. This was the 'great fair' of St Ives. People came here not only from all over eastern England, but also from overseas – from Flanders, Brabant, Norway, Germany and France. Many English towns enjoyed the right to hold an annual fair, but most served a local or regional market and lasted for only two or three days. The 'great fairs' which developed in the later twelfth century at Boston, Winchester, Lynn and Stamford as well as at St Ives were different. They lasted for several weeks. The fair held around St Giles's church outside the walls of Winchester lasted for sixteen days beginning on 31 August. They were open for business to all comers, free from the restrictions of trade that towns normally imposed to protect their own merchants and shopkeepers. This made them very attractive to foreigners of all sorts, including those who came from overseas. This enabled English producers of, say, wool and cloth to trade directly with foreign importers without going through London middlemen. St Giles' Fair was worth £100 or more a year to its lord, the bishop of Winchester, and a businesslike bishop such as

Peter des Roches often got royal permission to extend it by a week – to the irritation of the townspeople.

Another distinctive feature of the towns of 1215 was the presence in them of a number of Jews. So far as is known no Jews lived in Anglo-Saxon England. After 1066 French-speaking Jews from the flourishing community of Rouen crossed the Channel and some settled in London. The modern street name Old Jewry serves as a reminder of the medieval Jewry, not a ghetto in the strict sense of the word but a synagogue and a cluster of properties belonging to Jews, situated close to the busiest market in England, Cheapside; the Jewish cemetery lay outside the city walls, at Cripplegate. By 1215 there were small Jewish communities in at least twenty other English towns, the most important being in York, Lincoln, Canterbury, Gloucester, Northampton, Cambridge and Winchester. In total there may have been approximately 5,000 Jews in England, and until 1177 their bodies, no matter where they had lived, had to be brought to London for burial. In that year Henry II gave permission for Jews to create cemeteries outside the walls of every city in England. The cemetery at York, at a site still called Jewbury, was excavated in the 1980s, and the evidence recovered suggests that a community of about 250 had lived there.

In practice Jews were restricted to one economic activity: money-lending. With interest rates set at a penny, twopence or, occasionally, threepence per pound per week (i.e. 22 per cent, 44 per cent or 66 per cent per annum) this brought them great profits and, at times, even greater unpopularity. A Norwich monk, Thomas of Monmouth, accused the Jews of Norwich of the ritual murder of a young boy called William. His book on the subject launched the 'blood libel' against the Jews that was to leave a terrible scar on subsequent European history. William became a saint, much like the thirteenth-century boy 'martyr' 'Little St Hugh' of Lincoln. As a small, wealthy, exclusive and culturally distinctive minority, the Jews needed protection. The abbey of Bury St Edmund's had borrowed large sums from Jewish, as well as from Christian, money-lenders – this was in the feckless days before Samson became abbot – and in consequence when danger threatened the Jews, they were allowed to take shelter within the abbey – much to Jocelin of Brakelond's dismay.

'They came and went as they liked, going everywhere throughout the monastery, even wandering by the altars and shrine while Mass was being celebrated. Their money was deposited in our treasury. Most unsuitable of all in an abbey even their wives and children were allowed in.'

By far the most important protector of the Jews was the king. In legal terms they were 'in the king's peace' and, as King John observed in a letter of 1203, 'If we had given our peace to a dog, it should not be violated.' In return kings, certainly from Henry II onwards, exacted a heavy price, regulating Jewish business dealings closely and at times taxing them very harshly. In 1210 John demanded the staggering sum of £44,000 from the Jews, employing mass arrests and other brutal measures to enforce payment. According to one author, he extracted £6,666 from a rich Jew of Bristol by removing one of his teeth every day until he paid up. Since Jews themselves were in no position to enforce payment of debts owed to them, they had to rely on royal officials to do this for them. Debts owed to Jews who died intestate were taken over by the Crown. 'Jews are the sponges of kings', wrote an English theologian of the time. All this meant that landowners in debt to Jews constantly found themselves caught up in burdensome financial dealings with the Crown – an obvious cause of friction between king and barons that left its mark on Magna Carta. In Clauses 10 and 11 John was forced to promise that he would deal sympathetically with the widows and children of any landowner who died in debt to the Jews.

The king, however, could not always give the Jews the protection they bought at so high a price. In an anti-Semitic riot in London in 1189 several Jews were killed, while the houses of others were plundered and burned down. Richard I punished the rioters, hanging three, and he allowed a Jew who had pretended to convert to Christianity to escape death, to return to the faith of his fathers. But after the king left England for France, with the crusade as his goal, more anti-Semitic riots and murders occurred in 1190 in Lynn, Stamford, Norwich and Bury St Edmunds. Crusades, with their reminders of Christ's crucifixion, tended to stimulate anti-Jewish sentiment; a crusading vow was an expensive commitment and the plundering of Jews sometimes seemed an all-too-appropriate way of raising the cash. The killings of 1190 reached a climax at York. Jews took refuge, as they often did, in the royal castle, Clifford's Tower. A mob led by some of the local gentry, crusaders among them, and urged on by a fanatical hermit, mounted an assault on it. When the Jews realised they could hold out no longer, most of the men killed their wives and children, then committed suicide. Those families who did not opt for the ancient Jewish tradition of self-martyrdom surrendered when they were promised that their lives would be spared if they accepted Christian baptism. Once they left the castle they were killed. The mob then rushed to York Minster where the records of debts owed to Jews were stored and there, in the nave of the cathedral church, they made a bonfire of them. 'As for these people who were butchered with such savage ferocity', said the Yorkshire historian William of Newburgh, writing in the nearby priory of Newburgh, 'I unhesitatingly affirm that if they had truly wished to be baptised, then baptised or nor, they found acceptance in God's eyes. But whether their wish for baptism was genuine or feigned, the cruelty of those who murdered them was deceitful and utterly barbarous.' As far as it could – which wasn't very far – the government punished those responsible for the York massacre, and over the next few decades Jews returned to the city until, once again, it contained one of the richest communities in England.

Anti-Semitism and religious discrimination meant that the position of the Jews remained vulnerable everywhere in Latin Christendom. Philip II of France (usually known as King Philip Augustus) began his reign in 1180 by expelling Jews from Paris and confiscating their property. When he returned from crusade in 1192 he had eighty Jews found guilty of ritual murder and burned at the stake in Brie. In 1215 Pope Innocent III at the Fourth Latern Council in Rome decreed that Jews and Muslims were 'to be publicly distinguished from other people by their dress'. In 1218 the council governing England on behalf of the boy-king Henry III ordered 'all Jews to wear on the outer part of their clothing two strips on their breast made of white linen or parchment so that Jews may be distinguished from Christians by this visible badge'. This, it was argued, was to stop a person of one faith from unwittingly having sex with someone of another. A 'certain deacon', name unknown, certainly knew what he was doing, however, when he fell in love with a Jewish woman; he circumcised himself for her sake. He was defrocked on the orders of a Church council chaired by Stephen Langton, archbishop of Canterbury, held at Oxford in 1222, then taken outside the city walls and burned. In practice, the pope's rules on distinctive dress for Jews were commonly set aside in England. In return for money the king was happy to exempt individuals or communities from the obligation to wear the Jewish badge. On this and related matters his view was that churchmen 'have nothing to do with our Jews'. Before the end of the thirteenth century, though, the Crown's financial demands had pressed its Jewish sponges so hard that little more could be squeezed out of them. In 1290 Edward I expelled them from his kingdom, to general English applause. It was not until England had a new kind of ruler, in the shape of Oliver Cromwell, that they were allowed to return.

CHAPTER 4

School

Our heirs in perpetuity.

Magna Carta, Clause I

L ike nearly all babies born into royal and aristocratic families John was given to a wet-nurse. The authors of the time who discussed the care of babies and children preferred mothers to breast-feed their own children, and they advised them to feed on demand, not according to a rigid timetable. Yet nearly everyone who was rich enough to do so ignored them and hired a wet-nurse. She was a symbol of wealth and freed a busy, politically engaged mother, like Eleanor of Aquitaine, from domestic responsibility. John's wet-nurse was called Matilda.

His older brother Richard's was Hodierna, and we know a little bit more about her than we do of Matilda. Her own baby grew up to be an abbot of Cirencester and a famous scholar, Alexander Nequam. As a result of Richard's generosity she became a woman of property, well enough known to have a place named after her, Knoyle Hodierne in Wiltshire.

Henry and Eleanor were not expected to spend much time with their children. They were always on the move and travelling with a baby was not easy. In a poem by Marie de France, whom John may well have met, baby and wet-nurse had to stop seven times a day so that the infant could be fed and bathed. It was easier to leave royal babies and small children in some settled spot while their parents moved on. Other parents saw far more of their children than kings and queens did; the further down the social scale you were the more time you spent with them. 'Babies', wrote a thirteenth-century author, 'are messy and troublesome and older children are often naughty, but by caring for them their parents come to love them so much that they would not exchange them for all the treasures in the world.' It was with the expectation that their children would be a source of joy that many mothers faced the pains of labour.

During their earliest years all children remained in the care of women. It was from women that children learned how to behave, how to speak in a courtly fashion, and also the first rudiments of their letters. Small children would learn, everyone knew, by imitating adults. Their first steps and words were greeted with delight. This was also their playtime. Toys were already gender-specific. Boys had their soldiers, and girls their dolls' houses. In later life Gerald de Barri claimed to remember that when his brothers had built sandcastles on the beach at Manorbier, he had built churches; by temperament he was predestined to be a cleric.

In aristocratic households a sharp break came when children reached the age of seven or eight. While girls generally stayed at home, boys would be sent away. The author of

Tristan retained a vivid memory of this change in the pattern of a boy's life.

> 'In his seventh year he was sent away into the care of a man of experience. This was his first loss of freedom. He had to face cares and obligations unknown to him before, a stern discipline in the shape of the study of books and languages. He had tasted freedom, only to lose it.'

For this discipline John was sent to the household of Henry II's senior administrator, the justiciar of England, Ranulf Glanvil. It might have been from him that he acquired his interest in the law. The books which he possessed as king show that he could read Latin and French, and he may well have been able to read English too. The well-educated Englishman of 1215 was either bi- or tri-lingual.

Education in a noble household involved a great deal more than book learning. Above all, young people of both sexes were expected to learn courtesy – modest and polished manners. In order to appreciate the service he would receive during the rest of his life, it was an important part of a young lord's education that he should himself learn how to serve, both in the hall and elsewhere. For a handsome young man, serving at table on a major feast day when the hall was crowded with visitors and their wives was an opportunity to impress. When the sixteen-year old hero of *The Romance of Horn* served as cup-bearer,

> 'his well-cut tunic was of fine cloth, his hose close-fitting, his legs straight and slender. Lord! how they noticed his beauty throughout the hall! How they praised his complexion and his bearing now. No lady seeing him did not love

him and want to hold him softly to her under an ermine coverlet, unknown to her lord, for he was the paragon of the whole court.'

A popular twelfth-century work listed the seven spheres in which a well-taught knight was expected to shine: riding, swimming, archery, combat, falconry, chess and song-writing. Other similar lists include dancing. His sister would learn chess, music and dancing as well as the more specifically feminine accomplishments of embroidery and weaving. She, too, would learn to read, since as a wife or widow she might be expected to manage a household, and in that case it would be useful to be able to read documents and understand accounts. Many romances include scenes in which a daughter is shown reading to her parents and siblings.

In the character of Horn we have a portrait of the model product of late twelfth-century household education – the kind of training John himself received. 'No one could equal Horn when it came to handling a horse or a sword. He was similarly talented at hunting and hawking. No master craftsman was his equal; no one matched him in modesty. There was no musical instrument known to man in which he did not surpass everyone.' In this period, the accomplished young aristocrat was expected not just to appreciate music but to perform. In one scene in *The Romance of Horn* the king's sister played the harp, and the instrument was then passed to everyone in the room in turn. When the harp came to Horn, he sang a lay said to have been the work of a royal composer, Baltof of Brittany.

Then Horn made the harp strings play exactly the melody he had just sung. Having played the notes, he began to raise the pitch and made the strings give out completely different notes. Everyone was astonished at his skill with the harp, how he touched the strings and made them vibrate, at times causing them to sing, at times making them join in harmonies. Everyone there was reminded of the harmony of heaven!

John's elder brother, Richard I, was a celebrated song-writer – and at least one of his songs, *Ja nus hons prins*, 'No man who is in prison', the song he is supposed to have composed while a prisoner in Germany, can still be bought in music shops today.

The fashionable indoor game during John's lifetime was chess. It had been introduced into western Europe from the Arab world, and into England after 1066. As both men and women played chess, a quiet game in the corner of a room or in a window seat created opportunities for flirting. But not all chess games were quiet. Earlier board games such as backgammon or games with dice were essentially gambling games, so it was only natural that the new one, too, was often played for stakes. But chess was, above all else, a game of skill. Victory and defeat were no longer matters of chance, of good or bad luck. Alexander Nequam noted the intensity of the game, the loser's feeling of humiliation, the winner's pride. He watched the faces of the players go 'deadly white or fiery red, betraying the pent-up fury of an angry mind'. In an aristocratic household, budding chess-players were not only learning the moves, they were also learning restraint and how to control their emotions. King John often played backgammon with his courtiers, but there is no contemporary record of him playing chess. According to a later story, the *Romance of Fulk FitzWaryn*, 'one day John and Fulk were sitting alone in a chamber playing chess, when John picked up the chessboard and hit Fulk with it. Fulk hit back, kicking John in the chest so hard that his head crashed against the wall, and he passed out. Fulk rubbed John's ears so that he regained consciousness but was very glad that, apart from the two of them, there had been nobody in the room.'

The introduction of new rules into chess in the sixteenth century made it a much more complicated game than before. At the highest level it gradually turned into a game for professionals, not for the accomplished amateur, but throughout the Middle Ages skill at playing chess, like skill at playing music, was one of the measures of the well-brought-up young aristocrat.

In the village, children were expected to help their parents with the farmwork, weeding, stone-picking, looking after the animals, gathering berries, picking fruit, drawing and fetching water from the well. As they grew older girls and boys went slightly separate ways. Brothers and sisters stopped sharing a bed. Boys joined in their father's work, ploughing, reaping, building, or staying out in the fields with sheep and cattle. Girls stayed with their mothers, cooking, baking, cleaning, spinning and weaving. By the time they were fourteen both boys and girls had been trained for their future roles in life.

For those whose parents wanted them to be formally educated, but did not live in a noble household, there were schools. By 1215 all English towns would have contained at least one. This might not sound much to boast about, but it is in marked contrast with all earlier English history when nearly all schools had been in monasteries. From the twelfth century onwards town schools were open to all whose parents could afford the fees. By 1215 the demand for further education had led to the development of Oxford and Cambridge, the first two universities in Britain. Contemporaries were acutely conscious of living in an age of educational expansion. 'Are not teachers', one complained, 'nowadays as ubiquitous as tax collectors?'

This doesn't mean that most children went to school. Very few village children could have done, though occasionally a parish priest would teach the poor free of charge. But then, as now, there were ambitious parents who somehow found the money to pay school fees. According to Ranulf Glanvil, peasants sent their sons to school so that they could rise in the world by becoming clerics. This doesn't necessarily mean that they aspired to a career in the Church, but they did want to learn Latin and in this way gain access to the world of book-knowledge.

Children first went to school at about the age of seven. At what we might call 'primary' school, children learned their abcs – though some of them might already have been given their first lessons in reading by their mother. The earliest surviving manuscripts show the alphabet set down in three rows.

$$+A.a.b.c.d.e.f.g.h.i.k.$$
$$l.m.n.o.p.q.r.\imath.\int.s.t.$$
$$v.u.x.y.z.\&.9.\colon.est\ amen.$$

In other words the modern j and w omitted, v and u are alternatives, there are two forms for r and s, and it ends with the standard abbreviations for *et* and *con*, then three dots or tittles and lastly the words *est amen*. Sometimes

known as the 'crossrow', because of the way the top row
started, the alphabet was usually presented in this way until
the eighteenth century. Children then began to learn Latin
from a primer, a basic miscellany of prayers, or from a
psalter. From an early age they were familiar with the Latin
words of church services. They also learned how to write,
using a stylus to form letters on wax tablets. In medieval
Latin, writing (*scriptura*) and scripture (*scriptura*) were
synonymous. Many people learned to read without ever
learning to write. That they left to clerks – just as in recent
times many people left typewriting to typists.

A few girls attended primary schools, but almost none
went on to the next stage of education, the grammar schools
catering for eleven- to fifteen-year-olds. From now on
formal education was for males only. At grammar schools,
pupils worked on improving their Latin grammar, read Latin
literature, the scriptures, and usually picked up a little
science and law on the way. They worked hard. The school
day was a long one. It started at six or seven in the morning, and ended eleven hours later, with just two breaks of
an hour each. They were kept at it, contemporaries
observed, either by love of learning or by fear of the cane
– corporal punishment was taken for granted.

For most schoolmasters teaching was a way of earning
fees, so they did not always take kindly to competition.
The master of the cathedral school of St Paul's in London
acknowledged the permanent presence of schools attached
to St Mary-le-Bow and St Martin-le-Grand, but he was
entitled to excommunicate anyone else who dared to teach
in the city. There were, however, more than three schools
in London. According to William FitzStephen, 'many other
schools were allowed as favours to teachers celebrated for

their learning' – although these did not enjoy permanent institutional status. FitzStephen gives a vivid description of the regular London inter-school debating contests.

> On feast days the masters assemble their pupils at the churches whose feast-day it is, and there the scholars dispute. Some debate just to show off, which is nothing but a wrestling bout of wit, but for others disputation is a way of establishing the truth of things. Some produce nonsensical arguments but enjoy the sheer profusion of their own words; others employ fallacies in an effort to trick their opponents. Boys from different schools compete in verse, or in debates about the rules of grammar. Others use cross-roads humour to insult or mock their opponents, identifying them not by name but by teasing allusions to their well-known foibles – indeed, to general amusement, sometimes even their elders and betters are subjected to this treatment.

One of FitzStephen's enthusiasms was for school sports days. He describes at length the annual round of city sports, beginning with cockfights on Carnival (Shrove Tuesday) morning. The schoolboys of London were given the morning off from lessons to watch their favourite cocks do battle. Carnival afternoon was devoted to ball games. Schoolboys and guild apprentices played, while their seniors watched from horseback, recalling the days when they had been young and great ball players themselves. In the summer young Londoners went in for martial exercises such as sword fighting, archery and wrestling, and for athletic pursuits, like jumping, putting the shot, and throwing the javelin. In the winter, bull, boar, and bear-baiting provided amusement. When the great marsh adjoining the northern wall froze over, the ice quickly became crowded. Slides and toboggan runs were set up, 'while others, more skilled at winter sports, lash animal bones to their feet and striking the ice with iron-tipped poles propel themselves as swiftly as a bird in flight'.

So highly did the Church come to value education that in 1179 Pope Alexander III decreed that each cathedral should maintain a schoolmaster to teach its clerks and other poor scholars for nothing. Pope Innocent III elaborated on this decree in the 1215 Lateran Council, and diocesan statutes, such as those of Salisbury in 1219, show that his instructions were followed. 'When I was a boy,' wrote Alexander of Canon's Ashby around 1200, 'the ambition of nearly all teachers was to get rich by teaching, but now, by the grace of God, there are many who teach for free.'

Before 1066 virtually no Englishman went abroad to study. But all that changed after the Norman Conquest, partly because for two or three generations England's élites considered themselves French and it seemed natural to send the sons and nephews for whom they planned a clerical career to France. By the second quarter of the twelfth century Paris had become the acknowledged intellectual powerhouse of the Christian West, pre-eminent among a number of prestigious schools in northern France at Laon, Tours, Poitiers, Orleans and Chartres. Here the over-fifteens studied what was known as the arts course. This meant what were called the 'seven liberal arts', consisting of the *trivium* (grammar, rhetoric and logic) and the *quadrivium* (arithmetic, astronomy, geometry and music). In practice the greater part of their time was spent on the *trivium*, and most of all on logic. When the monks of Bury St Edmunds discussed the kind of person they would like to see as their new abbot, 'I', wrote Jocelin of Brakelond, 'said I would not agree to anyone becoming abbot who did not know some logic and how to separate truth from falsehood.' The full arts course usually took nine years, but many students stayed just a year or two, improved their Latin, learned some law and made some friends. Those who completed the whole demanding course were entitled to call themselves Masters of Arts (MAs). By 1215 half of the canons of Salisbury Cathedral were Masters.

In systematically organised debates, known as 'disputations', the students learned to apply the rules of formal logical reasoning and quick-witted verbal virtuosity in answer to questions posed by their masters. At popular debates known as disputations *de quodlibet* ('about anything at all') the questions could be put by the audience and might relate to current political controversies or subjects chosen for their humorous potential. If anyone ever debated 'how many angels can stand on the head of a pin?', it would have been during a joky *quodlibet*. The debating techniques honed in these sessions meant that the products of a school of advanced study had acquired skills which could be transferred to virtually any discipline. Most of them went on to careers as administrators, managers and consultants to kings, aristocrats and senior churchmen. Alexander Nequam remembered how he and a school friend had both vowed to enter a monastery, which he had, but his friend, his studies finished, was now working in the Treasury.

The most famous of the thousands of English students who travelled to the schools of France in search of the most advanced education Europe could offer was John of Salisbury, the author of *Policraticus*, The Statesman's Book. He studied at Paris and elsewhere from 1136 to 1147. The most famous of his teachers was the brilliant Breton, Peter Abelard, who taught him logic, but two others were Englishmen, Robert Pullen and Robert of Melun, later bishop of Hereford. The latter, according to John, taught that there was often no one right answer to the most interesting questions and was always willing to argue on either side of a question.

For students who wanted to study law, Bologna offered a prestigious alternative to Paris, especially if they were interested in Roman law – that is, civil law as opposed to the canon law of the Church. But the relevance of Roman law to English law was somewhat indirect, and there is no doubt that the vast majority of English students who went to the continent chose France. A study of the masters of the embryonic University of Paris has revealed that during the period 1179–1215 more than a third of those whose origins are known came from England. Among them was Stephen Langton, one of the key figures of 1215. He taught theology in Paris and it was he who introduced the present arrangement of the Bible into books and chapters. Another was Robert of Curzon, who returned to Paris in 1215 as a papal legate and cardinal and issued the first set of university statutes. Another English student at Paris, at least according to *The Mirror of Fools*, a satire written by Nigel Whiteacre of Canterbury, was Burnellus, an ass who decided to take the arts course. 'Then,' he daydreamed, 'I'll be Master Burnell, and the crowds will shout "Here comes the great Master Burnell".' According to Nigel Whiteacre, the English students at Paris were already, in the late 1180s, famous for their drinking and womanising. As for Burnellus, after seven years of study at Paris all he could say was 'hee-haw'.

By 1215, however, it was no longer quite so necessary to go abroad to complete your education. There were schools of advanced study in a few English towns: Exeter,

Lincoln, London, Northampton and Oxford. At this date Oxford was pre-eminent – though still much less prestigious than Paris or Bologna. When Gerald de Barri wanted to publicise his first major work, *The Topography of Ireland*, he gave readings from it on three consecutive days at Oxford 'because of all places in England that was where clerks were most numerous and most learned'. On the first day he entertained the poor, on the second, all the teachers as well as those scholars who had acquired some reputation, and on the third, the remaining students together with Oxford's knights and its many burgesses. 'It was', Gerald said with characteristic lack of modesty, 'a magnificent and lavish occasion.' By the 1190s Oxford was beginning to attract a few students from the continent. But at that time there was as yet no university, just an informal gathering of lots of teachers and students in a single town. The chronicler Roger of Wendover reported the bloodshed in 1209 that led to the creation of the university.

A certain clerk studying the liberal arts at Oxford by mischance killed a woman, and ran away on realising that she was dead. When her body and his absence were discovered the mayor of Oxford arrested three other clerks who had shared a rented house together with the fugitive. Although these three knew nothing whatever about the killing, they were imprisoned and a few days later, on the king's orders and in contempt of ecclesiastical privilege, were taken outside the town limits and hanged. At this all the clerks of Oxford, both masters and students, about 3000 in all, left so that not one of them remained behind in the town.

Some pursued their studies at Cambridge, others at Reading. The dispute between the town of Oxford and the clerks dragged on for years. Before a formal settlement could be reached, the clerks had to form themselves into a corporation, a body – like a borough – with legal rights and responsibilities: the 'university'. The English word derives from the Latin *universitas* meaning a corporation. Finally, in 1214, the town authorities agreed to do penance, to regulate the level of student rents and the price of food, and to make an annual payment to the university as financial assistance to poor students. Clearly, although Roger's figure of 3000 masters and students was an exaggeration, there had been enough of them for the withdrawal of their purchasing power to have a damaging impact on Oxford's economy. But the dispute had gone on for so long that one group of teachers and pupils had settled very comfortably in Cambridge. And there they stayed. Students lived in lodgings or rented houses like the unfortunates of 1209, but charitable benefactions from the later thirteenth century onwards meant that a few could be accommodated in colleges, of which the earliest was Oxford's Merton College.

In the advanced schools of Europe you could study law and theology as well as the liberal arts. As education came to be more formally structured, these subjects were seen as suitable for higher degrees, to be embarked on by the academically inclined after they had completed the arts course. Those who took a doctorate in law expected to be offered well-paid jobs when they finally left university, probably in their thirties. Those who studied theology were more interested in thinking out problems than in making money. Theologians liked to call their subject 'the queen of the sciences'. Law, by contrast, came to be known as one of the 'lucrative sciences'; the other was medicine, but anyone wanting to study that was better advised to leave England.

For them there was a choice between two prestigious schools: Montpellier and Salerno. Salerno, in particular, acquired a legendary reputation, as Marie de France's story, *The Two Lovers*, reveals. A king who could not bear to part with his daughter decided that only the man who could carry her to the top of a nearby mountain would be allowed to marry her. Many tried, but none got more than half-way up. As it happened, she fell in love with a young man and he with her but, not wanting to cause her father additional distress, she refused to elope. Fortunately she had a cunning plan.

> I have an aunt in Salerno, a rich woman who has been there for more than thirty years and who has practised the physician's art so much that she is well-versed in medicines, and knows all about herbs and roots. Go to her, taking a letter from me, and tell her your story. She will give you such electuaries and potions as will increase your strength.

He took her advice and when he returned from Salerno, he was much strengthened. (The rich aunt was probably based on Trotula, a woman who wrote a book on the medical care of women; Chaucer's Wife of Bath referred to her as 'Dame Trot'). He brought back with him a phial of a precious potion that would allow him to complete the Herculean task. She, meanwhile, trying to lose some weight for his sake, had had some success. When the time came for the test, she decided to wear nothing but her shift. He felt so invigorated by happiness that he carried her all the way without stopping once to take the potion, but at the top he collapsed and died. Burnellus the Ass was equally unfortunate. He went to Salerno in the hope of finding a specialist who could make his tail grow until it was as long as his ears. But on the way home, carrying ten jars of Salerno's finest tail-growing mixture, he was set upon by dogs and lost all the jars as well as half of his tail.

Salerno owed its reputation to a Tunisian Muslim, known in the West, after his conversion to Christianity, as Constantine the African, and his Latin translations of the Arabic medical treatises based on the writings of the great Greek doctor Galen. John of Salisbury was not impressed:

> Often failed students of science/philosophy go to Salerno or Montpellier, where they study medicine, and then their careers suddenly take off. They ostentatiously quote Hippocrates and Galen, pronounce mysterious words, and have aphorisms ready to cover all cases. They use arcane words as thunderbolts with which to stun the minds of their clients. They follow two precepts above all. First, don't waste time by practising medicine where people are poor. Second, make sure you collect your fee while the patient is still in pain.

His jaundiced words did little to impede the success of the new medicine. Kings of England employed the best doctors. At the beginning of the twelfth century Henry I's came from the Mediterranean – men such as the converted Spanish Jew Peter Alphonsi or Italians such as Grimbald and Faricius – who became abbot of Abingdon. But by the end of the century Richard I had doctors who were Englishmen such as Warin, abbot of St Albans

(1183–1195), and his brother Matthew who been trained at Salerno.

By 1200 the medical ideas of the school of Salerno were well known throughout the West. Its adherents saw the human body as having four principal members, each served by the appropriate network – the brain was served by nerves, the heart by arteries, the liver by veins and the genitals by the spermatic ducts. On this theory both men and women produced sperm. Without the first three members, the Salernitans said, the body would no longer function; without the fourth, the human race would cease to exist. They noted that although human beings looked more like monkeys than pigs, their internal organs were closer to those of pigs – an opinion not irrelevant to modern transplant surgery. There were also the four 'humours' – or, as we might say, principal components, corresponding to four elements: blood, which was hot and moist like air; phlegm, which was cold and moist like water; red bile or choler, hot and dry like fire; and black bile, cold and dry like earth. Hence, depending on which humour predominated, there were four 'complexions' or, as we might say, temperaments: sanguine, phlegmatic, choleric and melancholic. According to this school, good health depended upon a balance of humours. Analysis of a patient's urine, always bearing in mind their age and sex, was seen as a reliable guide to the balance of their humours and, thence, their health. On this subject a translation by Constantine the African of a treatise by a ninth-century North African-Jewish physician known as Isaac Judaeus was regarded as the authoritative book and remained so until the sixteenth century. When one of Henry I's doctors, Faricius, abbot of Abingdon, was proposed as a candidate for the see of Canterbury, there were churchmen who opposed him on the grounds that they did not want an archbishop who had been accustomed to examining women's urine. And, indeed, he was not appointed.

Many prescriptions recommended in the books of the time are simple enough, and not always dressed up in the pretentious Galenic theoretical language that John of Salisbury found so objectionable. Mugwort in wine, for example, was advised for the woman who had problems with menstruation. Steambaths were good for those who suffered from obesity. A swollen penis could be alleviated with a marshmallow compress.

> For deafness: take the fatty residue of fresh eels that appears after cooking them, the juice of honeysuckle, and house-leek, and a handful of ants' eggs. Grind them together and strain them. Mix the result with oil and cook it. After cooking, add vinegar so that the mixture penetrates better, or wine if preferred. Pour this into the healthy ear and stop up the afflicted ear. Have the patient lie upon their good side. In the morning take care to avoid a draught.

The confident tone of medical textbooks is noteworthy, grounded on the assumption that most conditions can be treated without recourse to miracles or magic. And miracle stories themselves suggest that most people shared this confidence in doctors. No theme in them is more common than that the saint healed when doctors had failed – which indicates that people went to the doctors before they went on a pilgrimage.

CHAPTER 5

Family Strife

*We have completely remitted and pardoned to all any ill will, grudge
and rancour that have arisen between us and our subjects.*

Magna Carta, Clause 62

T he turbulent family life of the royal dynasty into which
John was born would be familiar to viewers of television soap operas. Love, hatred and the desire for wealth
or power are commonplace emotions, capable of compli-
cating the lives of all families. The greater the wealth and
power at stake the more intense the love and hatred is apt
to be. The political successes and failures of John's parents,
Henry II and Eleanor of Aquitaine, of his brother Richard
the Lionheart, and of John himself were all, to a greater or
lesser extent, bound up with sex, love and sibling rivalry.

Sex, love and war were the three great themes of the
songs and romances of the age, of the stories on which
John would have been brought up. The *fabliaux* treated sex

with exuberantly bawdy humour. In one story a peasant is granted four wishes; when he allows his wife to have the first one, she wishes for him to be equipped with 'extra pricks' all over his body. Noblemen and noblewomen liked to think they were capable of finer feelings than this, of *fin amor*, usually referred to today as 'courtly love'.

The fashionable poetry of courtly love occasionally celebrated the joys and sufferings of platonic love, the kind of love that theologians envisaged in paradise when, as they put it, 'genital contact held no greater thrill than the clasp of a hand'. But far more frequently authors such as Hue de Rotelande (Rhuddlan) or the brilliant poetess Marie de France – who dedicated her songs to King Henry II – examined the pleasures and torments of sexual love, and of love in marriage, not just in adultery. In Marie's lay *Milun*, the unnamed heroine falls in love with Milun and, because she expects to marry him, sleeps with him – indeed they have a child. It does not work out, she has to marry someone else, but they find ways of staying in touch, and years later, when her first husband dies, they are married 'and lived happily ever after'. But it was not just writers of songs and romances who believed that there should be love in marriage. The English monk and chronicler Matthew Paris said that a married couple was joined by law, love and 'the harmony of the bed'.

The medical science fashionable at the time taught that conception only occurred when male and female sperm coalesced, and that women produced sperm only as a result of pleasure. This was why, men said, prostitutes did not get pregnant. Christian theologians and moralists disapproved of anyone doing anything for the sake of pleasure, but it does not look as though their disapproval carried much

weight, at any rate where sex was concerned. The earliest
surviving records of archdeacons' courts show that 90 per
cent of the offences brought before them were sexual,
mostly fornication. Thomas of Chobham, the author of a
handbook for confessors (written around 1215), described
fornication as 'the vice of everyone and excused by many'.
Gerald de Barri urged his readers not to listen to those
who said that fornication, far from being a mortal sin, was
only natural. But many did listen to those siren voices.
Many couples lived in long-term non-marital relationships. Church synods urged fornicators to marry – or, if
they would not, at least to pay a fine. Adultery was taken
much more seriously. The recommended penance for adul-
terers was that they should be whipped naked through the
streets. Thomas of Chobham allowed that a husband who
found his wife in adultery had the right to castrate her
lover, even in those cases where the lover was a clerk. On
this matter both Church and royal courts were of one
opinion.

But Daniel of Beccles would not have approved of such
a violent response by the husband. In his view, women
found it virtually impossible to resist any well-endowed
male, so wives were almost bound to be unfaithful. 'One
sinful act with her lover', he wrote, 'will please a wife more
than a hundred lawful times with her husband.' Although
he recognised the husband's right in law to punish the
adulterer, his advice to the civilised man was: pretend not
to notice. 'It is better to conceal your shame as a husband
than disclose the evil that brings a blush to your cheek and
grief to your heart.' He advised husbands not to beat their
wives. So far as he was concerned marriage was the relationship on which society was founded, and whatever your

wife did, or however much you came to dislike her, you should put up with it.

Daniel also advised you on what to do if your lord's wife made a pass at you. In his view it would end badly whether you accepted or spurned her advances. Your only hope was to pretend to be ill. And he pointed out that the stupidest thing you could possibly do was to tell your lord, out of loyalty to him, what his wife was up to. One of Henry II's courtiers, Walter Map, tells a story similarly based on the male notion that female sexual appetites were boundless. In this case when the queen made a pass at one of her husband's knights, he got out of this awkward spot by pretending to be gay. Which was fine – until the queen sent her serving-maid to test him out. The conventional male opinion that women were sexually voracious was doubtless the other side of the same coin as the equally conventional male opinion that when a woman said no she almost certainly meant yes.

The physicians who believed that pleasure was necessary for conception were also inclined to take a frank view of sex – disconcertingly so in the eyes of those churchmen who put a high value on celibacy. The anonymous author of a work known as the *Prose Salernitan Questions* wrote that nothing natural could be shameful and that only hypocrites shied away from discussing sexual intercourse. It seems clear that he was writing in the west of England around 1200 since he mentions five English physicians, three of whom have been traced in early thirteenth-century Hereford documents; indeed one of them, Master Hugh de Mapenore, became bishop of Hereford in 1216.

It should be noted that there are some who have a big sexual appetite but who, being choleric, can do little. There are those, such as Master Hugh de Mapenore, who have little appetite but can perform energetically; others such as Master Reginald de Omine can do little and indeed have little appetite, others such as Master Philip Rufus of Cornwall have big appetites but can manage very little; others such as Master John Burgensis and especially Master William Chers have both a big appetite and an impressive performance.

Doctors also reckoned that regular sex was good for your health. Long absence meant that crusaders were thought to be risking their lives in more ways than one if they remained faithful to their wives while they were away. According to Ambroise, the poet-historian of the Third Crusade,

> *By famine and by malady*
> *More than three thousand were struck down*
> *At the siege of Acre and in the town.*
> *But in pilgrims' hearing I declare*
> *A hundred thousand men died there*
> *Because from women they abstained.*
> *'Twas for God's love that they restrained*
> *Themselves. They had not perished thus*
> *Had they not been abstemious.*

John was born on Christmas Eve 1167 in the royal palace of Beaumont at Oxford. He was the youngest of eight, five boys, one of whom died young, and three girls, born to Henry and Eleanor in the first fifteen years of their marriage. His parents appear to have enjoyed the pleasure and harmony of their bed, and by this criterion at least their marriage had been a great success.

In a previous marriage lasting fourteen years, Eleanor had borne only two daughters. Her first husband, King Louis VII of France, had eventually decided that she was unlikely to bear the son he needed, and divorced her in 1152. For years before this the couple had been on bad terms. Eleanor was alleged to have had an eye for a handsome man, while Louis was deeply pious. He might have been influenced by those canon lawyers who taught that sex between spouses who had no affection for each other was a kind of adultery. In these circumstances it would not have been surprising that he should divorce Eleanor were it not for the fact that she was the heiress-duchess of Aquitaine. By divorcing her Louis risked losing a vast territory, roughly one-third of modern France, quite a high price to pay for a divorce.

In fact Louis VII belonged to the first generation of princes to face a new situation, one which created both great opportunities and awkward dilemmas. For the first time in European history women such as Eleanor, daughter of Duke William X of Aquitaine, were, if they had no brothers, inheriting counties, duchies and kingdoms. For this reason the twelfth century has been called the 'century of heiresses'. Geoffrey of Anjou, known as 'Plantagenet', had married one such heiress, Matilda, King Henry I's only surviving legitimate child, heiress to both England and Normandy. He had not got on at all well with Matilda, but chose to stay married to her. In previous centuries husbands had often repudiated their wives, but this was no longer an easy option for those who had married an heiress. When John was eight, Count Philip of Flanders, convinced that he had caught his wife in adultery, killed her alleged lover by hanging him upside down in a cess-pit. But his wife was the heiress to the rich county of Vermandois in north-eastern France, and he chose not to divorce her. By marrying Eleanor soon after her father died, Louis VII had enormously extended the territorial power of the king of France, but by 1152 the estrangement between him and Eleanor was so deep, and his desire for a son so great, that he chose divorce. Louis was not a ruthless man. He made no real effort to keep Eleanor under restraint either during or after the divorce proceedings. Eight weeks after the divorce she married Henry and transferred Aquitaine from her first husband to her second. This transformed the political shape of France overnight. Nominally Henry held his dominions in France as a subordinate of the king of France, but in reality he overshadowed him. Henry II was the most powerful king in Europe, richer even than the ruler of Germany, Emperor Frederick I, known as Barbarossa.

The prevalent modern idea that marriage in the Middle Ages was just a matter of political expediency is nonsense. In a world dominated by dynasties the political consequences of sexual incompatibility and marriage breakdown could be devastating, as Louis discovered. Nearly all marriages were arranged on the basis of political calculation, but whether or not the couple remained married, and whether or not they had children, was at least as much a question of love and sex as it was of politics. Anyone who said that the association of love and marriage was merely an ecclesiastical or literary convention, an illusion which existed only in the dream world of poets or the spiritual world of theologians, was living in a dream world of their own, an illusory land of neat and tidy categories. The real world was much more complicated.

It was King John's bad luck that in Philip II he had to

face a king of France who was a devious politician, ruth-
lessly determined to overthrow the Plantagenet empire and
take revenge for the humiliations that his father, Louis VII,
had suffered at Henry II's hands. But even so single-minded
a ruler as Philip allowed his sexual problems to jeopardise
his political ambitions. On 15 August 1193 he married
Ingeborg, daughter of the king of Denmark. According to
one French bishop, in beauty she was the equal of Helen
of Troy. Next morning, however, Philip tried to return his
wife to the custody of the Danish envoys who had escorted
her to France. They refused to take her back. Philip and
Ingeborg then fought a furious and prolonged legal battle
over what had – or had not – happened during the one
night they had spent together. Pope Innocent III told the
king it would not be enough to give her the public status
of a queen: he must also sleep with her, for 'nothing could
be more honourable or more holy'. Not until 1213, when
Philip was planning to invade England and wanted to be
sure that God would favour the enterprise, did he at last do
the decent thing. According to his court historian, the news
caused great joy throughout France. But for twenty years
Philip's political and diplomatic standing had been undermined by his attempt to secure a divorce that was recognised not just within his own kingdom – that was relatively
easy – but also by the other ruling families of Europe.

Compared with how little we know about other families of the time, we are amazingly well informed about the
family life of the Plantagenets. Young John must have
learned early just how complicated family life could be.
He was only five when, in 1173, his eldest brother Henry
rebelled against their father. Young Henry found a willing
ally in Louis VII of France, who was still smarting over the

loss of Aquitaine. Astonishingly, Eleanor decided to join the revolt. She sent her next two sons, Richard and Geoffrey, aged fifteen and fourteen respectively, to join their brother at the court of her ex-husband in order to fight a war against her present husband. Why she did this is unknown and unknowable. We cannot see into her heart, and do not know whether she was jealous of a mistress or mistresses that Henry may by now have taken, or whether she was politically frustrated, or whether it was a combination of sex and politics. What is certain is that she was angry. Sons, often frustrated by having to wait too long – as they saw it – before being allowed a share of their father's power, often rebelled. Henry understood this and was prepared to offer them terms. In his commentary on the revolt of 1173–4, the learned dean of St Paul's, Ralph of Diss, searched back through history, and found more than thirty examples of rebellious sons. But for a wife to rebel against her husband was extraordinary. Ralph of Diss did not call a single case to mind. Eleanor must have been very angry indeed.

The revolt of Eleanor and her sons triggered a greater war, since it was inevitable that rival rulers would seize the opportunity to cut Henry II down to size. The kings of France and Scotland, the counts of Flanders, Boulogne and Blois all joined in, and so did many nobles from Poitou, Normandy and England. Fortunately for Henry II, the war had hardly begun when his men captured Eleanor; allegedly she was wearing men's clothes. When the rebellion was over, he pardoned his three older sons and restored them to their former positions. Eleanor, however, he kept in custody or under close surveillance, mostly in Winchester, for the rest of his life.

In the war of 1173–4 all of Henry's sons – apart from John who was too young to be actively involved – were on the same side. But after that the quarrels between them became notorious. At stake was the family inheritance. When their father died, how was it to be divided up? Henry had not put together an empire that was intended to survive his death. He had built up a family firm, and was going to divide it between his sons. It had already been arranged that his eldest son, Henry, should inherit England, Normandy and Anjou, that Richard would have Aquitaine, and Geoffrey Brittany. Kings, of course, were also expected to provide for their daughters. If they did not wish to become abbesses – and it was not as easy now to push an unwilling girl into a nunnery as it once had been – they would be given in marriage, usually with a cash dowry, to a neighbouring prince. Thereafter the costs of supporting them were borne by their husband's family. In 1168 Henry married his eldest daughter Matilda to the richest of all German dukes, Henry the Lion, duke of Bavaria and Saxony. Eleanor was given to King Alfonso VIII of Castile in 1170; and Joanna to William II, king of Sicily, in 1177. At this stage only John was unprovided for. For this reason his father nicknamed him 'Sans Terre', Lackland.

In fact, John was only nine when his father betrothed him to Isabel, one of the three daughters of Earl William of Gloucester. He was too young to marry without a special dispensation from the pope. Canon law set the minimum age for marriage at fourteen for boys and twelve for girls, but betrothals between children too young to marry were common, and they rarely led to marriage. John's brother Richard was betrothed first to a daughter of the count of Barcelona, then to Alice, daughter of Louis VII by his second wife, but he married neither. As political circumstances changed, so new betrothals were arranged. In 1183 – when John was fifteen – it was rumoured that King Henry was thinking of arranging a marriage between Alice and John. Gossip said much more than this. Alice had been in Henry II's custody since 1169. For years both the pope and the king of France had been pressing him either to marry her to Richard at once or return her to the court of France. He never did. When he died in 1189 Alice was still in his custody, as she had been for twenty years. Henry's steadfast refusal to hand her over naturally gave rise to scandal. After his death the evidence that the king had seduced the young woman entrusted to his custody compelled her brother Philip Augustus to release Richard from the engagement. From then on Philip would not rest until he had brought down the family who had dishonoured his sister.

After Eleanor's rebellion, if not before, Henry II had a number of mistresses, most famously Rosamund Clifford. Even so, and despite the political difficulties it would inevitably cause, Henry had been unable to resist the temptation to seduce the young French princess in his care. The rumour that he planned to marry off his mistress to his youngest son reinforced the impression that the old king was thinking of an entirely new division of his empire. This exciting or alarming prospect set his sons quarrelling between themselves and sparked off new rebellions against their father, first by Henry and Geoffrey, then by Richard.

These civil wars within the family were not intended as wars to the death. On the contrary, the brothers only intended to bring pressure on their father to give them what they believed was their due. As the eldest son, Henry endured the permanent frustration of living in his father's shadow. That he had actually been crowned king of England during his father's lifetime did not help – if anything, it made things worse because it highlighted the contrast between his rank and his powerlessness. No king of England had carried through the coronation of his own heir before, and after the failure of Henry II's misguided experiment, none would in the future. Geoffrey joined his brother in rebellion because he wanted real control over Brittany – the duchy to whose heiress he had been married. After the deaths of his two older brothers Richard wanted his father to acknowledge him publicly as his heir, which Henry very publicly refused to do – predictably adding fuel to the rumours that he was planning a bright future for his youngest son.

In the event every one of the Plantagenet feuds of the 1180s ended with the death of one of the family. The rebellion of 1183, during which Henry II came close to being killed by an arrow, ended abruptly when his eldest son fell ill and died – to his father's intense grief. Geoffrey died suddenly in Paris in 1186 and was buried in Notre Dame. The war of 1189 ended with the defeat of the sick and exhausted Henry II by the combined forces of Richard and Philip Augustus. On 6 July, just a few days after his capitulation, the old king died. Many blamed Richard and John for their father's death. It was reported that when Richard inspected his father's body, blood flowed from the corpse's nostrils as a sign that the dead man recognised his murderer. Many thought that Henry had died because he had received the appalling news that John had deserted him. John had remained loyal to his father throughout the family feuds of the previous six years, but when he calculated that the old king's cause was lost he changed sides.

Henry died in despair, cursing the day he had been born. In his long reign he had made many enemies, Welsh, Scots, Irish, Bretons, the king of France, the pope, even his own archbishop of Canterbury, Thomas Becket, but none of these had been able to overcome him. What, in the end, brought him down was his own family.

Eventually John did marry Isabel of Gloucester – at his brother's insistence. After Richard came to the throne he had no intention of marrying Alice, but he didn't want John to marry her either. The archbishop of Canterbury prohibited the wedding on the grounds that John and Isabel were too closely related – he was a great-grandson and she a great-granddaughter of Henry I – but it went ahead anyway. John appealed against the archbishop's ban and the papal legate in England recognised his marriage as lawful pending the outcome of an appeal to Rome. Since John did not actually pursue the appeal, his marriage remained conveniently both legal and voidable. No doubt John preferred it that way. It is even possible that he never slept with Isabel. The new king of England was determined to go on crusade; if he were to die, John could expect to inherit the throne, and would then want a wife of higher status than an earl's daughter. Sex with Isabel would complicate an attempt to get the 'marriage' annulled. In any case for a king's son there was plenty of sex on offer elsewhere. John had at least seven illegitimate children, most probably born before he became king.

In dynastic politics the accidents of birth and death were crucial, and were themselves often the result of passion – or its absence. While on crusade Richard married Berengaria, a daughter of the king of Navarre, but the marriage turned out badly. They spent little time together

and had no children. In the second half of the twentieth
century it became fashionable to say that Richard was gay,
and this is still widely believed, although it derives entirely
from an anachronistic reading of the evidence. The well-
informed English chronicler Roger of Howden reported
that in 1187 Richard and King Philip of France shared a
bed, but it was common for people of the same sex to do
this then. It was an expression of trust not of sexual desire.
It was common then, too, for men to kiss or hold hands,
but these were political gestures of friendship or of peace,
not erotic passion. It is a mistake to assume that an act that
had one symbolic meaning eight hundred years ago carries
the same message today. Richard was accused by rebels
against his authority as duke of Aquitaine of 'carrying off
his subjects' wives, daughters and kinswomen by force and
then, when he had sated his own lusts on them, handing
them on for his soldiers to enjoy'. He had an illegitimate
son called Philip on whom he bestowed the lordship of
Cognac. If he was bisexual, as is also suggested today, it was
clearly a well-kept secret. His enemies – and he had plenty,
particularly at the French court – accused him of many
things, of murder, of disloyalty to the king of France, of
betraying Christendom in making peace with Islam, but
they never accused him of what they saw as 'unnatural
vice'. Since, however, he and Berengaria evidently did not
enjoy the 'harmony of the bed', he still had no legitimate
children when he was unexpectedly killed in April 1199.
It was this that finally brought John, the runt of the
Plantagenet litter, to the throne.

Richard, it was generally thought, had treated his younger
brother with remarkable generosity – far too generously, said
many. In England, in addition to the Gloucester inheritance,

he was given control of the counties of Derby, Nottingham, Cornwall, Devon, Somerset and Dorset, and in Normandy the county of Mortain. As soon as John heard that Richard had been taken prisoner in Germany while on his way back from crusade, he betrayed him. In January 1193 he made an alliance with Philip of France, promising to hand over to him strategic fortresses along the Norman border, and agreeing to ditch Isabel and marry Philip's sister Alice – this would surely have been a marriage of political expediency. But Alice was held by the counsellors, headed by his mother, Eleanor, who were governing in Richard's name and they were certainly not going to release her to marry a traitor. So nothing came of John's scheme to marry his father's ex-mistress. By January 1194 Philip had given John control of three major Norman frontier fortresses, Arques, Drincourt and Evreux, and in return had received John's promise that he would cede the whole of eastern Normandy to him. To offer to surrender lands that had been held by his ancestors for nearly three hundred years was a staggering betrayal, not just of his own crusader brother but of the whole dynasty.

No sooner had Richard been released than John changed sides again. Indeed, he did this so quickly and quietly that he was able to go to Evreux and have its French garrison killed while they still thought he was their commanding officer. He had now betrayed the king of France too. Treachery was a matter of deception and timing. It was one thing to oppose your father openly, and even – as Richard had done – to take up arms against him. It was quite another to pretend to be loyal but switch allegiance precisely at that moment when your support was most needed. John's record of treachery between 1189 and 1194 was such that William of Newburgh called him 'nature's enemy'. After 1194 he seems to have worked hard to recover his brother's trust and by 1197 he was regarded as heir presumptive to all of Richard's dominions. When a wound from a crossbow bolt turned gangrenous, Richard named John as his successor.

When John became king he divorced the childless Isabel and married Isabella of Angoulême, in August 1200. His new queen was young; she looked about twelve, observed one chronicler. Their first child, Henry, was not born until 1207, and hence was still far too young to play a political role in 1215. Had there been an active heir to the throne in 1215, those who opposed John would have turned to him; there would have been no Magna Carta.

In other ways too family politics played its part in the making of Magna Carta. It was believed that the two fiercest of John's baronial enemies, Eustace de Vesci and Robert FitzWalter, had personal reasons for taking up arms against him – even, John thought, trying to assassinate him. Eustace was angered by John's attempt to seduce his wife, Margaret, daughter of King William of Scotland. According to later gossip, the de Vesci honour was only saved by the device of placing a suitably disguised prostitute in the king's bed in place of Margaret. Robert FitzWalter announced far and wide that the king had attempted to rape his daughter. A monk of Waverley Abbey accused John of violating the wives and daughters of his barons. According to the author of the *Histoire des ducs de Normandie*, who was in the service of one of John's commanders, the king was 'a very bad man, cruel and lecherous'.

There was nothing unusual about a king having mistresses, including aristocratic mistresses; most of them did. Indeed,

William of Newburgh said that for a young king to remain celibate was a greater miracle than raising someone from the dead. But John's assaults on unwilling women of high status, the wives and daughters of his barons, was quite another matter. Whether true or not, as hostile propaganda these accusations of sexual harassment helped to establish the image of him as an immoral and bullying king who was unable to keep his desires under control.

CHAPTER 6

Tournaments and Battles

Immediately after concluding peace, we will remove from the king-dom all alien knights, crossbowmen, sergeants and mercenary soldiers who have come with horses and arms to the hurt of the realm.

Magna Carta, Clause 51

In 1215 the ethos of the English nobility and gentry was military. Their houses were often designed to look far more defensible than they really were. Fencing masters and weapons instructors trained young aristocrats to handle weapons, and these skills were much admired. A model knight such as Tristan 'learned to ride nimbly with shield and lance, to spur his mount skilfully on either flank, put it to the gallop with dash, wheel and give it free rein, and urge it on with his knees, all in strict accordance with the chivalric art'. The knightly art of fighting on horseback was extremely difficult to master – for horse as well as rider. Hunting helped to hone some of the necessary skills, but for real training in the art of chivalric combat, you had to go to the tournament, a serious war-game devised in the twelfth century.

A long poem written in French verse in England in the 1220s provides a superb insight into the aristocratic lifestyle, particularly tournaments: *L'Histoire de Guillaume le Maréchal* (The History of William the Marshal). William was the fourth son of a Wiltshire baron so although he had been born into aristocratic circles, as a fourth son he could not rely on inheriting an estate and would have to make his own way in the world. He made his way so successfully that he ended his life as earl of Pembroke, a great landowner with estates in Normandy, England, Wales and Ireland, and as regent of England during the minority of John's son, Henry III. The path he took began with tournaments, and it was here that he first made his mark. Not surprisingly the verse biography, composed soon after William's death, tells the story of his career on the tournament field with loving detail.

The tournament was, indeed, training for real war, not the formalised jousting of the later Middle Ages that film-makers have made so familiar. In the joust, knights carrying lances charged at each other. Each knight had to swerve at the last moment to avoid a head-on collision with his opponent, while at the same time couch his lance tightly to his side so that the blow was struck with all the weight and momentum of his horse behind it. If, in swerving aside, he moved his head or used his arm to thrust at his opponent, the blow had little or no effect. It was a technique that required split-second timing and horsemanship of the highest order – an ideal exercise for an exhibitionist knight.

In real war, lances might be used during the pursuit of a defeated enemy or during the opening stage – the joust, as it was called at the time – of a battle, but they soon splintered or were dropped. Most charges were delivered as flank attacks, not head-on as in the lists. In any event, very few battles were won by a massed charge of heavily armoured knights. The charge almost never worked against well-disciplined infantry. Horses are too sensible to risk impaling themselves on a hedge of spears. Battles nearly always turned into a series of mêlées in which both cavalry and infantry were involved, with victory going to the side that better co-ordinated the two arms. Consequently the mêlée was at the heart of the tournament. In major tournaments, foot soldiers armed with spears and bows could be used as a screen behind which the knights could withdraw and wait until they saw an opportunity to make another attack. Tournaments were not confined within enclosed lists but ranged over several square miles of ground, taking in villages, woods and vineyards, all of which were likely to suffer collateral damage.

In mêlées between knights, whether in battle or in the tournament, the overwhelming bulk of the fighting was done with sword and mace. It was William the Marshal's ability to take literally resounding blows on his helmet and return them with interest, like a woodcutter chopping down oaks, wrote the author of the *History*, that started him on the road to being a tournament champion. After one tournament he was found at the blacksmith's, kneeling with his head on the anvil while the smith beat his helmet back into shape so that it could be removed.

The kind of fighting that took place in tournaments and war was determined by the type of armour the combatants wore, in particular the expensive armour of the well-heeled knight. He wore a knee-length mail shirt, known

as a hauberk, made of interlinked metal rings, slit back and
front to facilitate riding and worn over a padded under-
garment, with mail mittens and mail leggings, known as
chausses. On his head he wore a padded cap; and over this,
to protect his neck, a mail hood and a helmet. If he was
technologically up to date this would be the great helm,
cylindrical and flat-topped. It had only a few narrow slits
for seeing and breathing, but gave the head much better
protection against missile weapons – above all arrows and
crossbow bolts – than did the old conical form of helmet
familiar from the Bayeux Tapestry. High-quality body
armour was becoming more widely available in the twelfth
century and it is this that explains the rise of the tournament. Without such armour it would have been an impos-
sibly dangerous war-game.

Although the knight was carrying a heavy weight of
metal, it was so well distributed that he could move freely
– at any rate, for a while. It did not take much exertion,
however, tightly encased as he was, for body heat and sweat
in his eyes to take their toll. Battles and tournaments tended
to be fought in bursts of activity, with long pauses for the
participants to catch their breath and plan what they might
do next. It was almost impossible to kill or even wound a
really well-armoured knight. The only way to do it was
with a sword or knife thrust through the eyehole of the
helmet or some other chink in the armour. In battle soldiers
used narrow killer-knives; in tournaments they did not. That
apart, the arms and armour used in twelfth century tournaments and battles were virtually identical. It was not until
the later Middle Ages that specially designed weapons for
tournament and joust became available. Despite all the high-
quality armour though, the tournament was a desperately

bruising business and the knight who participated was, like
a motor racing driver today, taking grave risks. If his horse
fell in a mêlée or he was knocked off by a rain of blows,
he was in danger of being dragged or trampled to death.
This was how King John's brother, Geoffrey of Brittany,
was said to have died at a tournament in Paris in 1186.
There were other risks in tournaments too. As in war, you
might be captured, and if you were then you lost your
horse and armour to the victorious knight. You might even
have to pay a ransom as well. It was thanks to his tournament winnings that the thick-skulled William Marshal won
fortune as well as fame.

But success in tournaments depended upon more than
good armour and a strong right arm. William was a master-
player in a team game. Victory and prizes were won not
so much by the jouster's display of individual prowess as
by groups of knights learning to fight together as a unit.
As in battle, the more knights in your team the more likely
you were to win. All was fair in the tournament, as in war.
If one knight became separated from the rest of his team
he might find four or five opponents bearing down on
him at once, and one of them might knock him down
with a blow from behind. If thrown from his horse, there
was no nonsense about letting him remount. It was thought
to be extremely clever tactics when one team pretended
not to be taking part in the tournament, and only joined
in late in the day when all the other knights, having played
on and off since soon after sunrise, were exhausted. William
became so skilful a team leader that he was taken on as
the player-manager of the team nominally captained by
Henry the Young King (as Henry II's eldest son was known).

Such strenuous war-games when so much was at stake

could easily degenerate into hot-tempered battles fought
in deadly earnest. Some kings worried about plotting and
rebellion when they saw knights meeting together in arms.
Henry II banned tournaments in England as a threat to
public order, so knights who wanted the exercise had to
go to the continent, to the borders of Normandy and
beyond, where there was reckoned to be a good tournament about once a fortnight. In England, during King
John's youth, the only sorts of tournaments were the
pseudo-jousts arranged every Sunday in Lent outside the
gates of London. Here the young citizens, on horseback
and armed with shields and blunted lances, could play at
being knights. If the court was in residence at Westminster,
then young courtiers, men attached to aristocratic households but not yet knighted, joined in, seeking every opportunity to show off. After Easter there came, according to
William FitzStephen, another chance to break a lance.

> A strong pole is set mid-stream and a shield tied to it. A
> young man with a lance stands at the prow of a boat which,
> powered by oars and the river's flow, is driven at the pole.
> If the lance splinters on the shield, he keeps his footing
> and has triumphed. But if his lance strikes the shield with-
> out breaking he is thrown into the river as his boat speeds
> on by. Although two rescue boats are on station to save
> him from drowning, his misfortune causes great mirth to
> the crowds watching from the galleries on the bridge.

In a cold winter, too, Londoners grabbed the chance to
stage an impromptu joust on ice. Two youths, armed with
poles, ran head-on at each other over the ice, to be sent
spinning and sliding away by the force of their collision,

lucky if they escaped with scrapes and bruises. Real knights probably watched such townsmen's entertainments with amusement – yet they may have contributed to London's ability to muster a substantial military force, of which William FitzStephen was justly proud.

When Richard I became king he encouraged the real thing in England. He designated five places as official tournament sites: the fields between Salisbury and Wilton in Wiltshire, between Warwick and Kenilworth in Warwickshire, between Brackley and Mixbury in Northamptonshire, between Stamford and Warinford (probably in Suffolk), and between Blyth and Tickhill in Nottinghamshire. According to William of Newburgh, 'the famous king Richard, observing that the extra training of the French knights made them more fearsome in war, decided that English knights should be able to learn from tourneying the art and customs of real war so that the French would no longer be able to insult them as crude and lacking in skill'.

Tournaments were repeatedly condemned by popes and other churchmen, but in Newburgh's words, 'knights were keen to acquire military fame and the favour of kings so they treated the Church's prohibitions with contempt.' When William Marshal was on his death-bed, in 1219, he was told by a priest that he would get to heaven only if he restored all his ill-gotten tournament winnings. The old warrior – he was now in his seventies – retorted that that was impossible: 'If because of this the kingdom of heaven is closed to me, I can do nothing about it, for I can't return those things. I can only commend myself to God, repenting my sins. Unless the clergy want my damnation they can ask for no more than that. But their teaching must be false, or else no one would be saved.'

The most famous battle of the age was fought in north-east France in 1214 at Bouvines, between Lille and Tournai. On one side there was an allied army composed of English troops commanded by John's half-brother, William Longsword, earl of Salisbury, with German and Flemish troops led by the German king and emperor, John's nephew Otto IV, and by the counts of Flanders and Boulogne. On the other side was the French army led by Philip Augustus. The allies had about 1400 knights and 7000 or so infantry. Philip had about as many knights and a thousand or two fewer foot-soldiers. In these circumstances a battle was the last thing Philip had wanted, but he was intercepted in a tactical situation which gave him very little choice. Reluctantly he decided to stand and fight.

As soon as the battle horns announced that fighting had started, King Philip's chaplain William the Breton and another royal clerk began to chant the psalm *Benedictus dominus deus meus qui docet manus meas ad proelium*. Other clerks took a more active part. On Philip's side the cleverest soldier and in effect the French battle commander was Guérin, the bishop-elect of Senlis. Philip's cousin, the bishop of Beauvais, was also present – by chance, said William the Breton. He happened – also quite by chance, William reiterated – to have a mace in his hand, and he used it to good effect. It was against canon law for a churchman to shed blood, so a mace was the 'clever' weapon to use. The bishop was a famously enthusiastic warrior, but as a churchman he should not have fought at all – hence William's insistence that his participation in the battle was entirely fortuitous.

Arms and armour were similar on both sides. Together with the mace, the beautifully balanced, tapered sword was the knight's main weapon. From the time the armies were within bowshot, both sides moved so quickly to engage hand to hand that there was little space or time for the archers to exercise their customary skills. Although not yet employed in the numbers that the English would later in the Hundred Years War, many of the bowmen of 1200 had bows as long and as powerful as those used to such devastating effect by their successors on the field of Agincourt (1415). At Bouvines the infantry used chiefly spears and knives, although William the Breton complained about the 'hooks' (presumably something like billhooks on long poles) used by some Flemish and German infantrymen to pull knights off their horses. Both armies used the skills and disciplines practised in tournaments. Cavalry contingents riding in close order under the banners of their lords charged the enemy lines whenever and wherever they saw an opportunity to disrupt them.

Because it was almost impossible to kill a well-armoured man, there were few fatalities among the knights at Bouvines. One, Stephen of Longchamp, was regarded as very unlucky when a knife thrust through the eyehole of his helmet pierced his brain. William the Breton accused the enemy of employing long, slender knives of a new design. In fact, both sides used them. It was difficult, though, to get close enough to your enemy to find the chinks in his armour. This is how William saw the killing of one Flemish knight, Eustace of Malenghin: 'The French surrounded him. One man grabbed his head holding it between his arm and chest, then ripped off his helmet, while another knifed him under the chin.' To kill a wealthy knight it was often necessary to wrestle him to the ground first – and then, naturally, you might prefer to spare his life in return for a fat ransom. At times indeed, as William the Breton makes clear, there would be moments of chaos as your own soldiers, almost oblivious to the battle going on around them, fought each other for possession of a rich prize.

The crisis of Bouvines came when a large force of German infantry, armed with spears and iron hooks, crashed into Philip's own division, fighting under the royal standard, golden fleur-de-lis on an azure field. The king was pulled to the ground. If it had not been for the superb quality of his armour, said William, he would have been killed then and there. One of his knights, Peter Tristan, jumped off his horse and covered the king with his own body, until more knights of the royal household arrived to kill the relatively poorly armoured German infantrymen. Then in a French counter-attack, Otto IV was nearly taken. A French knight grabbed the bridle of his horse. Another lunged at him with a knife. His first blow rebounded off Otto's armour; the second, as the emperor's horse reared up, went through the horse's eye. In its agony the horse broke away, carrying Otto to safety, before it collapsed. In this kind of fighting, and even though expensive war horses were now provided with armour, far more horses than knights were killed. According to one account, Otto had three horses killed under him during a ferocious mêlée.

The allied army, made up of its three separate contingents under their own commanders, was more easily driven into disarray than the French under unified royal command, and it was probably the better co-ordination of the French forces that decided the outcome of a bitterly fought battle. With great difficulty Otto managed to escape, but William Longsword and the counts of Flanders and Boulogne did not. They and dozens of other nobles on the losing side were carted off as prisoners. The count of Flanders was placed in the Louvre, Philip's newly completed great tower just outside the city walls of Paris.

The battle of Bouvines was an extraordinary event. Pitched battles such as this were very rare indeed. Although few knights were killed in battle, the king who committed his cause to battle was putting himself in jeopardy. William the Breton claimed that the allied leaders had sworn to kill Philip and had aimed their assaults directly at him. Since everyone knew that the surest way to win was to kill or capture the opposing commander, it must have felt like this. Commanders offered battle only when they were confident of the outcome, and in these circumstances their opponent was almost certain to avoid it. Philip Augustus fled from Richard I in 1194 and again in 1198, preferring the humiliation and the losses incurred in flight to the risk of total disaster that battle entailed. The standard handbook on the art of war in this period was the *De re militari* written by a late-Roman author, Vegetius. His advice on giving battle was quite simple: don't. 'Every plan is to be considered, every expedient tried and every method taken before matters are brought to this last extremity'. Successful commanders such as Philip followed Vegetius's advice. Battle was too chancy. A few hours, even a few minutes, of confusion or bad luck could undermine the patient work of years. Henry II never risked one. In Europe even so famous a soldier as Richard the Lionheart only fought in one. In a long lifetime of campaigning Philip too fought only one pitched battle, the battle of Bouvines.

Yet these were all kings who went frequently to war. If they were not seeking battle, then what were they doing?

Their aim was to win control of enemy territory, and first and foremost that meant capturing castles. Castles were, it was said, 'the bones of the kingdom'. Had Philip lost Bouvines but escaped, Otto and his allies would still have faced the problem of capturing his fortresses. New and better siege-engines called trebuchets, capable of hurling larger rocks, were being brought into use at this time, but castles remained hard to take. Even after their walls had been breached by artillery bombardment, casualties in a direct assault were so high that it was rare for troops to risk it – despite the incentive of the unrestricted plunder of castle or town that, should they succeed, they were allowed by the customs of war. A better way to win a castle was to take it by surprise. Another way was to capture the enemy commander, forcing him to surrender territory and strongholds in return for his release. But the best way to capture him was to take him by surprise. This was how King William of Scotland was captured at Alnwick in 1174, taken by surprise in the absence of most of his troops. In consequence he had to hand over Edinburgh, Roxburgh, Jedburgh and Berwick to English garrisons. This was how King John himself won his greatest success, at Mirebeau in 1202, when he captured Arthur of Brittany.

There was nothing unchivalrous about taking your enemy by surprise. On the contrary, this was exactly what the heroes of romances, idealised figures, tried to do. In the *Romance of Horn* many episodes illustrate the hero's cunning.

Horn led his young warriors into battle, leaving the old men behind on guard, for the old are tough and can endure great hardships when needed. Horn moved quietly along the bottom of a valley. He had ordered his troops to make no sound. The enemy had no inkling of the fight ahead of them. They heard Horn's battle-cry and were in the thick of it before they realised what had happened.

On another occasion Horn's skill was to lead the enemy into a trap.

> They came on with confidence, heading straight for where Horn's fleet was anchored. But when they saw it, they lost heart, like men who knew they were doomed. Then they realised that their deaths had been planned by Horn, for they saw that they were outnumbered, a few against many. If they could have found a way out, they would have taken it, but they were now surrounded.

In warfare speed of movement is vital. As Vegetius put it: 'Courage is worth more than numbers, and speed is worth more than courage.' But, obviously, you had to know in which direction to move – as Horn's enemies apparently did not. Good information was equally vital. If enemy forces were anywhere in the vicinity, it was crucial to send out frequent fast-moving reconnaissance patrols. They were so important indeed that the best generals, commanders such as William the Conqueror and Richard Coeur de Lion, chose to go on patrol themselves, despite the risks involved.

If there was no prospect of taking the enemy by surprise, then the tried and tested way of making war against him was to ravage his land – which meant destroying his economic resources, the fields and flocks of his people. According to Vegetius, this was the essence of war. 'The main and principal point in war is to secure plenty of provisions for oneself and to destroy the enemy by famine. Famine is more terrible than the sword.' The twelfth-century *Chanson des Lorrains* includes a vivid description of how it was done:

> The march begins. Out in front are the scouts and incendiaries. After them come the foragers whose job it is to collect the spoils and carry them to the great baggage train. Soon all is in tumult. The farmers, having just come out to their fields, turn back, uttering loud cries. The shepherds gather their flocks and drive them towards neighbouring woods in the hope of saving them. The incendiaries set the villages on fire and the foragers sack them. The terrified inhabitants are either burned or led away with their hands tied to be held for ransom. Everywhere bells ring the alarm. A surge of fear sweeps over the countryside. Wherever you look you see helmets glinting in the sun, pennons waving in the breeze, the whole plain covered with horsemen. Money, cattle, mules and sheep are all seized. The smoke billows and spreads, flames crackle. Farmers and shepherds scatter in all directions.

The term for this kind of raid into enemy territory was a *chevauchée*. Its purpose was well known: in the words of *The History of William the Marshal*, 'When the poor can no longer reap the harvest from their fields, then they can no longer pay their rents and this, in turn, impoverishes their lords'. As the description in the *Chanson des Lorrains* indicates, ravaging and foraging were operations which involved the dispersal of small bodies of troops over a wide area – 'the whole plain'. Troops so engaged were themselves highly vulnerable to attack, so once again it was essential to be well informed about enemy troop movements. Patrols had to be sent out on reconnaissance and to guard the foragers. In war a clash between opposing patrols, a dog-fight between small bands of cavalry, was the kind of fighting a knight was most likely to engage in. It was here that all his tournament practice paid off.

Even campaigns in which castles were the intended targets began with ravaging, an attack on the castle's economic base. This is how a late twelfth-century author, Jordan Fantosme, envisaged William of Scotland invading the north of Henry II's England as the ally of Louis VII.

> *Let him destroy your foes and lay waste their country*
> *By fire and burning let all be set alight*
> *That nothing be left for them, either in wood or meadow*
> *Of which in the morning they could have a meal.*
> *Then with his united force let him besiege their castles.*
> *Thus should war be begun: such is my advice*
> *First lay waste the land.*

The *chevauchée* alone was not enough. Ultimately wars were decided by sieges. It was in sieges rather than in battle that both archers and crossbowmen really came into their own – and sieges were many times more common than battles. When a siege was laid, some of the besiegers would entrench themselves in siege-works, but others would remain mobile. A rapid response force had to be ready to take immediate advantage of any opening created by a sortie by the defenders. The besiegers also had to send out well-armed patrols to guard their own supply lines and their foraging parties, all the more vital if the siege turned into a long drawn-out blockade intended to starve the defenders into surrender. Even this kind of struggle of attrition remained a war of movement, both in the preliminaries to siege and during the siege itself. In medieval warfare there were few pitched battles, but countless minor skirmishes in which small groups of brave men fought like teams in a tournament. William Marshal, the flower of chivalry, was an acknowledged master of this kind of war.

CHAPTER 7

Hunting in the Forest

All forests which have been afforested in our time shall be disafforested at once.

Magna Carta, Clause 47

During King John's lifetime nearly a third of England was forest. Only three counties, Norfolk, Suffolk and Kent contained none. It was possible to travel from the Wash to the Thames at Oxford, and from Windsor to the Hampshire coast without once leaving the forest. The whole of Essex was forest. But the fact that the whole county – towns, villages, farms, the lot – was so designated means, of course, that at that time the word 'forest' meant something quite different from what it does now. Some forest then we would recognise as such, the Forest of Dean, for example, or Sherwood Forest. Knaresborough Forest was described as 'a vast and terrifying solitude'. Such places were the refuges of outlaws – the 'Greenwood' of Robin Hood – and the homes of hermits. Here too were the last retreats of animals that were gradually being hunted to extinction, such as the wild boar and the wolf. And there were some tracts of forest, in this sense of the word, in Essex. No fewer than twenty-five wild boars and twelve feral cattle were recorded as having been taken in the county between 1198 and 1207. In law the wild boar was reserved for the king, but the wolf was regarded as vermin. King John offered five shillings for a wolf's head as an incentive to engage in the life and death struggle which the historian Robert Bartlett describes as 'the fight between human beings and wolves, England's fiercest and second fiercest mammals'.

But much of the forest was ordinary inhabited countryside. By declaring an area of land to be forest, the king created a royal monopoly over the management and distribution of resources previously enjoyed by local lords and tenant farmers. This process had started with the Norman Conquest. According to the Anglo-Saxon Chronicle, William the Conqueror 'set up great game-reserves and he laid down laws for them. Whosoever killed hart or hind was to be blinded. He forbade hunting the harts and the boars. He loved stags so very much, as though he were their father.' Condemning human beings to death or mutilation for the offence of killing wild animals seemed appalling to most thinking people, but ever since the Norman Conquest the kings of England had gained a reputation for tyrannical behaviour and nowhere more so than in the measures they took to protect their forests. William of Newburgh criticised Henry I for punishing poaching as severely as homicide. But in the Assize of Woodstock, a royal ordinance issued at Woodstock, one of his favourite hunting lodges, Henry I's grandson, Henry II, announced that in future forest offences would be punished not just by fines 'but by full justice as exacted by my grandfather'. The Assize of Forest, promulgated on Richard I's authority in 1198, set the penalty for killing deer as removal of the offender's eyes and testicles. According to the author of the *Histoire des ducs de Normandie*, in John's reign the deer felt so safe that when approached they merely ambled gently away. The records of forest courts suggest that in fact kings were much more interested in taking their subjects' money than their lives or body-parts. So lucrative, indeed, were the profits of forest justice that later kings continued William I's practice of declaring large tracts of land as forest. Henry II did this on a vast scale and by the end of his reign, 1189, the royal forest had reached its maximum extent.

A forest administration was established under a Chief Forester and his deputies. There were the foresters and verderers, officers responsible for policing the forest and attending forest courts; there were the regarders, who made inspections of the forest. All were supervised by the justices of the forest, who were sent round the country on 'forest eyres' to try offenders against forest law. Hunting without permission was forbidden. Dogs kept in the forest were 'lawed': three claws were cut off the fore paw so that they could not chase game. Clearing and cultivating land in the forest could be done only with permission – particularly exasperating in an age of rising population. A perpetual rent had to be paid to the crown for newly cultivated land. When one woman had an unauthorised ditch dug around her own land, it was confiscated, and it cost her a hundred marks to buy it back. (A mark was worth two-thirds of a pound, i.e., 13s 4d, or about 67p.) The right of local farmers to pasture their animals in the forest was strictly controlled and could be withdrawn at will. When the Cistercians offended King John he ordered his foresters to keep out their flocks and herds. In 1200 twelve Cistercian abbots prostrated themselves at the king's feet, begging him to allow their animals back in.

A landowner could chop down a tree so long as it was for his own use, and not for sale, but even then he had to be careful not to overstep the mark. According to Henry II's treasurer, Richard FitzNigel, 'If a man standing on the stump of an oak or other tree, can see five other trees cut down around him, that is regarded as "waste". Such an offence, even in a man's own woods, is considered so serious that even an officer of the Exchequer cannot be excused but will have to pay a fine proportionate to his means.' If an offence occurred and no offender could be identified and prosecuted, a whole community might find itself in trouble and forced to pay a fine. Whenever a king was in need of cash, he sent round another forest commission. In 1175 Henry II raised over £12,000 by this means alone – and that at a time when the total royal revenue audited by the English Exchequer rarely exceeded £20,000 a year. Forest officials were vilified, and it was taken for granted, apparently even by Henry II himself, that his Chief Forester, Alan de Neville, would go to hell. Lesser forest officials were also unpopular – but would themselves be in trouble if they did not do their job to the satisfaction of the justices of the forest. Even according to Richard FitzNigel, in forest justice it was not possible to say that something was truly 'just', but only that it was 'just according to the law of the forest'. Clearly this kind of justice was not thought of as just at all. When Henry II died, his widow,

Eleanor of Aquitaine, ordered that everyone held in prison for a forest offence was to be freed at once, and that everyone outlawed for forest offences was pardoned.

Richard I found other ways of making money out of the forest. In 1190 he 'disafforested' – declared no longer forest – 'that part of Bedfordshire that Henry I afforested' in return for £200. John took on this scheme and went even further. In 1204 he agreed to disafforest the whole of Cornwall for 2200 marks and the county of Devon for 5000 marks; and in 1207 Surrey for 500 marks. This could only have happened because people in those counties raised funds and petitioned for something they regarded as being of benefit to them all; such action helped to create county communities and was of great importance in paving the way for Magna Carta. It gave people experience of co-operative political action, of demanding reform and being prepared to pay for it. The Crown accepted that the extent of the forest could be a matter for negotiation – and this too would be a feature of Magna Carta. But both Richard and John continued to profit from the forests and forest eyres in the old ways. Indeed they and their foresters could not resist what looked like sharp practice. People who had paid to have their district disafforested could not have been happy with the order that those who lived outside the forest, but within two leagues of it, should none the less be required, on pain of fine, to attend forest courts. In Magna Carta Clause 44 John had to acquiesce in the ending of this practice.

At Runnymede in 1215 the baronial reformers demanded that forests should be taken back to the state they were in at the accession of Henry II together with the abolition of what they called the 'evil customs of forests and warrens'. This was a radical demand for the partial destruction of the royal forest, and for control of what remained. The iniquities of the royal forest system united rich and poor alike in opposition to the Crown. But even at Runnymede John was not prepared to concede so much. In Clause 47 of Magna Carta he agreed that all forests added during his reign were to be disafforested. But that was to give very little ground. It had been his father who had made the massive additions. Evidently the Magna Carta negotiations had involved some hard bargaining about the extent of the forest.

After John's death, a council governed the realm on behalf of the nine-year-old Henry III. It was largely composed of men who had been loyal to John – but on the subject of the forest they shared the views of those who had taken up arms against him. In 1217 they issued a charter dealing exclusively with the matter of the forest. In this charter they made a series of substantial concessions. All forests added by Henry II, Richard and John were disafforested; every freeman was to have the right to develop his own land within the forest so long as this did not cause damage to a neighbour; in future no man was to lose life or limb for taking the king's venison.

This last promise takes us straight into the world of Robin Hood, the outlaw hero who, in the words of the earliest surviving ballad, 'A Gest of Robyn Hode':

'alway slewe the kynges dere
and welt them at his wyll'

meaning that he did just as he liked with them. And what he liked was to set them before visitors, willing and unwilling, as 'fat vension', washed down with good red wine and fine brown ale. Sherwood Forest was already known as a haunt of robbers and poachers. When King John appointed Ralph FitzStephen to the forestership of Sherwood, he granted him, as one of the perks of the job, permission to keep for himself the chattels of all robbers and poachers taken within the forest bounds.

It was not, however, until the sixteenth century that a historian, John Mair, first expressed the opinion that the celebrated Robin Hood and Little John lived during the period of King Richard's absence on crusade and John's bid to usurp the throne. The earliest known ballads of Robin Hood place him in the reign of a King Edward. Whenever he lived – if he ever did – the ballads, by placing Robin Hood and his Merry Men in the 'Greenwood', create a world of sylvan liberty, of freedom from the oppression of corrupt officials and unjust laws. Yet nowhere was the contrast between tyranny and freedom sharper and more keenly felt than in the forest. In the imaginary world of the ballads the king himself was always portrayed in a good light. He goes into Sherwood in disguise and falls in with the outlaws. When, eventually, Robin recognises him, he kneels before him, and the king sets everything right. In the real world, the king fought hard to preserve intact the arbitrary power of forest law.

No one took greater pleasure in the freedom of the 'real' forest than the tyrant of forest law. In *The Dialogue of the Exchequer*, an earnest administrative handbook explaining the workings of the government's financial system, Richard FitzNigel wrote: 'It is in the forests that kings can forget for a while the nerve-racking stress of the court and breathe instead the pure air of freedom.' But these were pleasures and freedoms appreciated by many. The ballad 'Robin Hood and the Monk' opens:

> *In summer when the woods are bright*
> *And leaves are large and long*
> *It is full merry in fair forest*
> *To hear the birds in song.*

In a passage describing a hunt setting out on a winter's morning, the great medieval English poem *Sir Gawain and the Green Knight* conveys something of that same enjoyment of the open air.

> *Wonderfully fair was the forest-land, for the frost remained*
> *And the rising sun shone ruddily on the ragged clouds,*
> *In its beauty brushing their blackness off the heavens.*
> *The huntsmen uncoupled the hounds by a forest,*
> *And the rocks resounded with their ringing horns.*

Lords and even gentry possessed their own warrens, parks for small game such as hare and rabbit – the latter a recent immigrant, having arrived in southern England from the continent. They also had deer parks, enclosed within a combination of ditch, bank and fence, hedge or wall which allowed deer to jump into the park but not out of it. In 1215 there might have been as many as three thousand parks in the country. Lords were often granted the right of 'free warren', that is to say the exclusive licence to kill the lesser game on their own estates; the lesser game meant foxes, wild cats, otter, badger, squirrel and roe deer as well as hares and rabbits. But no one except the king, his guests and his foresters were allowed to touch fallow or red deer, or wild boar. Forest law was designed as much to reserve the pure air of freedom for the exclusive use of the king and his friends as it was to fill the royal coffers.

Not all nobles and kings loved hunting. John's brother Richard I had little time for it, and John's son, Henry III, little taste for it. Even so, Henry III still maintained, as did all kings, a large hunting establishment for the supply of meat to his household. For Christmas 1251 Henry III ordered his huntsmen to send to York 430 red deer, 200 fallow deer, 200 roe deer, 200 wild swine from the Forest of Dean, 1300 hares, 395 swans, 115 cranes – and much smaller game besides. John's father, Henry II, had been a passionate huntsman, off at the crack of dawn for a day on horseback. A cynical courtier, Walter Map, reckoned that Henry was afraid of getting fat. (He also alleged that Henry's judges encouraged him to go hunting so that, unchecked by the king, they could get on with the business of fleecing litigants.) John, too, was addicted to the pursuit. On 6 March 1204 he gave orders that wild animals should be trapped in the New Forest and sent to Normandy with his horses, dogs and falcons so that when he got there he could be sure of good hunting. The intended purpose of his trip was to drive out invading armies, but evidently that did not mean, so far as he was concerned, that he would be giving up his hunting.

The wealthy kept packs of hunting hounds, as well as hawks and falcons. They hunted deer either on horseback with hounds, which pursued the quarry to its death, or had game driven into enclosures known as 'hayes' or 'deer hedges', and then used bow and arrow to bring them down. Hunting arrows had triangular heads with long, heavy barbs, designed to cut through muscle and tissue, wounding and fatally weakening even a powerful stag. The bloody excitement of the kill comes across powerfully in *Sir Gawain and the Green Knight*:

Lo! The shimmering of the shafts as they were shot from bows!
An arrow flew forth at every forest turning,
The broad head biting on the brown flank.
They screamed as the blood streamed out, sank dead on the sward,
Always harried by hounds hard on their heels,
And the hurrying hunters' high horn notes.

Hunting wild boar was less one-sided, though it was commonly the hounds, not the huntsmen, who lost their lives. A confrontation between Richard I and 'a very fierce wild boar armed with very long tusks', as described by the chronicler Richard, prior of Holy Trinity, London, makes it clear that training in handling weapons and horsemanship was among the uses of hunting.

'At the king's shout, it retreated a little then turned to face its pursuer. Foaming at the tusks, with its raised hairs bristling and ears erect, it worked itself up into a fury. The king shouted, but it did not move. It held its ground, spinning round to face the admiring king as he rode around it. The king attacked, thrusting a lance into it as though it were a hunting spear. The lance snapped and the boar, maddened by the wound, made a powerful charge. The king, having virtually no space or time to manoeuvre, put spurs to his horse and it jumped across the boar's charge so that only its rear trappings were hit. They attacked each other again. As the boar charged, the king cut into the back of its neck with his sword. He then spun his horse round again, and cut the boar's throat.

Hunting, whether with dogs or birds, had long been regarded as a pursuit in which the practitioners could demonstrate great skill and learning. For King Alfred the Great, the art of hunting came second only to the art of government. King John's son-in-law, the Hohenstaufen Emperor Frederick II, was so dedicated to falcons and falconry that he wrote a Latin treatise on the subject, *De Arte Venandi cum Avibus*, On the Art of Hunting with Birds. In this he claimed that falconry was nobler even than other forms of hunting because of the greater difficulties encountered and skills required if the birds were to be cared for, handled and trained to return to the falconer's wrist.

According to Frederick, the taming of a newly caught falcon began with it being carried around for twenty-four hours without feeding it until it was exhausted. Most kings and aristocrats employed professional falconers to train and take charge of their birds. Henry II, for example, bought some property in Winchester and had it converted into mews with rooms for the falconers. The highest prices were paid for birds imported from Norway, Ireland and Scotland. All experts agreed that birds hatched in captivity were nowhere near as good as those born in the wild and trained to hunt by their parents. John was a keen falconer. He regularly went hunting on Sundays and saints' days and then gave alms to the poor, the wealthy man's comfortable – and useful – penance. On one occasion he went hawking on the Feast of Innocents, 28 December, and paid penance at the rate of feeding fifty poor people for each crane his birds brought down; on that day he did penance for seven cranes. He cared, too, about the feeding of his birds of prey, ordering that his favourite falcon, Gibbun, was to be 'well fed with plump goats and good hens, with hare once a week'.

King Henry I was so expert a hunter that he was said to be able to tell the number of tips on a stag's antlers by examining its hoofprint. According to John of Salisbury, Thomas Becket's intellectual friend who became bishop of Chartres, the science of hunting was the only science the aristocracy knew. It was a science with its own laws, 'the rules of the chase', and with its own fashionably fluctuating terminology. We get a flavour of this in the early thirteenth-century poem *Tristan*. The hero was still just a precocious boy when he interrupted a huntsman on the point of carving up a newly killed hart:

> 'How now, master, what is this? In God's name stop! What are you at! Whoever saw a hart broken up in this fashion?'
>
> The huntsman fell back a pace. 'What do you want me to do with it then, boy?'
>
> 'In my land they excoriate a hart'.
>
> 'Dear boy, what is "excoriate"? I have never heard the word, and unless you show me I shan't have the slightest idea what it means.'

Tristan proceeded to demonstrate his mastery of the art of butchering venison 'according to the rules of the chase', allowing the poet to demonstrate in great detail his own mastery of the arcane jargon of hunting.

The English aristocracy objected to the forest as an arena for exploitative royal jurisdiction, but they undoubtedly did like it as a game reserve and hunting ground. In the 1217

Forest Charter Henry III's minority council allowed a freeman to clear land in the forest, but placed a significant
condition on that freedom. He was not to do it if it involved
destroying cover in which game lived. The Forest Charter
also specifically stated that archbishops, bishops, earls and
barons travelling through the forest in answer to a summons
to court were permitted to kill one or two beasts, and in
the cases where there were no royal foresters nearby to see
what they were doing, they were to sound their horn to
give notice that they were openly taking what was permitted. Even when discussing great affairs of state and the
reform of the realm, they made it plain that they intended
to have their hunting.

CHAPTER 8

The Church

The English church shall be free, and shall have its rights undiminished and its liberties unimpaired.

Magna Carta, Clause 1

In Magna Carta's first clause King John proclaimed that 'We have granted to God and by this our charter have confirmed, for us and for our heirs in perpetuity, that the English church shall be free, and shall have its rights undiminished and its liberties unimpaired'.

In 1215 the phrase 'the freedom of the English church' meant freedom from secular power and, above all, from the power of the Crown. For many centuries, most churchmen had in practice been appointed by laymen. It had been laymen, whether kings, nobles or lords of a manor, who had given the land on which churches were built, and who had often paid for the building. Unless churchmen were prepared to give up their estates, which they were not, it seemed to laymen only right that they should retain some control over the selection of those who were going to enjoy the fruits of their generosity.

In the eleventh century a group of ecclesiastical reformers, many of them monks, had begun to argue vehemently that churchmen should be 'freely' chosen by other churchmen. The reformers argued that the soul was more important than the body and so priests, who looked after people's souls, were more important even than kings since kings ruled only over people's bodies. If churchmen were to have the rights they demanded, freeing them, as it were, from the control of lay society, then they should be able, the reformers argued, to show that they were superior to laymen. Priests should do this by keeping themselves sexually 'pure'. Yet for centuries most priests had had wives and children, and many were themselves sons of priests. When a reforming archbishop of Rouen told a meeting of his clergy that they should give up their wives, he was answered by a hail of stones. Wives and laymen, those who cared for bodies, held strong cards and at first nearly everyone regarded the reformers' assaults on long-held assumptions about sex, property and power as absurdly unrealistic. But, very slowly, the reformers began to achieve parts of this astonishingly radical programme. One of the churchmen who campaigned hardest for the celibacy of priests and for what they called the 'liberty of the church' was Pope Gregory VII (1073–1085). In consequence the reformers, especially the hard-line ones, are usually known as Gregorians.

In England the most dramatic episode in the struggle for the liberty of the Church had come soon after John's birth: the murder of Thomas Becket on 29 December 1170. By the middle of the twelfth century men of goodwill had come to realise that Church–State relations bristled with intractable problems that could only be managed in a spirit of compromise. But in 1162, in an uncompromising demonstration of traditional royal power, Henry II had pushed through the selection of his trusted friend and adviser Thomas as archbishop of Canterbury. In the eyes of respectable churchmen, Becket, who had been chancellor since 1155, did not deserve the highest ecclesiastical post in the land. He had enjoyed a notably extravagant lifestyle and he had led troops into war. This was no way for a man with his mind on higher, spiritual things to behave.

But no sooner had Thomas been 'freely elected' than he set out to prove, to an astonished world, that he was the best of all possible archbishops, a true Gregorian. Right from the start he went out of his way to oppose the king. For example he objected to the marriage of Henry's younger brother to a wealthy heiress on the grounds that they were too closely related. Naturally Henry felt betrayed, and an angry Henry was not a pretty sight. On one occasion when he thought another servant had betrayed him he 'fell into his usual rage, flung his cap from his head, pulled off his belt, threw off his cloak and clothes, grabbed the silken coverlet off the bed, and started chewing pieces of straw'.

He chose the issue of 'criminous clerks' as the one on which to settle accounts with Thomas. Like many laymen, Henry resented the way in which clerks who committed felonies could escape capital punishment by claiming trial in an ecclesiastical court. He demanded that they should be unfrocked by the Church and then handed over to the lay courts for punishment. Becket's resistance to this only made Henry press harder for a definition of royal rights over the Church. He summoned Becket before a royal court to answer trumped-up charges. In 1164 Becket fled to France and appealed to the pope. He stayed in exile for five years, but when Henry wanted to secure the succession by having his eldest son Henry crowned, a new urgency entered the seemingly interminable negotiations between king, pope and archbishop. Becket returned to England, and was greeted by cheering crowds. In a rage Henry spoke the words that caused four of his knights, William de Tracy, Reginald FitzUrse, Hugh de Morville and Richard le Bret, to ride off to do what they felt sure he wanted: silence the archbishop.

On the afternoon of 29 December 1170, after an alcoholic lunch, they were shown into his chamber in the archiepiscopal palace at Canterbury. Becket, sitting on his bed, did not rise to greet them, although he knew they had come from the king. After a shouting match they stormed out and armed themselves. When they attacked the palace, Becket's advisers managed to move him into the cathedral, but he would not have the door barred. A church was not a castle. With swords in their right hands and axes, for breaking down doors, in their left, the four knights entered, shouting, 'Where is the traitor?'

'Here I am. No traitor to the king but a priest of God. What do you want?' Reginald FitzUrse tried to arrest him, and Becket resisted, calling FitzUrse a pimp. The knights struck out at the archbishop's head with their swords. After the murder they searched the palace, looking for documentary evidence of treason, and helped themselves to all the loot they could find.

The deed shocked Christendom. Overnight Becket's tomb became the most popular shrine in England, visited each year by thousands of pilgrims, such as those described two hundred years later in Chaucer's *Canterbury Tales*. The murder proved to be wonderfully inspiring for the makers of pilgrim badges: badges depicting the sword that struck him down or the head which received the fatal stroke, badges in the shape of a T for Thomas, badges showing the ship in which he had returned from exile. The variations were endless. No other shrine matched Becket's Canterbury for the sheer numbers of souvenir badges it produced, or for the inventiveness of their designs. In 1173 Pope Alexander III declared Becket a saint. This was canonisation in record time.

No doubt Henry deeply regretted what had happened. He certainly had little choice but to say sorry. In 1174 he arrived to do penance at Thomas's tomb in Canterbury Cathedral. The bishop of London explained to all present why the king was there: 'Our lord the king declares before God and before the martyr that he did not have Saint Thomas killed, nor did he command that he should be assaulted, but he freely admits that he did use words that resulted in Thomas being murdered.' Garnier of Pont-St-Maxence tells us what happened next.

'The king took off his cloak, and thrust his head and shoulders into one of the openings of Saint Thomas's tomb. He would not, however, take off his green tunic so that I do not know if he was wearing a hair shirt underneath. Then he was flogged, first five strokes of the whip from each of the prelates present and then three lashes from each of the 80 monks. When he had been disciplined and by atonement was reconciled to God, he withdrew his head from the tomb and sat down on the dirty ground with no carpet

or cushion under him, and he sang psalms and prayers all
night, without getting up for any bodily need.'

At first sight it seems that the medieval church had the
capacity to humiliate even kings of England. But we should
be careful before we jump to conclusions. We might think,
for example, that anyone, even a head of state, responsible
for a murder should be punished, and that, if anything,
Henry II was being treated lightly – especially since he did
not have to take off his green tunic. According to one of
Henry's household clerks, Peter of Blois, many knights were
ashamed to do penance in public, believing it showed either
weakness on their part or hypocrisy. On the other hand,
for a politician then, as now, to apologise occasionally can
be a shrewd move, and no politician ever said sorry more
theatrically than Henry II. Few have been able to exploit
their penance more cleverly. On 13 July, the day after
Henry's penance, his great enemy, King William of Scotland,
was captured while leading an invasion of England. It
seemed that, once again, Henry had God on his side.

In theory, twelfth-century kings of England conceded the
Gregorian principle that bishops and abbots should be freely
elected by the canons of a cathedral chapter or the monks
of an abbey, but in practice they continued in their old
ways, controlling appointments just as before. That kings
wanted to control ecclesiastical appointments is hardly
surprising, given how wealthy and well integrated into society the Church was. A conservative estimate of total annual
ecclesiastical income in England puts it at about £80,000.
Although churchmen themselves were forbidden to take
part in war, the bishoprics and major Benedictine abbeys
were required to provide the Crown with contingents of

troops, amounting to about one-seventh of the total service owed by English landowners.

The practice, as opposed to the theory, of appointment was expressed in the writ allegedly sent by Henry II to the monks of St Swithin's Priory, the cathedral chapter of Winchester, in 1173: 'I order you to hold a free election; nevertheless I forbid you to elect anyone save Richard my clerk.' As this writ indicates, the electors were expected to wait until they had received the king's permission before they proceeded to choose a new bishop or abbot. In the meantime, the Crown collected a church's revenues during the period of the vacancy. Not surprisingly, there was a tendency for vacancies to be prolonged. After the death of Hugh of Lincoln in November 1200, John kept the see vacant until July 1202, making a net profit of £2649. Generally, the electors chose the kind of men the king wanted. It was, after all, very much in the interest of cathedral canons and monks that their churches were governed by men who had the king's confidence. Thus Richard had been able to secure the free election of his trusted counsellor, Hubert Walter, as archbishop of Canterbury – the supreme embodiment of the civil servant-prelate and generally considered one of the ablest royal ministers of all time, the man who sent Longbeard to the scaffold. When John came to the throne he appointed Hubert as chancellor, and relied on him to administer England while he tried to keep Philip Augustus at bay in France. When Hubert died in June 1205 John is said to have remarked, 'Now I can be king at last.'

After Hubert's death who was to be the next archbishop of Canterbury? Both the monks of Canterbury and the bishops of the province of Canterbury claimed the right to participate in the election, and appealed to Rome. John persuaded both parties to agree to a postponement of the election, but a group of monks went ahead and secretly elected their sub-prior, Reginald, who at once set off for Rome. Then, in the king's presence, the monks remaining at Canterbury thought better of it, and in December 1205 elected John's candidate, John de Gray, bishop of Norwich. Innocent III rejected the bishops' claim to have a voice in the election of their archbishop, but ruled both elections invalid, and invited the monks at Rome to hold another election. With the monks still split between Reginald and Gray, Innocent proposed a new candidate, Cardinal Stephen Langton. The Canterbury monks at Rome acquiesced. John, however, refused his assent. As he saw it, the traditional royal right of patronage had been infringed, and Stephen's long career as a teacher of theology at the embryonic university of Paris meant that he was guilty of association with his greatest enemy, the king of France. Both sides dug their heels in. Innocent consecrated Stephen as archbishop; John refused to allow him into England and seized the estates of Canterbury. Innocent responded by imposing an interdict on England in 1208. It lasted until 1214. For those six years no church bells rang out over England. This eerie silence carried a message. The clergy were on strike.

The papal interdict meant that the regular church serv-ices on Sundays and feast days were banned, and that no one could be buried in consecrated ground. Horror stories were told of corpses being put into coffins and hung from trees in the churchyard until they could be buried later on. New burial grounds had to be opened up in the expecta-tion that they would be consecrated when the interdict was over – as indeed they were, eventually. But it was not a general strike. Parsons were instructed to continue to baptise infants and give confession and absolution to the dying. In 1209 the pope allowed monasteries and nunneries to celebrate mass once a week – although it had to take place behind closed doors, and with no ringing of bells. In an impressive demonstration of papal authority Innocent III's orders were carried out. There is no record of any priest celebrating Sunday mass – the only regular religious ritual most people attended.

Churchmen put a high value on mass: 'The value of this sacrament is beyond all estimation', wrote the Cistercian Baldwin of Ford, who became archbishop of Canterbury in 1184 and died on crusade in 1190. The regular Sunday sermon was thought to be vital for the religious instruction of parishioners. Yet during the six years that the interdict lasted there is not a shred of evidence that any lay person protested. Not a mouse squeaked. There are no recorded petitions begging John to end his quarrel with the pope so that the churches might be re-opened. To all appearances no one – except the clergy – gave a damn.

In fact, parsons continued to provide important services uninterrupted by the interdict. Priests continued to hear confessions, which should have helped them reconcile village enemies. They probably continued to bless animals and crops – and curse caterpillars. Miracles recorded at the tombs of the bishops of Lincoln, Salisbury and Worcester suggest that many shrines remained open, and that pilgrims continued to visit them. Tithes continued to be paid; in each parish the government appointed four men to guard church barns. Church courts continued to sit. Church building continued.

The history of marriage shows clearly the extent and

the limitations of the interdict. Marriage had originally been a purely secular affair – one for arrangement between the two families concerned – but it was one that the Church was now increasingly trying to influence. In 1200, for instance, an English church council held at Winchester decreed that no marriage should be contracted without a public announcement in church on three occasions and that no one should be joined in matrimony except publicly in front of the church and in the presence of a priest. The custom was that the banns should be read on the three Sundays preceding the wedding, and that the wedding itself would take place at the church door. It has been suggested that the magnificent porches of some churches were built so that the wedding party could keep dry on a rainy day. During the wedding ceremony the husband handed his wife a symbolic object, a knife for example, to signify that he was giving her a dower. The wedding itself was now over, and it was only at this point that the wedding party went into the church to hear mass. During the mass the newly-weds lay prostrate before the altar, while the altar cloth was held over them. During communion the husband would give the kiss of peace to the priest and afterwards kiss the bride.

The interdict meant that for six years there were no marriage services in church, but this did not prevent weddings taking place. The decrees of the Council of Westminster tell us how the Church would have liked marriages to be celebrated, but that is all. In fact the Church had already decided that what made a marriage valid in law was the freely given exchange of marriage vows between two people of age (that is, twelve or over) who were not within the prohibited degrees. Twelfth-century canon law defined the prohibited degrees of kinship as meaning that any couple who were within seven degrees, that is who shared great-great-great-great grandparents, could not enter into a valid marriage. However, this created an absurd situation in which virtually every marriage was vulnerable to the charge of incest. At the Lateran Council of 1215 Innocent III tackled the problem by reducing the number of prohibited degrees from seven to four. Much later, in 1537, the papacy reduced them again to two for South American Indians, then for blacks in 1897, and finally for the Roman Catholic population at large in 1917.

For a marriage to be valid it did not matter where the vows were exchanged. It did not have to be at the church door, though doubtless most people liked a traditional wedding. It could just as well have been in a garden, in a shop, in a tavern or in bed. No witnesses or public ceremony were necessary. The couple who freely exchanged vows did not need, though it was undoubtedly desirable, the consent of their parents, guardians or lords. The canon law of marriage – the lover's charter, it has been called – remained the law in England until 1753, when Parliament decided that all marriages had to be performed by a clergyman and that no one under the age of twenty-one could marry without the consent of parents or guardians. After 1753 the young eloped across the border to Gretna Green where the old law remained in force. During the interdict perfectly valid marriages continued to be contracted, maybe even at the church door. It is just that there could be no wedding mass.

Indeed, in most ways church business went on as usual. It was just the regular celebration of mass that came to a standstill. Churchmen lamented what they saw as the people being cut off from the way to salvation. But there is no evidence that laymen saw it like this. The mass itself centred upon the consecration of bread and wine by the priest and the doctrine of transubstantiation meant that in the eucharist Christ's body and blood were literally consumed. But there was no doctrine that produced more scepticism than this. Many had doubts. The reason Thomas Becket raced through mass, according to his friend and biographer Herbert of Bosham, was to minimise the sceptical thoughts that tended to trouble him at that point. This, of course, in Herbert's eyes, was proof of just how important transubstantiation was: it was precisely at this moment that Lucifer chose to send his sharpest darts.

In any event the eucharist – the sacrament commemorating the Last Supper, in which bread and wine are consecrated and consumed – for all its theoretical importance, only rarely involved the laity. Priests who suggested that lay people should take communion three times a year, at Easter, Whitsun and Christmas, were unusually keen. At the Lateran Council in 1215 Pope Innocent III decreed that all adults should take communion at least once a year, at Easter – which suggests that many were in the habit of taking it less often. Evidently it was not hard to be deprived of so occasional a ritual. It looks as though during the six years of the interdict, priests continued to perform the services the laity valued, and stopped doing only those about which ordinary people cared little. One preacher, Alexander Ashby, complained that at what was supposed to be the most solemn moment of Mass, the hush as the priest prayed silently before consecrating the eucharist, a hubbub of gossip and joking commonly broke out among the congregation.

In many ways the interdict suited John well. He confiscated all the assets of the clergy on the grounds that since they weren't doing their job they had no right to enjoy their endowments. In practice it would have been impossible for the government to take over the direct administration of so much property all at once, so he allowed the clergy to buy back the privilege of managing their own lands. He arrested and imprisoned the wives and mistresses kept by many, then released them back into the custody of their 'husbands', again in return for cash – and to the amusement of many who were diverted by the spectacle of theoretically celibate priests being willing to pay up so that they could continue sinning.

In 1209, when the pope saw that the interdict was having no effect, he excommunicated John. Excommunication, with a ritual extinction of lighted candles, was intended to be awesome, and certainly frightened some. John's pious son, who became Henry III, would have been frightened – but John was indifferent; many of his friends and allies on the continent were themselves excommunicate. All the bishops except for Peter des Roches of Winchester left England in obedience to papal commands rather than have dealings with an excommunicate, but John could govern without them. 'He neither feared God nor regarded man; it was as if he alone were mighty upon earth,' wrote a Canterbury monk at the time. Negotiations between king and pope continued in a desultory fashion but were broken off in 1211. By this time, with no less than seven bishoprics and seventeen abbacies vacant, John's profits from the English Church were so great that he preferred being excommunicate to reaching a settlement. In 1213 when a settlement was reached at last, he agreed to compensate the

Church for the financial loss it had suffered. This was assessed at 100,000 marks (approximately £66,666). The English clergy – inevitably – said this was an underestimate, and in any case it excluded the king's income from vacancies. In the event only about a third of the sum was ever paid, but from John's point of view the interdict had been wonderfully lucrative.

So why did it end? Why did John finally give way and accept Langton as archbishop of Canterbury? It was because King Philip of France was massing troops and a fleet in north-east France in preparation for an invasion of England and John thought that if he submitted to the pope, then the pope would tell Philip not to invade. Having decided to give way, John did it in style. On 15 May 1213, near Dover and in the presence of a papal legate, he swore allegiance to Pope Innocent III, and promised to pay the papacy an annual tribute for England and Ireland:

> Being in great need of God's mercy and having nothing but ourselves and our kingdoms that we can worthily offer to God and the Church, we desire to humble ourselves for Him who humbled Himself for us even unto death, we offer and freely yield to God, to his holy apostles Peter and Paul, to the Holy Roman Church our mother, and to the lord pope Innocent and his catholic successors, both the whole kingdom of England and the whole kingdom of Ireland.

These were more than mere words. The public ceremony of submission in the presence of most of the baronage of England was looked upon by many at the time – as well as by many more in the centuries since – as a humiliation.

'To many it seemed an ignominious and monstrous yoke of servitude,' wrote the well-informed Barnwell chronicler.

But John was quite right in his anticipation of the pope's response. Innocent was delighted. He ordered the king of France not to invade the dominions of so obedient a son of Holy Church. And, indeed, there was no French invasion of England in 1213. Which is why many historians have described John's submission to the pope as a Machiavellian masterstroke of policy. But Philip's plan for an invasion of England required that he first of all deal with John's ally, the count of Flanders. He went ahead with this, but his invasion hopes were dashed by an English fleet that destroyed and looted his own fleet as it lay at Damme, the port of Bruges. Rather than risk seeing more of his ships fall into English hands, he burned those that remained and called off the invasion. It was this naval action, not the pope, that saved England in the summer of 1213. What the story of interdict and invasion shows is that the pope could command his clergy – they obeyed the interdict – but that he had no power in secular politics. When Stalin asked his famous question: 'How many battalions does the pope have?' he knew the answer. Kings such as Philip of France knew it too, and even John would discover it in 1215 and 1216 as, first, his barons rebelled against him, then French troops invaded his kingdom, both in defiance of papal prohibition.

CHAPTER 9

King John

John, by the grace of God, King of England, Lord of Ireland, Duke
of Normandy and Aquitane, Count of Anjou.

Magna Carta, 1st paragraph

On Ascension Day 1199 John, under a canopy held by four barons, was led in procession into Westminster Abbey. On his knees before the high altar he swore, as his brother had ten years earlier, a triple coronation oath: to observe peace, honour and reverence towards God and the Church all the days of his life; to do good justice and equity to the people entrusted to his care; to keep good laws and destroy any bad laws and evil customs that had been introduced into the land. He was then undressed down to his underpants and shirt, his chest bared. The archbishop of Canterbury, Hubert Walter, anointed him with consecrated oil – known as chrism – on head, chest and hands. (Until Victoria all subsequent monarchs were anointed in this way. She was anointed only on head and hands.) To protect the sacred oil on his head and keep it there for the next seven days, John wore a coif held in place by straps tied under his chin. When his coffin was opened in 1797 the antiquaries who inspected his remains were puzzled to find him wearing what they took to be a monk's cowl; more likely he was buried wearing his coronation 'coif of unction'. It was the act of anointing that conferred upon the new ruler the divine sanction for his kingship, and it was this, rather than the crowning, which lay at the heart of the coronation service.

> *Not all the water in the rough rude sea*
> *Can wash the balm from an anointed king.*

Next John was dressed in the royal robes and handed the sword of justice by the archbishop. He was then led back to the high altar where the archbishop adjured him not to receive the crown unless he truly intended to keep the oaths he had sworn. John replied that, with God's help, he intended to observe them all. Then the archbishop crowned him. The crown was so heavy that the king could wear it only with two earls helping to take the weight. Finally the archbishop gave him the sceptre and the virge, a rod of office, and John mounted the throne. He sat there while Mass was celebrated. When it came to the offertory the bishops led him again to the high altar, on which he placed one mark of the purest gold, then returned him to his throne. Mass over, still wearing the crown and carrying the sceptre and the virge, he processed back to the palace for the coronation banquet. For that he was permitted to wear a lighter crown and robes. Twenty-one fat oxen had been purchased in

Worcestershire and driven to Westminster in time for the banquet.

King Philip of France invaded Normandy the moment he heard that Richard I was dead. The leading barons of Anjou had rejected John and declared in favour of his nephew Arthur, the posthumously born son of Duke Geoffrey of Brittany. After some hesitations the barons of Normandy and England decided to follow Richard's recommendation, and his mother's urging, and recognise John as their ruler. The one plausible alternative, Arthur, was still only twelve. But after the way in which John had betrayed his father, his brother and his allies, it is hard to see how anyone could have welcomed his accession or trusted him. While he rushed from Normandy to England to be anointed and crowned king, he left his affairs on the continent in the capable hands of his mother, Eleanor of Aquitaine (the older she got the more influential she became). She had helped secure Richard's release from his German captivity; now she helped her youngest son to the throne. John was in a hurry: he had landed on the Sussex coast on 25 May and his coronation took place just two days later, on the twenty-seventh.

Once back in Normandy at the head of a large army drawn from English resources, John held the upper hand. His strongest card lay in the network of alliances built up by Richard's diplomacy and which remained intact. In August 1199 at an assembly at Rouen, no fewer than fifteen French counts, headed by Flanders and Boulogne, pledged their support for John. Richard's influence and financial help had secured the throne of Germany for his nephew Otto of Brunswick, and Otto too was ready to support him against Philip of France.

Arthur drew the obvious conclusion: his bid for power beyond the borders of Brittany was going nowhere, so in September he and his mother, Constance, met John at Le Mans and submitted to him. No sooner had they done this than they changed their minds. During the night they slipped out of Le Mans and fled to Philip's court. Someone had warned them that John was planning to seize them and throw them into prison. Since they had been welcomed by him and were now protected by the 'peace of the king's court', it would have been a gross breach of accepted political convention for him to arrest them – yet they evidently believed the near incredible. What could have led them to believe John capable of such deceit? Presumably someone had reminded them of his record of treachery. And whatever he had or had not planned in September 1199, the sudden night flight of Arthur and Constance from Le Mans must have reminded everyone of his past and reactivated fears that had lain dormant.

In the next few weeks the coalition that had seemed so powerful began to crumble. The count of Flanders led a large group of nobles who now decided that they would go on crusade rather than be drawn into a war as John's ally. Soon only Otto IV was still prepared to support him. With the resources of England at his disposal, John at least remained strong enough to persuade Philip, in the treaty of Le Goulet, sealed in January 1200, to withdraw his support for Arthur – but only by surrendering strategically vital territories, including Evreux, and the alliance with Otto. This was a high price to pay for peace and the resolution

of the succession dispute in Anjou. As early as the first year
of his reign John's reputation for unreliability had cost him
dear. From now on if he were to rule his possessions in
peace he depended upon the trustworthiness and benevo-
lence of the king of France – who had learned to despise
him. It is significant that Philip's first action on hearing of
Richard's death had been to send an army to reoccupy
Evreux, the town in which John had massacred French
soldiers a few years earlier. Two years later he invaded again,
and this time he did not call a halt until he had occupied
Normandy, Anjou and Poitou.

Most contemporaries believed that the seeds of this disaster lay in John's decision to marry Isabella of Angoulême.
On John's accession to the throne he persuaded some bishops to dissolve his marriage to Isabel of Gloucester, and
sent an embassy to Portugal to negotiate for the hand of
a Portuguese princess. On 24 August 1200, however, and
before his envoys had returned, he married the daughter
and heiress to Audemar, count of Angoulême. This came
as a surprise to many – and above all to Isabella's then
fiancé, one of the most powerful lords of Poitou, Hugh de
Lusignan. In view of the great strategic importance of the
semi-autonomous county of Angoulême there was much
to be said, from John's point of view, for a marriage to
Count Audemar's daughter. Suitably compensated, the
Lusignan family might have been reconciled to their loss
of Angoulême, but John had not the slightest intention of
placating them. His scornful treatment of their pleas for
justice led them to appeal for help to King Philip, who
was delighted to seize the opportunity.

Did John simply make a disastrous political calculation?
Or had sexual desire come into his sudden decision to marry

Isabella? Some chroniclers believed that John had been capti-
vated by her beauty. She cannot have been more than fifteen,
and was more likely twelve or less: the well-informed chronicler Roger of Howden tells us that Hugh de Lusignan had
postponed his wedding to Isabella because she was not yet
sexually mature. But in August 1200 John would not wait,
even though this meant placing his envoys to Portugal in
an embarrassing and potentially dangerous position.

King Philip summoned John to appear before his court
– not, of course, as king of England, but as duke of Normandy
and Aquitaine – to answer the charges brought by the
Lusignans. His refusal to attend eventually resulted, in April
1202, in Philip pronouncing the confiscation of all the lands
he held in France. Philip offered Poitou, Anjou, Maine and
Touraine to Arthur and arranged for him to marry his daughter Mary. While Philip and the count of Boulogne advanced
into eastern Normandy, Arthur and the Lusignans trapped
Eleanor of Aquitaine at Mirebeau in Poitou.

John was at Le Mans when he heard the news. Le Mans
and Mirebeau were over eighty miles apart – but John
covered the distance in forty-eight hours. Arthur and his
followers were enjoying a relaxed breakfast – pigeons were
on the menu that day – confident that Eleanor could not
hold out for much longer and that her son was still far away,
when their quiet meal was interrupted by John's sudden
arrival. Arthur and more than two hundred barons and
knights were taken prisoner. On 1 August 1202 John had
defeated his enemies more emphatically than ever his father
or brother had been able to do. 'God be praised for our
happy success,' he wrote, in exultation. But his greatest military victory led rapidly to his greatest political mistake.

His triumph had been possible only with the help of

two of the most powerful barons of Anjou, Aimeri of Thouars and William des Roches, yet he denied them any voice in deciding what should be done with the prisoners. Worse still, he treated all his prisoners badly. According to *The History of William the Marshal*, 'He kept his prisoners so vilely and in such evil distress that it seemed shameful and ugly to all those who were with him and who witnessed this cruelty.' Since there was hardly a noble family in Poitou who did not have a kinsman or friend among the knights taken at Mirebeau, John offended a whole province. Within a month Aimeri of Thouars and William des Roches had switched sides. As in September 1199, the reminder of what John was capable of had led to a swift change of heart. In October 1202 Aimeri and William captured Angers, the chief city of Anjou. In January 1203 John withdrew into Normandy leaving Philip to sail, unchallenged, down the Loire and take possession of Anjou, Maine and Touraine.

Soon John's reputation came under further attack as rumours spread about the fate of his nephew, Arthur of Brittany. What happened to Arthur cannot be known with certainty, but almost certainly he was murdered on John's orders. Some believed that John himself carried out the murder when drunk. If he did have Arthur killed, he committed a heinous crime by the chivalrous political standards of his day, and even if he did not, the fact that it was alleged that he had and that he could not or would not dispel these rumours undermined his defence of Normandy.

John stayed in the duchy throughout most of 1203 and great barrel-loads of English silver were sent across the Channel to him. But it did little good. Few trusted him and in return he trusted almost no one. *The History of*

William the Marshal portrays an obsessively suspicious king desperate to ensure that no one knew in advance where he was going next:

> When he left Rouen he had his baggage train sent on ahead secretly and silently. At Bonneville he stayed the night in the castle, not in the town for he feared a trap, believing that his barons had sworn to hand him over to the king of France . . . in the morning he slipped away before daybreak while everyone thought he was still asleep.

Unable to trust his barons, the only people he half-trusted were those who depended upon him for their pay, the bands of mercenaries commanded by professional soldiers such as Girard d'Athée and Louvrecaire. But it was not enough to have professional forces at his disposal; to defend Normandy he needed the support of the Norman political nation, and that he did not have. Indeed, his reliance on mercenaries only made things worse. 'Why', asked the author of the *History of William the Marshal*, 'was John unable to keep the love of his people? It was because Louvrecaire maltreated them and pillaged them as though he were in enemy country.'

Although John tried to organise the defence, he did so from a safe distance, never prepared to go where the fighting was. In December 1203 he sailed to England, leaving Normandy to its fate. The strategically vital castle of Château-Gaillard surrendered in March 1204; Rouen, the capital of the duchy, followed suit in June. When, on 31 March 1204, Eleanor of Aquitaine died in her early eighties, the lords and prelates of Poitou rushed to Philip's court to pay homage to him. The king of Castile sent in an army to overrun Gascony. In the south-west of France it was as if John did not exist. He talked about returning to Normandy, but in fact during the first six months of 1204 he sent very little money and did nothing effective. Who could feel confidence in such a king, or wish to risk life and limb for a man so patently reluctant to risk his own? As a contemporary troubadour put it,

> No one may ever trust him
> For his heart is soft and cowardly.

Despite the one stunning success at Mirebeau, his overall military record in those years earned him a new nickname: Softsword. He was believed to be capable of murdering his nephew, but not of committing himself to the defence of his ancestral possessions. And so he lost them.

One explanation offered by contemporaries for John's feeble defence of Normandy in 1203 cited his relationship with his wife. According to Roger of Wendover, at Christmas 1202 John made no preparations for the coming struggle, despite the desperate military situation on the Norman frontier, but preferred to enjoy sumptuous feasts with his queen, then stay in bed until lunch-time. When the king of France's armies invaded Normandy in 1203, John took no counter-measures but stayed in Rouen with his queen, acting as though he were bewitched. According to the well-informed author of the *Histoire des ducs de Normandie*, when the French captured John's strongholds, he 'acted as though he did not care, and devoted himself to the pleasures of hunting, falconry and to the queen whom he greatly loved'. Even so, the same author believed John could not resist teasing her with references to the gossip that it was his marriage that lay at the root of his political misfortunes: "You see, lady, what I have lost for your sake!" To which she retorted, "And for you I have lost the best knight in the world." In all she bore John five children between 1207 and 1215. After his death, Isabella returned to Angoulême, and in 1220, now about thirty, she married again. This time she chose her own husband: Hugh de Lusignan, the son of the Hugh to whom she had been betrothed twenty years earlier.

In 1205 John made an effort to restore his authority. He assembled a large fleet at Portsmouth, but the English barons refused to sail with him, forcing him to cancel the expedition, which showed just how low his reputation had sunk. He did better in 1206, managing in June to take a fleet to La Rochelle. Philip had moved to defend Normandy when he heard John was preparing to sail, and this gave John a free hand to consolidate his hold on Angoulême – Isabella's father had died in 1202, so the county was now hers – and drive the last Castilian troops out of Gascony. In September 1206 he marched north to ford the Loire and ravage Anjou. But as soon as news came that Philip was advancing towards him with an army, John beat a hasty retreat. In October the two kings agreed on a truce based on the status quo. Something had been salvaged from the wreck of empire, but the territories John had recovered – Gascony and the south-west of Poitou – were ones in which Philip had shown no interest. From now on Normandy and the Loire Valley, the heartlands of the Plantagenet empire, remained firmly under the control of the kings of France.

The loss of these dominions was a disaster for John. He had come to the throne in 1199 as ruler of the most powerful state in Europe. For almost two hundred years England had been just one country within a wider empire: first a part of Cnut's North Sea empire; then, after 1066, a part of the cross-Channel empire established by William of Normandy; and from 1154 onwards a part of Henry II's still wider empire. John had inherited vast dominions that stretched from Ireland and the Scottish border in the north to Gascony and the Pyrenees in the south. Hence the opening words of Magna Carta, and the opening words of all charters issued by King John: 'John, by the grace of God, King of England, Lord of Ireland, Duke of Normandy and Aquitaine, Count of Anjou.'

But by 1215 this list of titles had a hollow ring. Although he still claimed to be the rightful ruler of Normandy and Anjou he had lost them. Although he still claimed to be duke of Aquitaine, he had lost much of the duchy. In the history of English kingship the losses of 1203–4 marked an important turning-point. Until then Henry II, Richard and John had been French princes, who also ruled, and occasionally visited, England. After 1204 the centre of gravity shifted. John and his descendants became kings of England, who occasionally visited Gascony. For this reason many English historians in more recent centuries have looked upon the defeats of 1203–4 as a 'Good Thing'. To influential authors, such as Thomas Macaulay, the French possessions were an encumbrance that endangered the sound development of a truly English state and culture:

Had the Plantagenets, as at one time seemed likely, succeeded in uniting all France under their government,

it is probable that England would never have had an independent existence. The revenues of her great proprietors
would have been spent in festivities and diversions on the
banks of the Seine. The noble language of Milton and
Burke would have remained a rustic dialect, contemptu-
ously abandoned to the use of boors. England owes her
escape from such calamities to an event which her historians have generally represented as disastrous.

It was, as the Victorian historian William Stubbs put it, 'the
fortunate incapacity of John' that enabled England 'to cut
herself free from Normandy'. (Ironically for French historians too, 1203–4 has been regarded as a 'Good Thing':
authors such as Michelet saw Henry and his sons as rulers
of an 'English empire', as Englishmen who had to be driven
out of France. This kind of language is often found in
guidebooks for tourists in France even today.)

What really mattered in the eyes of historians like
Macaulay and Stubbs were events that took place in England:
the murder of Thomas Becket, the making of English
Common Law, Magna Carta. But no one should think that
John and his advisers breathed a sigh of relief and thanked
God that they could now concentrate on the 'real business'
of a king of England. On the contrary, John became an
English king of England only by defeat and against his will.
In his own time 1204 represented a catastrophic loss of
reputation. His attempt ten years later to restore his repu-
tation led directly to the making of Magna Carta.

For five years after 1206 John concentrated on extending his authority within the British Isles and on raising and
hoarding money. If he were ever to recover his reputation
and the lost dominions he had to build up a massive war

chest. By 1212 he had something like 200,000 marks (£133,333) stored away safely in royal castles such as Bristol, Gloucester, Devizes, Marlborough and Corfe. This was well over 30,000,000 silver pennies, perhaps as much as half of the total of coin normally in circulation. It was time, he decided, to recover his lost empire. He set about rebuilding the coalition he had sacrificed in 1200. Barrel-loads of silver were sent to the Low Countries and Germany. In the Rhineland it was said to be 'raining sterling' thanks to his largesse. A fleet and an army began to assemble at Portsmouth. But in July 1212 John's optimistic plans were shattered by a Welsh revolt. To counter this he shifted the muster of his naval and land forces from Portsmouth to Chester. He was at Nottingham on 14 August when he learned of a plot against his life. Trusting no one, he ordered his army to disband. An Exchequer official, Geoffrey of Norwich, was arrested and died in prison. Two barons, Robert FitzWalter and Eustace de Vesci, were clearly implicated in the plot and fled abroad. From those he suspected, especially the barons and knights of the northern counties, he took guarantees of loyalty in the shape of hostages and castles. A popular preacher, Peter of Wakefield, caused a stir by prophesying the imminent end of the reign. In a bid for popular support John promised to reform abuses of power by his sheriffs and forest officials. But he continued to treat English landowners with his usual cat-and-mouse mix of bribery and coercion, and from now on he went everywhere with an armed guard of crossbowmen.

John postponed his expedition to the continent to 1213, but was forestalled by Philip who announced that he would invade England that April. As the king of France prepared for the riskiest enterprise of his reign, he decided to set his life in order. 'The one thing for which he could justly be blamed', wrote his chaplain, William the Breton, 'was the fact that although he had treated his wife Ingeborg, daughter of the king of the Danes, honourably, he had not slept with her for more than sixteen years. Now that his invasion fleet was ready, the magnanimous king took her back into his grace. At this news all France rejoiced.'

To secure the backing of Pope Innocent III John decided to subject England to papal authority and pay Rome an annual tribute of 1,000 marks. At Innocent's insistence he agreed to allow FitzWalter and de Vesci to return to England. In order to meet the threat from France, he stationed a large army in Kent from 21 April. Thus, virtually the whole baronage witnessed the ceremony at which he surrendered his kingdom to the papacy on 15 May 1213 at Ewell near Dover. For those who believed the prophet John's reign ended here. But at least he was still on his throne on the anniversary of his coronation, 27 May, and he celebrated by having Peter of Wakefield and his son hanged.

A few days later he had even more to celebrate. With the loss of Normandy and its Channel ports to Philip Augustus, the once peaceful waters between England and France had been turned into a theatre of naval war. John had responded by continuing the work, initiated by his brother Richard, of building a war fleet and establishing a naval base at Portsmouth. The commanders of Philip's invasion fleet discovered this to their cost when English ships, commanded by William Longsword and Count Renaud of Boulogne, caught them as they lay at anchor in the harbour of Damme. Hundreds of French ships, heavily laden with stores and the personal belongings of many of Philip's barons, were plundered and set on fire. 'Not since the days of King Arthur had so much booty been seen in England,' wrote one author. And not only that: this naval victory cleared the way for John to return to France.

In June John ordered his army to sail with him to Poitou. But, as in 1205, the magnates refused to go, and the expedition had to be postponed again. Some northern barons, led by de Vesci, claimed that, as tenants-in-chief of England, they did not owe military service in Poitou. This group, increasingly prominent in the opposition, came to be known as 'the Northerners'. In February 1214 John disembarked at La Rochelle while William Longsword took an army to Flanders where he was joined by Otto IV and by the counts of Flanders and Boulogne. The strategy was a good one. A two-pronged attack from the south-west and the north-east was to force Philip to divide his forces. But John was gambling. Failure abroad could only add to the opposition he faced in England. Hence, the reports he sent back to England made the most of every success he achieved. In one he triumphantly announced that his old enemies the Lusignans had decided to submit. In reality he had persuaded them to change sides by making them an offer they could hardly refuse. He granted them the rich land of Saintonge and the strategic Isle of Oléron off the western coast of France, and he betrothed his daughter Joan to Hugh de Lusignan's son – also called Hugh. (It was this selfsame younger Hugh who, six years later, would marry his fiancée's mother, Isabella of Angoulême.) The extraordinarily high price John paid for Lusignan support in 1214 did at least mean that he could advance into Poitou and beyond. On 17 June he entered Angers unopposed.

Only two weeks later he was in flight. All it had taken was for Prince Louis of France to bring an army to close quarters for John to beat a hasty retreat. His version of events was that he had been betrayed by the Poitevins, and it might well be true that they were reluctant to risk life and limb for him. Despite this humiliation he had at least managed to keep his western army intact and so prevented the French from reuniting their forces. Unfortunately for John, this strategic success counted for nothing when his allies engaged Philip Augustus in battle at Bouvines on 27 July 1214 and were disastrously defeated. In the opinion of the author of *The History of William the Marshal*, forcing Philip to stand and fight had been a terrible mistake. Philip was now free to join his son and confront John in Poitou. All John could do was to sue for terms. On 18 September the two kings agreed on five years' truce. Allegedly it cost John 60,000 marks.

When he returned to England in October 1214 his coffers were empty. Moreover, the reforms he had promised in 1212 and 1213 resulted in a huge drop in royal revenue. His income in 1214 came to less than half of the amount collected in 1212; his days as a wealthy king were over. The battle of Bouvines had been decisive. Its political consequences were far-reaching in the Holy Roman Empire (Germany and Italy) as well as in France and England. Had John's troops and allies won, he would have returned to England in triumph, ready to launch a new expedition to reconquer his ancestral lands in France and punish those barons who had refused to help his war effort. Now he was in no position to do either. The gamble of taking the war to France while he was facing unrest in England had failed. In the words of the historian Sir James Holt, 'The road from Bouvines to Runnymede was direct, short, and unavoidable.'

CHAPTER 10

The King's Men

*To the archbishops, bishops, abbots, earls, barons, justiciars, foresters,
sheriffs, stewards, servants and all his officials and faithful subjects,
greetings.*

Magna Carta, 1st paragraph

At the heart of royal government was the king. 'Kings
are like God to their subjects,' wrote Henry of
Huntingdon, 'so great is the majesty of this earth's highest,
that people never weary of looking at them, and those that
live with them are looked upon as being above the rest of
mankind. No wonder crowds of women and children rush
to gaze at them, so too do grown men, and not only men
of a frivolous type.' Kings gave their subjects plenty of opportunity to gaze. They were constantly on the move, travelling incessantly, criss-crossing their dominions. This enabled
them to return the gaze, to keep an eye on local officials,
to hear complaints or requests from the local aristocracy
and clergy. In this way many of the king's subjects, in many

different places, got a direct sense of their ruler's will and personality.

John's father, Henry II, had put together a much larger empire than any earlier king of England. He was as much at home in Bordeaux, Poitiers, Angers, Le Mans, Caen and Rouen as he was in Winchester or London. Indeed, until John lost control of Normandy and Anjou in 1203–4, Henry and his sons spent more time on the roads of northern and western France than they did in England.

After 1204 John acquired more houses in England. By 1215 he had over fifty residences, castles, palaces and hunting lodges – about twice as many as his father and brother. He spent plenty of money having them extended and refurbished, and he moved rapidly from one to another, rarely staying more than two or three days in one place. During the king's absences – which, for many of his residences, was virtually all the time – his houses were looked after by a keeper, usually paid a penny a day, although keepers of the more important palaces were paid substantially more. At Westminster he was paid over £10 a year, while the keeper of the house and park at Woodstock received a salary of £15.

Take, for example, the month of March 1207. From the first to the third of the month John was at Geddington in Northamptonshire, a royal hunting lodge. On Saturday 4 March he was at Kimbolton in Huntingdonshire, the next day at Southoe and the next at Huntingdon. On the seventh he moved to Cambridge. By 9 March he was in Newport, Essex, on the tenth at Bardfield in Essex. He spent two days at Hallingbury (also in Essex), and on the thirteenth he went through London to Lambeth, then for two days, the fifteenth and sixteenth, he was at Farnham in Surrey.

He was at Freemantle in Hampshire for three days, then for another three days, the twentieth to the twenty-second, at Winchester. He spent a further three days at Clarendon and three days at Cranbourne in Dorset. He was at Poorstock in Dorset on 29–30 March and ended the month at Exeter. That month he stayed in sixteen different places. This was not unusual. He moved from one place to another around fifteen times every March, and averaged over thirteen moves a month throughout his reign. He spent only one month in England without moving, in November 1215 when he laid siege to Rochester Castle at the start of the war that followed Magna Carta.

Some of the places he stayed at in March 1207 he knew well. He visited Winchester about sixty times during his reign, Clarendon over forty times and Freemantle nearly as often. He averaged about a visit a year to Geddington, Farnham and Cranbourne. By contrast, so far as we know, he only visited Southoe, Huntingdon, Newport and Hallingbury the once, in March 1207. He sometimes expected one of his courtiers to put him up. At Kimbolton he enjoyed the hospitality of the justiciar, Geoffrey FitzPeter. At Southoe it was the turn of Saer de Quincy, newly made earl of Winchester. At Farnham, he stayed in the palace of Peter des Roches, the ultra-loyal bishop of Winchester. His love of hunting helped to keep him on the move. Geddington, Clarendon, Freemantle, Cranbourne, Poorstock were all hunting lodges – though Henry II's building work had turned Clarendon from a lodge into a hunting palace.

The king did not travel alone. Everywhere he went he was followed by courtiers, officials, servants, traders, petitioners and hangers-on of every description. At the centre of this crowd was the king's household. In part, this was an elaborate domestic service: cooks, butlers, larderers, grooms, tent-keepers, carters, packhorse drivers, and the bearer of the king's bed. This meant dozens of packhorses and a baggage train of ten or twenty carts and wagons, carrying his wardrobe, tents, kitchen equipment, barrels of beer and wine, his chapel and plenty of money. Chamberlains and chamber clerks looked after the money and treasures. Then there were the household menials – laundresses, chambermaids, scullions, footmen and grooms. Household knights and officials were paid an annual fee and daily wages according to the number of days they served. When in attendance on the king they were accompanied by their own friends and servants. Then there were the men who looked after the royal hunt: the keepers of the hounds, the horn-blowers, the archers – perhaps fifty or more on the hunting staff alone.

All of this took a great deal of organisation. Harbingers had to be sent ahead to arrange billets for the night, with two of the king's four bakers who had to make bread at the next stop. Arrangements had to be made for food and wine to be sent to the right place, or bought in the locality. King John, for example, had tuns of wine stored in fifteen castles; his butler was responsible for ensuring that a tun or two was waiting for the king wherever he stopped. It was not a case of the king's household travelling to where the provisions were and consuming them on the spot. On the contrary, huge quantities of food and drink had to be transported to wherever the king was heading next. When they knew in advance where the royal household was going, merchants could arrange to be there with their wares. In 1207 when the king left Exeter on 1 April, he turned east again, and after brief stays at Sherborne, Gillingham, Cranbourne, Clarendon and Freemantle, reached Reading on 11 April. Hugh de Neville, the Chief Forester, was travelling with the king and Hugh's own officials saw to it that his men and their horses were looked after. Hugh's clerks recorded the purchase of the following items at Reading:

Bread 3s 1½d; beer 1s 6½d; wine 1s 3d; herring 8d; whiting 9d; salmon 9d; hay 1s 1d; litter 1s 1½d; oats 2s 7½d; firewood 2½d; charcoal, 3d; shoeing the horses 9d.

Household purchases had a dramatic effect on local food-stocks and prices. The arrival of the royal household always caused disruption, but it was, on the whole, good for the local economy – so long as it did not stay too long in a place without the infrastructure to support it. A letter survives in which Edward I announced that he intended to spend Easter at Nottingham, and asked that local people should be comforted by his promise to leave as fast as he had come.

In theory the king's itinerary was planned in advance and well publicised. But events or simply the king's mood might cause a change of plan. Then all hell broke out. One of Henry II's courtiers, Peter of Blois, described the chaos that could occur:

If the king has promised to remain in a place for a day, and particularly if he has got a herald to make a public announcement of his intention, he is sure to upset all the arrangements by departing early in the morning. As a result you see men dashing around as if they were mad, beating the packhorses, running their carts into one another – in short it's hell. If, on the other hand, the king has ordered an early start, you can take it for granted that he'll sleep until midday. Then you'll see the packhorses loaded and waiting, the carts ready, the courtiers dozing, traders fretting and everyone grumbling. People go to ask the maids and doorkeepers what the king's plans are, for they are the only people likely to know the secrets of the court. Many a time the message would come from the king's chamber mentioning a city or town he planned to go to, and though there was nothing certain about it, after hanging about aimlessly for so long, we would all be roused up and comforted by the prospect of good lodgings. At once there would be such a clatter of horse and foot that all hell seemed let loose. But when our courtiers had gone ahead almost the whole day's ride, the king would turn aside to some other place where there was just enough accommodation for himself. I hardly dare say it but believe he takes a delight in seeing what a fix he puts us in. After wandering three or four miles in an unknown wood, often in the dark, we think ourselves lucky if we stumble upon some filthy little hovel. All too often there is a bitter quarrel over a mere hut, and swords are drawn for possession of lodgings that pigs would shun.

On one occasion Geoffrey de Mandeville, son of the earl of Essex, killed a servant of William Brewer, one of John's senior officials, in a brawl over lodgings in Marlborough. William complained to John, who swore that by God's teeth he would hang the killer. But Geoffrey was the son-in-law of the powerful Robert FitzWalter, lord of Dunmow in Essex and of Baynard's Castle in London, and he fled to him for protection. When Robert interceded on his son-in-law's behalf a blazing row broke out between king and baron, during which Robert told the king that if Geoffrey were to be hanged, two thousand knights would lace up their helmets and go to war. A few years later Robert became the commander of the rebels fighting for Magna Carta.

The king's household always included a number of barons, men such as William Brewer. Servants in the king's household, they were also the lords of great estates and masters of their own households. Through their influence, the authority of the Crown was carried into the localities. This informal power system was reinforced by the appointment of members of the king's household to local offices. In the early years of John's reign, for example, the sheriff of Nottingham was William Brewer, and at different times he was sheriff of eight more counties. Household knights, too, were often appointed as sheriffs or as constables of royal castles. They also constituted a rapid-response force capable of dealing with trouble that blew up unexpectedly. In the event of war the military department of the household was dramatically increased in size as more and more troops were brought on to the payroll and employed to garrison key castles. A household cavalry composed of knights and mounted archers was used as a main field force, while other household knights acted as captains of supplementary forces.

In his coronation oath, when John promised to do good justice and equity to the people entrusted to his care, there is no doubt that in theory this meant all of his subjects. But it meant especially those who had attended his coronation, and their friends and relatives. If a king could win the approval of the few dozen baronial families who constituted the small but powerful élite of medieval England, he would be a successful ruler. These families were not only his subjects, they were his tenants. In legal jargon they were tenants-in-chief: they held their estates from the king. In return for their tenancies, they were expected to serve and aid him. Essentially this meant they were to support him politically and, in time of war, give him military service and financial aid. A tenant-in-chief's heir had to pay a kind of inheritance tax, known as a relief, to take up his inheritance, while if he – or she – were under age, the king took both the minor and their estates into his custody to do with very much as he pleased. In these circumstances he controlled his ward's marriage. If there were no direct heirs then, after provision had been made for the widow – whose own remarriage was also subject to Crown control – the king could grant the land to whomever he wished. He had at his disposal not only offices such as those of sheriff or constable of a castle, but also heirs, heiresses and widows.

From Henry II's time lists were kept of the widows and wards in the king's gift, together with information that allowed the king to assess their market value and to check that the estates in his custody were being efficiently managed. Here, for example, is the first entry on a roll known as the 'Roll of ladies, boys and girls in the king's gift', a government record drawn up in 1185.

The widow of Everard de Ros, who was the daughter of William Trussebut, is in the gift of the lord king, and is 34

years old, and has two sons, of whom the first born is 13.
And the land is in the custody of Ranulf Glanvil. And her
dower land in Stroxton is worth £15 a year with this stock,
two plough-teams, 100 sheep and 3 pigs and one horse.
Not possible to increase its value.

This degree of control over the inheritances and
marriages of the richest people in the realm meant that
the king's powers of patronage were immense. When
Richard I came to the throne one of his first acts was to
give his father's old servant, William Marshal, the hand of
Isabel de Clare, heiress to immense estates in Normandy,
England, Wales and Ireland. At the time Richard and
William were standing at the foot of Henry II's still
unburied corpse in the church of Fontevraud in the Loire
Valley; as a fabulously wealthy ward Isabel was held for
safe-keeping in the Tower of London. On hearing the good
news from the king's own mouth, William rushed to get
the girl before anything could go wrong or the king could
change his mind. In his haste to board a ship at Dieppe
he fell off the gangplank, but he made it to London and
he got his bride. The king had, in effect, the power to
make a trusted servant a millionaire overnight. No head
of government in the West today has anything remotely
approaching the power of patronage in the hands of these
kings of England. This was why the royal court was the
focal point of the whole political system, a turbulent, lively,
tense, factious place in which men – and a few women –
jostled each other in desperate attempts to catch the king's
attention.

One of the clichés of the age was that life at court was
hell. According to Walter Map, Henry II was advised by

his mother Matilda to treat the business of political patronage like training a hawk.

> He should keep posts vacant for as long as possible, saving
> the revenues from them for himself, and keeping aspirants
> to them hanging on in hope. She supported this advice by
> an unkind parable: an unruly hawk, if meat is often shown
> it and then snatched away or hid, will become keener, more
> attentive and more obedient.

One inescapable problem was that in the nature of things
there were never enough offices, heirs, heiresses and widows
to go round. For every William Marshal who had reason
to be satisfied, there were bound to be several who were
disappointed. Every single act of royal generosity thwarted
someone else's hopes. Even so, at the mouth of this hell,
there were always hundreds desperate to enter.

It had long been standard practice for kings to use the
patronage system as a handy source of income. Ambitious
men offered money to obtain the good things the king
had to offer: office, succession to estates, custody of land,
wardship or an advantageous marriage. All these were to
be had at a price, and the price was negotiable. At times
there was a lively auction, and although the king was
certainly not required to accept the highest bid, it was an
area in which he could, if he chose, raise more money by
consistently driving harder bargains. John drove some very
hard bargains indeed. Geoffrey de Mandeville agreed to pay
20,000 marks for the hand of John's former wife, Isabel of
Gloucester. A northern baron, Nicholas de Stuteville,
offered 10,000 marks for the succession to his brother's
estates. Both Geoffrey and Nicholas felt that they had been

pushed too far. Both would be among the rebels of 1215. Magna Carta (Clause 2) addresses this source of tension.

> If when any of our earls or barons or other tenants-in-chief holding by knight service dies, his heir is of age and owes relief, then he shall have his inheritance on payment of the traditional relief, namely £100 for an earl's or a baron's barony, £5 at most for a full knight's fee, and anyone who owes less than the service of one knight shall pay less in accordance with the ancient custom of fiefs.

The importance of this issue is indicated by the fact that it was dealt with so early in the charter. Clauses three to seven tackle other aspects of the king's control over inheritance, wardship and marriage. Iconic statements about the freedom of the subject before the law or the king's duty of justice come in Clauses 39 and 40. In 1215 they counted for much less than the content of Clauses 2 to 7.

Clearly, patronage could be used as a way of squeezing the rich, but it was often more useful as an instrument of political control. Generally, the Exchequer made little or no effort to collect the sums offered by men seeking advancement. Often, indeed, the greater the sum owed, the less was actually paid. This was not slack government. It was a way of ensuring that many rich and influential people were permanently in debt to the Crown. The expectation that the Exchequer would not press too hard for payment meant that the politically ambitious sometimes offered more than they could afford. This gave them a powerful motive for serving faithfully; if the king came to distrust them, he might demand immediate payment of the debt – and if they could not pay up, their lands might be forfeit to the Crown.

All twelfth and thirteenth-century kings used this system to a greater or lesser extent, but none as blatantly as John. Because he was always suspicious of men's loyalty, he consciously set out to compel them to be loyal. In 1213 John de Lacy, constable of Chester and lord of Pontefract, agreed to pay 7000 marks in order to succeed to his father's lands. In setting out the terms of the agreement, John made open use of both carrot and stick. He gave de Lacy three years to pay, and agreed to let him off 1000 marks if he gave loyal service: the carrot. As a pledge for the payment de Lacy had to surrender his two most important castles to the king: the stick. In 1214 de Lacy went on the expedition to Poitou with John when many barons refused to do so. One castle was restored. In March 1215 he was one of the very few barons to vow to go on crusade with John; the next day all his debts were cancelled. In consequence John no longer had a financial stranglehold over him; at last he had some freedom of action. Two months later he joined the rebels. King John was now paying the price for having reduced the time-honoured bond of good lordship and faithful service to nothing more than a calculation of profit and loss.

Early in the reign, William de Briouze, one of John's closest associates, had offered 5000 marks for the lordship of Limerick in Ireland. For seven years he paid virtually nothing. Then he fell out of favour, and the Exchequer came knocking at his door. When he couldn't pay up immediately, John ordered one of his military captains, Girard d'Athée, to occupy William's estates in south Wales. The king then pursued him and his family to Ireland. William managed to escape to France but his wife and eldest son were captured — and disappeared from view. It was generally believed that they starved to death in one of John's prisons. According to John's own account, all this was merely 'action for non-payment of debt in accordance with the custom of our kingdom and the law of the Exchequer'. These words were hardly calculated to reassure the many other landowners in debt to him. From now on, too many members of the political élite saw his style of government as a threat to themselves and their families.

The élite were those people described in Magna Carta (Clause 14) as the 'archbishops, bishops, abbots, earls and greater barons', who received letters addressed to them individually when summoned to play their part in giving the king 'the common counsel of the realm'. One of the tasks Magna Carta imposed upon the sheriffs was that of ensuring that all the rest of the tenants-in-chief would be summoned too. Clearly assemblies at which the king received 'the common counsel of the realm' were envisaged as occasions of the greatest political importance, at which all the tenants-in-chief represented the whole nation. What were they expected to talk about? They were to be summoned, said Clause 14, 'for the assessment of an aid or scutage'. 'Aids' and 'scutages' were two forms of tax. Kings had always had the right to request or demand – it was not always easy to tell the difference – financial help, or aid, from their subjects in situations of exceptional need. Scutage, which meant something like 'shield-tax', was levied on the king's tenants in place of actual military service, and was meant to help meet the costs of war. Clause 12 spelled matters out further:

> 'No scutage or aid is to be levied in our realm except by the common counsel of the realm, unless it is for the ransom

of our person, the knighting of our eldest son or the first
marriage of our eldest daughter; and for these only a reasonable aid is to be levied.'

Who was to say what was 'reasonable'? Who was to say on
which occasions, other than the three special cases specified in Clause 12, the king was entitled to raise a tax? Who
was to say whether or not any particular war was either
justified or sensible? Who was to say whether or not a situation of exceptional need had arisen? These questions must
have been asked many times before, but it was only in
John's reign that they came to be asked with such frequency
and insistence that the upshot was the creation of a mech-
anism for establishing an assembly that would give answers,
disguised in the form of advice. This was a significant step.
Such assemblies were not yet called 'parliaments' and the
make-up envisaged for them in 1215 was clearly different
from that of later thirteenth-century assemblies, which were
called 'parliaments', when men were summoned to represent individual constituencies – counties and boroughs.
None the less in Magna Carta, Clauses 12 and 14, we can
see a kind of parliament in embryo.

This radical development took place because John had
managed to combine consistent military failure with
frequent and heavy taxation, particularly in the form of
scutage. During his reign royal revenue soared. In the five
years from 1199 to 1203 when money was desperately
needed for war against Philip of France, revenues audited
at the English Exchequer averaged just over £27,000 a
year. In 1210 and 1212 the same sources produced roughly
twice as much as that and in 1211 three times as much.
Moreover, in these same years, large sums were paid directly

into the king's chamber – his household financial office – and were not subject to the regular Exchequer audit. A recent calculation estimates John's total revenue from England in 1211 at a staggering £145,000 – six times as much as the Crown's average annual income at the beginning of the reign. Hardly surprising that he was described as 'the plunderer of his subjects'. Something had to be done about this kind of government. In the event that 'something' turned out to be rebellion and Magna Carta.

CHAPTER II

Trial by Ordeal

To no one will we sell, to no one will we deny or delay right or justice.

Magna Carta, Clause 40

As the king's coronation oath makes plain, governments then, as now, were expected to deal with problems of law and order. Generally this was left to the agents of local government. At their head were the sheriffs – shire-reeves – responsible for the counties and county courts. If the role of the sheriff of Nottingham in the Robin Hood ballads shows just how crucial the character of the sheriff was in setting the tone of local government, so too does Magna Carta. Five of its clauses (4, 24, 26, 30 and 48) seek to limit the sheriff's powers in some way, and Clause 45 limits the king's freedom to appoint as sheriff anyone he liked.

Below the sheriffs came the bailiffs in charge of the divisions of the shires known as hundreds. Forgotten today, the hundred courts had a long history, emerging in the tenth century and only abolished in 1867. Indeed, as late as 1886 the hundred was liable in law to make good damage caused by rioters. Below the hundreds came an administrative unit too small to have a court of its own. This was the vill or township, with its constable responsible for policing the area. There was, it must be remembered, no police force at this time. It was up to the victim of crime him or herself to raise the 'hue and cry'. On hearing it, every able-bodied man in the district had to turn out as quickly as possible and do the utmost in his power (*pro toto posse suo* – from which comes the word 'posse' of American cowboy films) to chase and apprehend the accused. Most cases were dealt with routinely in spring and autumn sessions of the hundred courts presided over by the sheriff or his deputies. Serious crimes went to the county courts. Thus, if a woman was raped, she had to go at once to the nearest vill, show her injuries, blood and torn clothes to reliable men there, then go to the hundred bailiff and do the same, and lastly proclaim it publicly at the next meeting of the county court.

Then, as now, fear of crime led, every now and then, to high-profile government initiatives, crack-downs on crime, often with particular targets in mind. One such drive, launched by Henry II against churchmen who committed serious crimes and used their clerical status in order to escape proper punishment, led directly to the king's dramatic confrontation with Archbishop Becket. Another, launched in 1166, just a year before John's birth, resulted in a series of major innovations that amounted to a trans-formation of the whole English judicial system: a public prosecution service, the growth of a legal profession, the establishment of a central court of justice at Westminster, and a system of sending royal judges out from the centre to go on circuits through the counties. These developments ensured that, as far as serious crime and property law were concerned, there would be a single framework of law covering the whole country – the Common Law – instead of a number of different regional customs.

Magna Carta reflects this revolution in the administration of justice. In Clause 18 the king promised to send to each county four times a year two judges whose job it would be, sitting together with four knights from that county, to hold assizes in the county court. In fact, the government was never able to send judges round so frequently. Clause 18 is an extraordinary clause. As a rule Magna Carta set limits to what the king could do; but in this one clause he was required to give more rather than less government. The demand for royal judges to hold county court sessions four times a year was the product of a longing for law and order, for the settlement of property disputes. When the charter was reissued in 1217 the requirement was changed to a more realistic once a year – although even that proved to be beyond the organising capacity of the government. But something the government was doing was clearly right: people wanted more of it.

Clause 18 spelled out that the judges were to hear the assizes of novel disseisin, mort d'ancestor and darrein presentment. What this dauntingly obscure legal jargon means is that they were to hear civil actions about the possession of property. If someone felt that they had recently been 'disseised' – that is, dispossessed of property that was properly theirs – they could go the royal chancery and pay for a clerk to write out a writ of 'novel disseisin'. Writs of mort d'ancestor were for people who claimed to be the lawful heir of a dead person's property; and darrein present-ment was for people who disputed patronage over churches. Like all writs, these were written royal commands. Writs had been around for centuries, at least since the time of Alfred the Great, three hundred years earlier, but what was special about the new writs established during the reign of Henry II – writs such as novel disseisin, mort d'ancestor and darrein presentment – was that they set a whole machinery of justice in motion. Previously a complainant had been expected to draft a writ himself and then deliver it to his opponent – which might well be risky – but these new-style writs were addressed to the sheriff of the relevant county and ordered him to take action to get the dispute heard in court. The sheriff had to arrange for a jury to decide the case on the basis of their local knowledge when the king's judges next visited the county. Although it was still up to the plaintiff to take the writ from chancery to the sheriff, the later stages of the system had, as it were, been automated. The first stage too had been made much easier once a branch of the chancery had settled perma-nently at Westminster, as it had by the 1170s. Previously English people who wanted royal writs had had to find either the king or, if he was abroad, his representative, the justiciar, and since they kept moving around the country, this was sometimes frustratingly difficult. It helped, too, that the new writs were standardised in form – which meant they could be obtained for a comparatively modest fee. For the system to work efficiently it was important that the king's judges made frequent circuits of the counties.

The expectation that the king would punish criminals reinforced the demand for more active royal judges, and Henry II responded. In 1176, for example, he divided the country into six circuits. In 1179 he sent out twenty-one judges in four circuits. These circuits were known as judicial eyres – the word derived from the Latin *errantes* meaning 'travelling'. The result was that some men were so frequently appointed as justices in eyre that they became professional judges, specialists in the law. In view of the common belief that in the Middle Ages only churchmen could read and write it is worth noting that the overwhelming majority of this new class of judges were laymen, men learned in a law which depended for its regular functioning upon documents. Everywhere they went these judges applied the same laws, a common law all over England, which is why the king who sent them out is commonly regarded as the founder of the Common Law.

What happened then, when a serious crime was committed? Let's look at a particular case. In 1217 George, lord of the manor of Northway in Gloucestershire, accused Thomas of Eldersfield of burglary and wounding him with an axe when he tried to prevent him making off with stolen goods. Thomas's story, of course, was completely different. He said that relations between him and George had long been tense because he had once had an affair with George's wife – although this had been while she was married to her first husband. He had refused to marry her after her first husband died, so she had grown to hate him and had poisoned her second husband's mind against him. Despite this he and George had spent Whitsunday 1217 in an alehouse together and had left it much the worse for wear. On the way home George suddenly hit him over the head with a heavy stick, and wouldn't stop until Thomas tried to ward off the blows with the axe which he just happened to be carrying. As a result George was slightly

wounded in the arm, and ran home shouting that innocent blood had been shed. On reaching his house, George
blew his horn to raise the 'hue and cry' and then concocted
the burglary story so that he could bring a private prosecution (known as an appeal) against Thomas. George's
appeal amounted to a charge of a breach of the king's
peace, and this meant that a trial would have to be adjourned
until it could be held before royal judges. In fact, it was
not until 1221 that the justices next visited Gloucestershire.
During the interval George had Thomas arrested several
times, and although Thomas always managed to get himself
out of jail, it was an expensive business.

In court at Gloucester, Thomas formally denied the
appeal, but a jury of neighbours decided that there was a
case to answer. (No doubt they bore in mind that the lord
and lady of the manor of Northway were people of influence in the neighbourhood.) The justices ordered that a
trial by battle should be held before them when they
reached Worcester. Trial by battle had been introduced into
English law by the Normans after 1066. In this case it took
the form of a duel between the two men in front of a
large crowd on the meadow known as Kingsmead near the
cathedral. The two combatants were armed with clubs and
shields, but used every weapon at their disposal. They fought
– as did nearly all in their predicament – literally tooth
and nail, biting and gouging. Thomas was thrown to the
ground and his right eye was almost completely gouged
out. At this point he cried 'Craven' – that is, he conceded
defeat. Since an omnipotent God was believed to be capable of giving victory to the party with the lesser duelling
skills and strength, the court now concluded that Thomas
was guilty. The judges could have ordered him to be hanged

there and then. Instead they decided to be merciful, and merely ordered him to be castrated and have his eyes torn out. It was up to George's kinsmen to carry out the sentence – which, supervised by court officials, they did with enthusiasm. Thomas's testicles were thrown to boys who kicked them to and fro among the girls in an impromptu game of football.

Within a few years of this case, the author of *Bracton's Notebook*, an important treatise on English law, wrote: 'Every corporal punishment, even the slightest, is more severe than any financial penalty, no matter how great.' The savagery of the corporal punishment Thomas suffered, though certainly less definitive than the death sentences carried out by many modern states, had its purpose. It was intended to create fear. Fearing for their lives if defeated in the duel, the parties in a dispute were under pressure to come to terms before matters came to so horrifying a dénouement. In this particular case, if Thomas had offered large enough compensation for wounding George, the latter would have dropped his appeal. In this sense the system of appeal, duel and corporal punishment suited both those who were after compensation and those who wanted retribution. Naturally many were allowed to have champions to fight for them: women, the young and old, the sick and the maimed. A class of professional champions evolved, men such as Duncan the Scot who fought duels in Dorset and Middlesex in 1229 and 1230. Husbands and wives, however, were regarded as one flesh, so it was laid down in Magna Carta, in Clause 54, that the only appeal of homicide that a woman could make was for the death of her husband.

There were other ways of tackling crime than by the dangerous path of private prosecution. Henry II had in effect created a public prosecution service. In 1166 he ordered that the sheriffs had to empanel a jury in every hundred whose job it was to present – that is, name – those of their neighbours whom they believed guilty of murder, robbery, theft or receiving stolen goods and other serious offences. In this we see the origin of the jury of presentment, the grand jury still in use in the USA. Those who had been named were then to be arrested by the sheriffs and brought to trial before the king's judges. Sheriffs were ordered to build jails. Court records make plain that most of the accused fled the county, or went into hiding, often in the forests. Hence the most common sentence was outlawry, imposed in their absence. If they appeared before the king's judges and were found guilty, they were punished by the Crown. They might be hanged, mutilated or fined – but they did not pay compensation to the victim. Only if victims themselves or their relatives chose to go down the old path of the appeal did they have a hope of receiving compensation. But the juries of presentment did at least mean that criminals who belonged to families too poor to pay compensation were now subject to a public judicial machinery. And some kind of check was kept on presenting juries by judges who fined them if they decided that they had made frivolous or malicious presentments.

The judges had clerks who kept brief records of court proceedings, and compiled lists of the fines they imposed. At intervals these lists were sent to the Exchequer, now based at Westminster. The judges found that they had so much business that after they returned to Westminster they continued to sit there, in Westminster Hall, as a central court of justice, the King's Bench. Increasingly litigants or defendants needed the advice and help of legal specialists.

Rich landowners had long retained the services of legal experts to look after their interests, but so great was the increase of legal business to be dealt with, and especially in and around Westminster, that by 1200 a new class of lawyers had arisen, a group of attorneys, based in London, who were willing to represent any client in return for a fee. The legal profession was born, and the suspicion grew that justice was a money-making operation, fees for clerks and lawyers, sweeteners for judges, fines for the Crown.

In these trials how was guilt or innocence determined? Take a case recorded by the clerks of the justices sitting at Launceston in Cornwall in 1201.

Walter Wifin was burgled and boots were found in the house of Lefchild de Ranam. Walter identified them as boots of his taken in that burglary. Lefchild said that he bought them in Bodmin market for twopence halfpenny, but does not know from whom. Further, Walter claims that 11 yards of linen and other goods were stolen in that burglary, and were sold in Lefchild's house. Lefchild denies. The jurors were then asked, and they said that they suspect Lefchild of receiving. Therefore let Lefchild purge himself by water according to the assize.

'Purging himself by water according to the assize' meant that Lefchild would be bound and lowered into a pit of cold water. If the water received him, he was innocent; if it did not, he was guilty.

Before Lefchild was put to the ordeal, he would have been taken to a church with which he was not familiar, and spent at least a day and a night there, fasting and praying in the company of a priest he did not know – and who, no doubt, all too often drew his attention to the church's finest painting of the Last Judgment, with its lurid depiction of the hellish fate to which the souls of sinners were condemned. Immediately before the ordeal the atmosphere would be further charged as the priest blessed the water, calling upon God to harm the guilty and spare the innocent. If the water received the accused he was deemed innocent and pulled out. If he seemed to stay on the surface, probably struggling and thrashing about, he was adjudged guilty. There was evidently room for interpretation here, with different witnesses seeing different things.

The same was true of the other form of ordeal imposed by English courts, the ordeal by iron. In another case heard at Launceston in 1201, Osbert of Reterth appealed Odo Hay for assault on his way home from Bodmin market, and for wounding him badly. Odo denied it, but because Osbert was undoubtedly maimed and unable to fight a duel, the court decided that Odo would have to 'purge himself by the judgment of iron'. In this case the accused would have to pick up a piece of red-hot iron, walk three paces, then put it down. His hand would then be bandaged and sealed. Three days later the bandages would be removed. If his hand was healing cleanly, he was innocent; if it looked unclean – if there was suppuration – he was guilty. In this decision too there was room for flexibility.

What happened to Lefchild and Odo Hay we do not know, but there is no doubt that some people were cleared at the ordeal, and others found guilty. In the case of the rich Londoners who went in for housebreaking, one of the richest, John Old, was found guilty in trial by water and was hanged, despite offering the king the huge sum of fifty marks for his life. As a general rule London citizens enjoyed the privilege of not being subject to the rigours of ordeal or duel unless they chose to. But then, and in many societies before and since, people offered to go through the ordeal as a way of clearing their name. Significantly, Henry II laid down that those who were presented by local juries and found innocent at the ordeal still had to leave the country. God had cleared them of the particular accusation, but had not changed the fact that their neighbours looked upon them as troublemakers. Exiling them was a way of dealing with those persistent offenders who had enough coolness of nerve to get through the ordeal.

What Lefchild's case also demonstrates is that the courts did not rush to send the accused to the ordeal. They followed the procedure outlined in a lawbook attributed to King John's former tutor, Ranulf Glanvill.

> The truth of the matter shall be investigated by many and various inquiries and interrogations in the presence of the justices, taking into account the probable facts and possible conjectures both for and against the accused, who as a result must either be cleared or made to go to the ordeal. If the ordeal convicts him of the alleged crime, then judgment over life and limb depends, as in other cases of felony, upon royal clemency.

Whenever they could the judges preferred to proceed on the basis of testimony and evidence. Trial by ordeal was used only as a last resort. But in the centuries before forensic science, fingerprints, DNA, there was often no evidence, especially where crimes had been committed stealthily, at night for instance, or in cases of murder – as distinct from the open killing of homicide. In such cases the judges asked the jury to decide whether or not the accused should go though trial by ordeal. Defendants in such cases swore to their innocence, using words such as 'as God is my witness', so, in the absence of conclusive evidence and as a last resort, it is not surprising that God should be called upon to use his miraculous power of telling truth from falsehood to decide the case.

But at the end of John's reign the whole system was thrown into chaos. In 1215 at the Fourth Lateran Council Pope Innocent III prohibited priests from taking part in the ordeal. This was an academic decision. At schools and universities many more people than ever before were studying law and theology. The study of Roman law made them aware of a much-admired system that had functioned without ever using the ordeal. For Christian theologians there was no doubt that God could work miracles. He could, for example, make a guilty man's body stay on the water's surface. The problem was, however, that the basis of the ordeal was that God was required to work a miracle every time he was asked to do so, but since a miracle was surely a free act of God, this was theologically unacceptable unless the ordeal was, like the Mass, a sacrament. In the Mass a miracle occurred each time a priest said *Hoc est corpus meum*. But how could the ordeals of iron and water be sacraments? The Church had not instituted them. There was nothing about them in the Bible. By 1215 most educated churchmen had decided that ordeals were wrong. In some ways Innocent III's decision was a remarkable one. Priests were paid fees for the work they did in making ordeals work. For many churches, their possession of an ordeal pit and of consecrated irons was a privilege that gave them dignity and influence in the neighbourhood. The high-minded pope was requiring that they surrender an important and lucrative right. And they did so.

When the English government first faced up to the problem posed by the papal prohibition, it had no immediate solution. 'We leave it to your discretion,' they instructed the judges. 'Proceed according to your good sense and conscience, ascertaining as far as you can the character of the individuals involved, the nature of the crime and the truth of the matter.' What the judges eventually came up with was trial by jury. A new kind of jury was invented, not to present a list of names of suspects, but to decide guilt or innocence in particular cases. As one observer remarked, 'Before the war [the civil war of 1215–17] they had the ordeal of fire and water; now there is empanelling of juries.' The choice made by the judges was by no means inevitable. Indeed throughout Europe people faced the same dilemma and it was only in Denmark and England that the jury was introduced. What normally happened in hard cases in which there was suspicion but no useful testimony or evidence was that the authorities tried harder to get the accused to confess. Elsewhere in Europe people turned increasingly to torture – that is to say they went down the path of Roman law, for the law of Rome, which knew nothing of the ordeal, was very familiar with the torture of both suspects and witnesses as a way of getting at 'the truth'. In England torture was authorised in cases of alleged treason, but not otherwise. By contrast the use of torture became a normal judicial procedure throughout almost the entire continent of Europe during the later Middle Ages and early modern period.

In English cases where the right to land was at issue the

procedure was trial by battle. The combatants swore oaths that they were fighting for the right, and it was then up to God to decide the right, to test the truthfulness of the contradictory oaths. In this sense the judicial duel was also an ordeal, a bilateral one, but it was a much less religious event than the unilateral ordeal, and did not require the presence of a priest. For this reason trial by battle continued after 1215, and only very gradually declined. Indeed the possibility of an appeal leading to trial by battle remained on the Statute Book until 1819. In another important innovation, known as the Grand Assize, Henry II had granted permission for defendants in a case of right to land to choose trial by jury instead of trial by battle. Glanvill explains the procedure to be adopted in empanelling the jury.

> The knowledge required from jurors is that they shall know about the matter either from what they have personally seen and heard, or from what their fathers told them in circumstances such as make them bound to believe them. If none of the twelve knows the truth of the matter, and swears this in court, then others shall be found. If some of them declare in favour of one party, and some in favour of the other, then further jurors are to be added until at least twelve agree.

What was wanted was a jury of twelve who spoke unanimously, who had – like God – 'one voice'. Although this verdict-giving jury was clearly required to act very differently from a modern British jury, this original mind-set was to be tremendously influential. Until very recently indeed the jury was required to reach a unanimous decision.

When a verdict in such cases had been reached, the matter was closed, and could not be brought to court again. Trial by ordeal had also been intended to produce a final decision (and was often swiftly followed by a hanging), so when the judges presiding over the trial of criminal cases after 1215 pondered the problem of how to replace the ordeal, they opted to follow the formula of the Grand Assize. This had allowed a defendant to choose between battle and jury. So after 1215 the judges allowed a defendant in a criminal trial the choice of whether or not to go before a jury. If he chose not to, he was simply kept in prison. But this was soon felt to be unsatisfactory, and so he was pressured to 'put himself on the country' – to choose to be tried by a jury. First, a statute of 1275 specified that the imprisonment should be *forte et dure*, and then it was decided that the accused should suffer *peine forte et dure* until they 'saw sense'. The classic form of *peine forte et dure* was for heavy stones to be placed on the accused's chest and the weight gradually increased. In this way, a form of torture was introduced into the English legal system by the side door. Stubborn defendants had the option of being pressed to death rather than go before a jury.

The most famous case of this occurred in the Salem witch trials in Massachusetts in 1692 when Giles Cory chose to die rather than be tried. He did this because he believed he would be found guilty, with the consequence that not only would he be hanged but all his property would be confiscated as well. By being pressed to death, he died innocent and his family inherited his property. It was not until 1722 that the accused's choice was finally removed. From then on refusal to plead before a jury was regarded as an admission of guilt. This lasted until 1827 when the present formula was adopted. Now if defendants refuse to plead, a plea of 'Not Guilty' is imposed upon them. In 2002, in England and Wales, we still live with the convention that when a jury has given a verdict, the case cannot be re-opened. Perhaps not for much longer.

CHAPTER 12

A Christian Country

For the honour of God and the exaltation of Holy Church.

Magna Carta, 2nd paragraph

The England of 1215 was a very Christian country, as were Ireland, Scotland and Wales. Apart from a few thousand Jews, living in towns as far north as Newcastle and as far west as Exeter, everyone else was treated as a Christian. Heresy was regarded as a serious problem by the Church authorities on the continent but was virtually unknown in England. In 1166 a group of twenty religious enthusiasts who arrived from the continent were identified as heretics – they denied the sacraments of baptism, Mass and marriage – branded and left to die. A few more heretics arrived in 1210, and were arrested and burned. By such drastic methods the strong-arm royal government co-operated with the Church at keeping this island, as they saw it, uncontaminated by heresy.

A Christian people, the English were baptised as babies,

and went to church throughout their lives on Sundays and great feast days, such as Easter and Christmas. They paid tithes to the Church, and nearly all were buried in church-yards. There were no official charges, but the custom of making offerings to the priest for baptism, marriage and burial was hard to avoid. Learned clerks, with characteris-tic sophistry, explained that it was acceptable for priests to receive voluntary gifts *at* such ceremonies, though not – be it understood – *in return* for them.

Every parish church had its own landed endowment, usually a decent-sized farm. The rector of the parish also received tithes, one-tenth of all agricultural produce. This was deeply unpopular, and tithe avoidance was thoroughly respectable behaviour. So was tithe evasion. Pope Innocent III ruled that it was not permissible to deduct expenses incurred in running a mill or fishery before paying tithes on income. The Church fought hard to keep its tithes. When the rector of Sempringham found out that one farmer had evaded the tithe-collectors, he removed a tenth of the grain stored in the farmer's barn, and then burned it in the village street. He was not a greedy man, was the message of the flames, but the law of the Church must be upheld. The richer churches collected tithes on such a scale that special barns had to be built. Substantial churches, generating large revenues, were much sought-after, so inevitably many rectors were influential men who had no intention of devoting themselves to pastoral work in the parishes. Non-resident rectors appointed vicars to do the work for them, and some vicars subcontracted it to sub-vicars. This was a system wide open to abuse, and bishops were meant to see that there was a priest (either the rector or his vicar) in every parish. In 1222 the minimum salary for vicars was fixed at £3 a year – about threepence a day at a time when you could buy an ox for about eighty pence.

England was well provided with churches: there were some 9000 parish churches with at least as many chapels situated in new suburbs and markets, or on the private property of the powerful, as well as in less populated parts of the countryside. The clergy were everywhere. As many as one in every twenty adult males was a clerk. Most clerks, however, were not intended for the priesthood or anything like it. A clerk was a man – there were no women clerks – with a tonsure; that is, the crown of his head had been shaved. He was also expected to renounce beard and moustache, colourful clothes, weapons and visits to taverns. He was expected to have some education. It was their clerical education that meant that clerks could act as administrators and secretaries, which is what most of them did. Very few became priests. Many were not 'ordained' at all, and many others took only 'minor orders', which meant that they stayed on the lower rungs of the clerical hierarchy, as cantors, doorkeepers, and lectors. They were allowed to marry. Marriage was forbidden only for those in major orders, subdeacons, deacons and priests.

By 1215 the English Church had been thoroughly organised. At the top of the hierarchy were the two archbishops of Canterbury and York, and below them their bishops. New bishoprics had been established at Ely in 1108 and Carlisle in 1133, but since then there had been no changes in diocesan structure – and there would be no more until the Reformation of the sixteenth century. Each cathedral had its own chapter, either of monks, as at Canterbury and Winchester, or – more commonly – of canons, each holding a portion of the cathedral's revenues as his own individual stipend, known as a prebend. Valuable prebends became

highly desirable objects of patronage and were often held
by men who preferred to remain close to centres of power
– the royal court, for example – and who certainly had no
intention of performing cathedral services themselves. The
usual arrangement was for non-resident canons to employ
vicars choral to do their singing for them.

In the years since 1000 a whole new network of archdeaconries had been set up in each diocese. Archdeacons were
responsible for enforcing moral standards on both lay and
clergy; not surprisingly they were often deeply unpopular.
No archdeacon, it was alleged, would ever get to heaven.
Below the archdeaconries came the rural deaneries and within
them the parishes. The parish system, a kind of administrative grid covering the whole country, had hardly existed at
all in 1000 and was still being built up in 1215. There was
now a network of ecclesiastical courts in which the Church's
own law, canon law, was applied with increasing precision
and subtlety. The system required resources and bureaucrats
to run it; there was plenty of work for clerks here. Critics
said the Church was ruled not so much by law as by lawyers.

In England there were around seven hundred religious
houses catering for about thirteen thousand men and
women who had taken vows, roughly three times as many
men as women. Since there were approximately six hundred
houses for men and only a hundred for women it is evident
that a male-dominated society made much better provision for men. Both monks and nuns had taken a vow to
dedicate themselves to God by living a life of prayer, poverty,
chastity and obedience to their head of their house, abbot,
abbess, prior or prioress. They were there, as they saw it,
not just to save their own souls, but also to fight for the
spiritual welfare of the whole kingdom, and especially for

those who had founded or endowed their community. As one twelfth-century monk put it:

> Strenuous is the warfare which these castellans of Christ wage against the Devil. Who can recount the vigils, hymns, psalms, prayers and daily offerings of masses with floods of tears which monks perform? And so, noble earl, I most earnestly advise you to build such a castle in your country, manned against the wiles of Satan by monks who crucify themselves so that they may please God.

As trained and dedicated soldiers of Christ, the monks and nuns in every house chanted each day the full cycle of prayer, the monastic office: Matins, Lauds, Prime, Terce, Sext, Nones, Vespers and Compline.

Monks and nuns may have given up sex – though, inevitably, there were a few notorious exceptions – but it sometimes seemed as though they had given up no other pleasures or comforts. Although their vow of poverty meant that they were supposed to have no property of their own, they lived in property-owning communities. In a rich monastery they were poor in name only. Since the Benedictine houses were the most ancient and had accumulated vast estates, Benedictine monks tended to live like rich landowners, even keeping horses and going hunting with hawks and hounds. They acquired a reputation for gluttony. Gerald de Barri claimed that when he visited the cathedral monastery of Christ Church at Canterbury he saw that for lunch (the main meal of the day) the monks were served sixteen dishes, one after the other. On the basis of fifteenth-century monastic kitchen accounts, the earliest to survive, it has been calculated that the monks of Westminster

Abbey were allowed two pounds of meat on a meat day, up to two pounds of fish on a fish day, plus a daily ration of two pounds of bread and a gallon of ale. Wine was reserved for the sick and for feast days – of which there were a hundred or so in the year.

The meat allowance is especially revealing. According to the Rule of St Benedict, the flesh of quadrupeds was not allowed in the monks' refectory (the dining room). Hence the classic monastic diet consisted of poultry, fish, eggs, cereal and vegetables. But by the twelfth century the word 'meat' had been interpreted to mean fresh meat cut from the joint, while entrails, offal and meat that had been salted or precooked, were regarded not as meat but 'meatish'. Hence bacon, fritters (using precooked meat) and 'umbles' (sheep's entrails cooked in ale and breadcrumbs, the origin of the phrase 'humble pie') were all allowed. Moreover since the Rule banned eating meat in the refectory, close analysis of the text revealed a loophole. Plainly it was permissible to eat whatever you liked in some other room, just so long as there were enough monks eating in the refectory to main-tain the sense of a community observing the Rule. Special dining rooms known as misericords were provided.

In some houses the monks' interest in food and drink threatened to become an obsession. At Bury, when a fire damaged the shrine of St Edmund, causing pilgrims to put off visiting it, Abbot Samson blamed the disaster on the sinfulness of his monks, and especially, he said, their constant complaints about the quality and quantity of food and drink. When he suggested they cut back on food to save money to repair the shrine, the monks decided that, since he was a saint, Edmund could perfectly well restore his own shrine without their help.

Some monks reacted to their fellows' lax ways and sought a less comfortable way of life. They abandoned their old Benedictine communities and either joined a group of hermits or set up new monasteries. One new monastery, at Citeaux in Burgundy, became the well-spring of a new order, the Cistercians, who saw themselves as the only true followers of the Rule of Benedict. In every way they aimed at a more austere lifestyle in less luxurious accommodation. They gave up the linen underwear and black woollen top garment (or 'habit') of the Benedictines, the Black Monks, and wore nothing but an undyed woollen habit. They became known as the White Monks. To avoid collecting rents from their estates, they farmed them themselves – or rather, they took in people much poorer than the gentrified Benedictines would accept, and allowed them to take the vow and wear the habit in return for working as ploughmen, shepherds and carpenters. These 'lay brothers' lived in separate buildings. According to a chronicler from the first Cistercian house founded in England, Waverley Abbey in Surrey, by 1187 his monastery contained seventy monks and 120 lay brothers. The Yorkshire Cistercian houses of Fountains and Rievaulx were even bigger than this. The austerity of Cistercian life impressed potential benefactors and the new order rapidly became an immensely popular order all over Europe. Seven Cistercian abbeys in 1118 had become well over 500 by 1200. In 1205 King John himself founded a Cistercian house, at Beaulieu in Hampshire.

By this time there were other recently established religious orders from which an aspiring monk or nun could choose: Augustinian, Carthusian, Templar, Hospitaller, and Gilbertine. In 1066 there had been only about fifty religious houses in England, all of them following – more or less – the Rule of

St Benedict. By 1215, in addition to more than two hundred and fifty Benedictine houses, there were over four hundred other religious communities offering a wide choice of different rules, each with its own particular emphasis.

The most dramatic development was the abandonment of the system of 'child oblates'. In 1066 and earlier the ancient Benedictine houses had recruited their monks largely from children handed over or offered – in Latin *oblatum* means offered – by aristocratic parents. Usually a gift of property accompanied the child in order to cover the cost to the monastery of bringing him or her up. Most monks and nuns were, in effect, child conscripts who had known no other way of life. But the Cistercians prohibited entry to anyone under the age of sixteen and insisted upon a year's novitiate. In this they were followed by the other new orders, and by the end of the twelfth century even the Benedictines had been forced to abandon their age-old system. Conscripts had been replaced by volunteers – and there were now many thousands more volunteers than there had ever been conscripts. In the religious life of the nation, more people had the freedom to choose and a greater variety to choose from.

Some volunteers were prepared to give up everything to live a life of Christian poverty. Francis of Assisi, the son of a wealthy cloth merchant, started a brotherhood, the Franciscans, which owned nothing. The brothers, known as friars, were to wander the world, preaching penance and begging for their daily food. In 1210 Francis went to Rome and obtained Innocent III's approval of his way of life. A Spanish priest called Dominic, impressed by his radical step, founded a similar order of his own. Many thousands of idealists all over Europe joined the new orders, often to the dismay of well-off parents who were shocked to see their children begging. Both orders used houses known as friaries as bases from which to preach and beg. In 1221 the Dominicans reached England, where they became known as the Black Friars. Three years later the first Franciscans, the Grey Friars, arrived. The earliest friaries were in London, Canterbury and Oxford. Whereas the Cistercians had 'fled the world' by locating their houses far away from people, in the Yorkshire moors, for example, the friars went straight for towns, where their preaching was badly needed – and where begging was easier. By 1300 there were around 150 friaries in England, eighty in Ireland, more than twenty in Scotland and nine in Wales. In the history of religious institutions the twelfth and thirteenth centuries were indeed an age of faith.

Of all these new orders only one, the Gilbertines, founded by Gilbert of Sempringham, had its origins in England. Twelfth-century Christianity was organised on a pan-European basis and the English Church was just one part of the Latin Church under the pope. The other new orders were brought to England from the continent, and some of them, the Cistercians, Dominicans and Franciscans, were conceived on an international basis from their inception. All Cistercian houses were dedicated to the same saint, Mary, the mother of Christ. Representatives of each house were obliged to travel to an annual chapter at Citeaux. All of the houses of the Military Orders, the Templars and Hospitallers, no matter where they were in Europe, were intended to be parts of two great networks of assistance for the crusader states in Palestine and Syria.

For many centuries pilgrims had gone to Rome to pray. The pope had long been the guardian not only of the shrines of St Peter and St Paul but also of those of hundreds of other early Christian martyrs. During the twelfth century, however, he also became the effective head of the Latin Church in the sense that from now on churchmen throughout the West looked to him to decide local quarrels. Litigation took English churchmen to the papal court, usually at Rome, time and time again. Having finished his education, John of Salisbury entered the service of the archbishop of Canterbury. His job was to represent the interests of Canterbury and, to some extent, the interests of the whole English Church, at the papal court. This involved him in frequent journeys to and from England and the curia. Gerald de Barri went to Rome three times between 1199 and 1203 in the hope of persuading Innocent III that the church of St David's should be freed from its subordination to Canterbury and become an independent archbishopric of Wales.

Litigation was expensive. All too often it seemed as though the only people who profited from it were the Romans. The officials of the papal curia won for themselves an unenviable reputation for avarice. 'Money is the root of all evil.' In Latin this was, as Walter Map pointed out, *Radix omnium malorum avaritia* – R. o. m. a. A twelfth-century satirical parody of the scriptures made the point nicely:

> Here beginneth the Gospel according to the Mark of Silver. And it came to pass that a certain poor clerk came to the court of the Lord Pope and cried out, saying 'Have pity upon me, O doorkeepers of the Pope, for I am poor and needy and therefore I beseech you to succour my misfortune and my misery.' But when they heard him they were filled with indignation and said, 'Get thee behind me, Satan,

thou hast not the flavour of money about thee. Verily, verily, I say unto thee, thou shalt not enter into the joy of thy Lord till thou hast paid to the uttermost farthing. So the poor man departed and sold his cloak and his tunic and all that he had, and gave unto the cardinals and the door-keepers and the chamberlains. But they said, 'What is this among so many?' and they cast him out, and he went out and wept bitterly and would not be comforted.

Then there came into the curia a certain rich clerk, who had waxed fat and grown thick, and had committed murder in the insurrection. He gave, first to the door-keepers, then to the chamberlains, then to the cardinals. But they thought among themselves that they should have received more. Then the Lord Pope, hearing that the cardinals and servants had received many gifts from the clerk, fell sick nigh unto death. But the rich man sent him a medicine of gold and silver, and straightway he was healed. Then the Lord Pope called unto him the cardinals and the servants and said to them, 'Brethren, see to it that no man deceive you with empty words. For, lo! I give you an example. Even as I receive so receive ye also.

Despite this, litigants continued to go to Rome and often decisions made in cases taken to the curia became in effect papal legislation for the whole Church. Likewise papal councils, often held in the Lateran Palace in Rome, became councils for the whole Church. And none more so than the Fourth Lateran Council summoned by Innocent III in 1215. This was attended by hundreds of prelates from all over Latin Christendom, including nine English bishops and eleven heads of English religious houses, among them Alexander Nequam as abbot of Cirencester. The decrees promulgated at this Council dealt with virtually every aspect of the Church's teaching and organisation, and did so in ways that had profound consequences for its future structure. Papal authority over churchmen, however much they might complain or joke about it, had become extra-ordinarily effective. And through it all the city of Rome remained a place of pilgrimage. Despite the failure of his litigation in the papal court, Gerald de Barri went there again in 1206, this time as a pilgrim.

For those who love medieval cathedrals and parish churches it cannot but seem that this was, as it is often called, an 'Age of Faith'. Why else should people have spent such huge sums in erecting and furnishing churches? Yet the rich and the powerful spent far more money on building and decorating houses to live in than on churches to pray in. It is just that the churches survive while their houses do not. It is easy for us to imagine medieval people at prayer. Apart from the Jews, everyone throughout Europe was supposed to be taught the Lord's Prayer (beginning *Pater noster*, 'our father') and the Creed beginning with the word 'Credo' – 'I believe'. But many may have been careless or indifferent. One preacher complained that people repeated the creed like magpies, not knowing what they were saying. Some may have been agnostic or even atheist. According to the prior of Holy Trinity, Aldgate, Peter of Cornwall, writing around 1200:

There are many people who do not believe that God exists, nor do they think that the human soul lives on after the

death of the body. They consider that the universe has
always been as it is now and is ruled by chance rather than
by Providence.

What did Peter of Cornwall mean by 'many people'? How
many believed in a steady-state Godless universe? We cannot
tell.

In some respects the Christian laity allowed the Church
to organise their life. They allowed, for example, jurisdiction over wills and marriage, the question of what made a
marriage valid or invalid, to pass to Church courts. But
when it suited them the laity could dig their heels in.
According to canon law, the children born out of wedlock
were legitimised by the subsequent marriage of their
parents. In 1236 at a meeting at Merton, Surrey, the barons
rejected a proposal made by some bishops to bring English
law into line with canon law. 'We will not change the laws
of England,' they declared. Under English law, once a
bastard, always a bastard. On the other hand English
common law happily accepted the canon law dictum that
a priest's child was necessarily illegitimate.

Very many, probably a majority of the population,
resented having to pay tithes. A story told by a twelfth-
century canon of St Paul's Cathedral reveals another cause
for resentment: the Church's rule against working on
Sundays and holy days. When a man working on the feast
day of London's St Erkenwald was reproached for doing
so, he 'belched out his poisonous brew of insults':

> You clerics have so much time on your hands that you
> meddle with what's none of your business. You lot grow
> fat and soft with idleness, you don't have a real job, your

life is just a game or a play. You clerics with your ever-
lasting useless dirges despise us, though we are the ones
who do all the real work. And then you go and bring in
some Erkenwald or other to justify your idleness and to
try to stop me doing the job that I need to stay alive. You
might just as well tell me I can live without eating as tell
me to stop working. Why should I pray alongside drones
like you? When we've made a bit of money, enough so we
can eat – and a bit more too, so we can drink – then we
have a holiday, and a good time dancing and singing. You
keep your festivals, your mouldy old tunes and your
Erkenwald to yourselves. Leave us alone.

As is inevitable in stories such as this, the critic had no
sooner finished his diatribe than he was struck down dead.
In this case he staggered under the heavy weight of timber
he was carrying, tripped over a half-buried skull in St Paul's
churchyard and fell on his head. The author was delighted
by the swiftness of God's justice, but even he acknowledged that not everyone who witnessed the fatal accident
interpreted it in the way he did.

In 1199 a charismatic preacher named Eustace de Flaye
came over from Normandy and drew large crowds. His
favourite subject was Sunday observance. According to the
historian Roger of Howden, the people of York were
impressed by his preaching and swore not to work on
Sunday and not to sell anything on that day, except food
and drink to travellers; even then from every five shillings
they took in payment, they were to put a farthing into the
church box for the burial of the poor. But after Eustace
had returned to France, Howden noted, people returned
to their old ways, holding Sunday markets just as before.

Critics of the clergy had plenty of material to hand. Priests were supposed to be celibate, but many 'lived in sin'. Gerald de Barri described the house of the typical parish priest as 'full of bossy mistresses, creaking cradles, newborn babies and squawking brats'. Learned men criticised the poor quality of education of country priests. But ordinary people may have taken a different view of the alleged priestly shortcomings. Other evidence suggests that learning could erect a barrier between a parson and his flock, that what they needed was a man who could bring comfort and the sacraments to the dying, and who could, with good sense and tact, help to resolve local feuds. For these tasks the experience of farming and of family life that he shared with his parishioners might well have been of more use than a knowledge of Latin. Understanding human relationships might have been more helpful than a 'correct' understanding of the mysterious relationship between the three persons of the Trinity.

Many learned churchmen argued that illness was God's punishment for sin, and the more unpleasant the disease the worse the sin. Since the fifth century leprosy had often been interpreted as the reward for sexual excess. One of the early Norman bishops of London, Hugh d'Orival, chose to be castrated in the hope of obtaining a cure but, according to William of Malmesbury, the only result was that he spent the rest of his life a eunuch as well as a leper. Doctors, of course, explained leprosy as the result of an imbalance of humours. Undoubtedly leprosy was a real scourge in King John's England. Archaeological evidence has proved that Hansen's disease, as leprosy is now termed, was present in several forms including lepromatous, the most virulent and disfiguring. One of Bishop Hugh of Lincoln's claims to sanctity was his habit of kissing lepers; the more unpleasant their appearance the more tenderly he embraced them. When challenged by a learned master of the schools of Lincoln to follow the example of St Martin of Tours and heal one of those whom he kissed, Hugh replied that it was not the leper but himself who was being healed: kissing them dissipated his own 'sickness of spirit'. In 1200 King John helped to carry Hugh's coffin, and in 1220 the bishop was canonised.

To have dealings with lepers was a sign of true humility. When Henry II was on his way to do penance at Becket's tomb, he stopped just outside the walls of Canterbury to pray at the church of the leper hospital founded by Lanfranc at Harbledown. Whatever we may think of his motives, he made a lavish donation to the hospital in Becket's memory. The foundation of no less than three hundred leper hospitals between the Norman Conquest and 1250 was a huge philanthropic achievement, however mixed the motives behind it might have been.

CHAPTER 13

The English and the Celts

We will restore at once the son of Llywelyn and all the hostages
from Wales and the charters delivered to us as security for peace.
We will treat Alexander, King of the Scots, in the same manner
in which we will act towards our other barons of England.

Magna Carta, Clauses 58 and 59

England, in the view of English writers of the time, was 'a land of untold riches' where 'no one who wanted to make money need ever die poor'. The English saw themselves as prosperous, urbanised, enterprising, peaceful and law-abiding. They admitted to only one serious fault. They were, wrote Richard FitzNigel, 'natural drunks'. Certainly they impressed the inhabitants of other countries with their hard drinking.

'God! how handsome Englishmen are!' was the first thought of a French princess as she gazed at the man she was falling in love with – or that at least was what the patriotic author of a narrative poem written during John's reign imagined she would think. The poem is the *Roman de Waldef* and was written in the variety of French known to scholars as Anglo-Norman. *Deus! tant sunt Engleis beles genz!* are the actual words. In another Anglo-Norman work composed at about the same time, its author, Chardri, compared England to a fair meadow covered with flowers, and went on:

> England surpasses all the kingdoms that exist. Let me count
> the ways. In all pleasures and in nobility. If the women in
> England are well brought up, you should not wonder, for so
> are the knights, and all the others that follow them are valiant,
> courteous, and noble – except in this one respect, the great
> harm that drinking too much does to their fair life.

Works like this show that, by John's reign, English patriotism could be expressed in French. Indeed the earliest known history in the French language was written in the 1130s by an author called Geoffrey Gaimar and – remarkably – it was not a history of France, but of England, the *Estoire des Engleis*. Figures such as Hereward the Wake, leaders of the resistance against the Norman Conquest, are portrayed as heroes of the nation. Just as today intense Irish patriotism can be expressed in English, the language of the former colonisers, so too English patriots at the time of Magna Carta could think and speak in French.

This means that the picture of England created by Sir Walter Scott in *Ivanhoe* is entirely wrong. According to Scott:

> Four generations had not sufficed to blend the hostile blood
> of the Normans and Anglo-Saxons, or to unite, by common
> language and mutual interests, two hostile races, one of

which still felt the elation of triumph, while the other
groaned under the consequences of defeat.

Thanks to film and television, Scott's portrayal of English
society around 1200 as having been bitterly divided
between English and Norman still lingers in the public
imagination. In this scenario English freedom fighters such
as Robin Hood – Scott's Robin of Locksley – still roamed
the forest, doing their best to save the poor from Prince
John's tyranny and the bullying of the Norman sheriff of
Nottingham. Indeed there had been English freedom
fighters in the forests and wild lands in the years immediately after 1066, but that had been – as Scott noted – four
generations ago, and now there were none. Nor was there
any longer, as there once had been, an ethnic divide between
English and Norman. Apart from the royal family and a
handful of other aristocrats, everyone who lived in England
felt themselves to be English. Everyone spoke English, and
everyone who wanted to be someone in culture or in politics learned to speak French as well. French gave the English
easy access to a very cosmopolitan world, for in 1215 French
was a fashionable language not just in Britain and Ireland
but also in Spain, Germany, Italy, Sicily, Greece,
Constantinople, Cyprus and Syria. Those who spoke
Parisian French were proud of their 'good' French and
mocked the Anglo-Norman dialect. For instance, they
enjoyed the confusion that arose when ordering a roast
dinner from the English inability to make a clear difference in pronunciation between *anel*, donkey, and *agnel*, lamb.

The mother-tongue of those who lived in this bilingual
society was enormously enriched as a result of their intense
familiarity with French. By 1215 French words such as

'baron', 'feast', 'noble' and 'servant' had entered the English language, and over the next two hundred years many more came in. By 1400 there were about ten thousand French loan-words in English. Chaucer, for example, used nearly five hundred words borrowed from French in the 858 lines of the Prologue to *The Canterbury Tales*. Sometimes the old word was driven out. The word *stow* meaning 'place' for example no longer exists – except in some place-names such as Godstow, the nunnery where Henry II's mistress, Fair Rosamund, was buried. More often both the English and French words for something continued simultaneously in use, with the English generally retaining a more common or garden sense, as in English 'house' and French 'mansion'. Sometimes spelling changed. For instance the spelling of the modern word 'queen' comes from the French combi-nation of letters *qu* replacing its English equivalent *cw*. Also of French origin is the convention, exasperating and confus-ing, of using *c* instead of *s* for the ess sound in words such as cell or circle.

For centuries the English had shared Britain with other peoples and other kingdoms. This had not prevented one of Henry II's courtiers, Walter Map, referring to Britain as 'the English island' and 'our island England', though he was by no means the first and certainly not the last to confuse the identities of England and Britain in this typically English fashion. In the west there were the people of Wales, proud of their descent from the Britons against whom Julius Caesar had fought. At any one time there were usually several Welsh princes in Wales, rulers of old kingdoms such as Gwynedd, Powys and Deheubarth. There was only one king of the Scots, but his authority did not reach as far as the Scandinavian and Irish peoples of Caithness, Argyll and the Isles, where virtually autonomous chiefs held sway under the loose overlordship of Norway. It was not until 1266 that the king of Norway sold his rights over the kingdom of Man and the Western Isles to the Scottish Crown in the 'closing down sale' that marked the end of the 'Viking period' of Scottish history. And it was not until 1469 that the Scottish Crown acquired possession of Orkney and Shetland.

During the course of the twelfth century the English came to look upon the Celts with new, condescending eyes. Writing in the 1190s both the dean of St Paul's, Ralph of Diss, and the Yorkshire historian William of Newburgh referred to the Welsh, Irish and Scots as barbarians. By this time their views of the Scots were a little old-fashioned: according to the English historian, William of Malmesbury, King David I of Scotland (1124–53) had offered tax-breaks to his subjects if they would learn 'to live in a more civilized style, dress with more elegance and eat in a more refined manner' – they had, in other words, to be more like the English. By 1200 economic development and the foundation of new towns such as Berwick, Edinburgh, Stirling, Perth, Glasgow and Aberdeen by the Scottish kings meant that Lowland Scotland had in fact come to look very much like England. But the Welsh, the Irish-speaking Highland Scots and, still more, the Irish themselves continued to be classified – and vilified – as primitive, savage and immoral. They were, for instance, often accused of being addicted to adultery and incest. Welsh and Irish marriage law allowed divorce, remarriage and marriage with cousins. So, too, had English marriage law in earlier centuries, but no longer. Now Celtic marriage customs seemed, to English and continental European eyes, a licence for wife-swapping and every kind of sexual immorality.

Also, while in Lowland Scotland there was just one king,

in Ireland and Wales there were many kings and princes, fiercely independent rulers who fought among themselves with what seemed, to English eyes, stomach-turning brutality. Irish and Welsh kings and princes appeared to have no compunction in the open way they killed, blinded and castrated their rivals, especially their own kinsmen. By contrast King John could not deal with his nephew and rival, Arthur of Brittany, in the same fashion. If he was responsible for his nephew's death – as he probably was – he carried out secretly what he knew he could not possibly do openly. The rumour that he was to blame decisively damaged his reputation in the crucial years when he lost control of Normandy and Anjou.

Gerald de Barri accompanied the young Prince John on his expedition to Ireland in 1185, and used his experiences to write two remarkable and hugely influential books on Ireland and the Irish. He painted a picture of Ireland as a country rich in natural resources but undeveloped owing to the lack of industry of the natives, as a land of gold and rain-forests, where the savages whiled away their lives in war, sex and laziness, an Eldorado awaiting colonisation by enterprising and clean-living Englishmen. He envisaged a ladder of evolution of human societies with Ireland still on the bottom rung.

Mankind usually progresses from the woods to the fields, and then from fields to settlements and communities of citizens, but the Irish have not advanced at all from the primitive practices of pastoral farming. They scorn to work the land, have little use for the money-making of towns and despise the rights and privileges of civil society.

It is noticeable how much weight Gerald and other contemporary observers gave to towns and the market economy. They associated towns with a civilised lifestyle, and claimed to be civilised themselves.

These perceptions helped people feel comfortable with their invasions of Wales and Ireland. They were confident that they were introducing a morally better, economically more advanced and socially more sophisticated way of life to the natives. Soon after their conquest of England, Norman 'marcher lords' to whom William I had given estates in the 'marches', as the frontier zones were known, invaded Wales, occupying the more fertile parts, the coasts and river valleys, especially in the south. They built castles and towns such as Chepstow, Monmouth, Cardiff, Brecon and Pembroke, and filled them with English settlers. The biographer of King Stephen wrote: 'They vigorously subdued the natives, imposed law upon them in the interests of peace, and made the land so productive that it could easily have been thought to be a second England.' In his mind this was just as well since he saw native Wales as 'a country of wood and pasture, abounding in deer and fish, milk and herds, a land which breeds men who fight against each other like animals'. As far as the English were concerned, the Welsh did not change. In Gerald's words, 'they ate very little bread and paid no attention to commerce, shipping or industry.' English commentators undoubtedly exaggerated the extent to which the economy of Celtic peoples, including the Welsh, relied upon pastoral farming, but the fact remains that they continued to exaggerate, and in consequence looked down upon their neighbours. It was with this attitude that, towards the end of the thirteenth century, Edward I embarked on the final conquest of Wales.

Soon after his accession to the throne of England, Henry II discussed plans for an invasion of Ireland. He may even have received a bull from Pope Hadrian IV granting him Ireland, on the grounds that the Irish were not good Christians, and they needed a decent, upright king like Henry to go in there and set them straight. Hadrian IV, whose original name was Nicholas Brakespeare, was an Englishman, the only one ever to sit on the throne of St Peter. In fact this papal bull, known from its opening word as *Laudabiliter,* might have been a forgery; scholars still argue the point. Forgery or not, it undoubtedly reflected views current in twelfth century Rome. In the event King Henry changed his mind and it was not until years later, after an Anglo-Norman magnate, Richard de Clare, better known as Strongbow, answered an appeal for help from an Irish king, Diarmait Mac Murchada of Leinster, that English soldiers first entered Ireland in force. This was in 1169, known in Irish history as 'the year of destiny'. Two years later Henry II came to Ireland with an army and an armada of four hundred ships. When the English invaded Ireland or Wales, they came with the military resources of a much more highly industrialised power behind them. In terms of armour, arms and ammunition – crossbow bolts and arrow-heads – they were able to out-produce any Welsh or Irish ruler many times over.

From the moment of Henry's arrival he acted as though he were the lord of all Ireland, come – he claimed – to stop the Irish slaughtering each other. Most of the more powerful Irish kings submitted to him. Henry kept the most important ports of Dublin, Waterford and Wexford for himself, and handed out Irish estates to his followers. In 1177 he designated his son John as king of Ireland, and asked Pope Alexander III to provide a crown. It never arrived, but John assumed the title 'Lord of Ireland' and actually visited the country in 1185 – his first political command. English courtiers became great landowners in Ireland, although some never went there, remaining absentee landlords. English – and a few Welsh and Flemish – settlers, farmers, craftsmen, traders and labourers did, however, cross the Irish Sea. In the south and east of Ireland, from Cork to Carrickfergus, where most of the immigrants settled, a massive change in the man-made landscape occurred: villages, mills, bridges and new towns were built. The countryside here became anglicised and, on the whole, permanently so. The Irish were pushed back into uplands and bogs, the poorest areas. As William of Newburgh, writing in the 1190s, remarked: 'This marked the end of freedom for the Irish, a people who had been free since time immemorial. They had not been conquered by the Romans, but now they fell into the power of the king of England.'

According to Gerald de Barri, the Irish kings and chiefs who came to the Christmas dinner Henry II gave at Dublin in 1171 were made to eat crane, a bird they had never before thought of as a delicacy. It was a demonstration of the *nouvelle cuisine* that identified the French-speaking English as members of a cosmopolitan west European civilisation. The Italian pope, Alexander III, wrote to the Irish clergy expressing joy at hearing that the 'unlawful practices of a barbarous and ignorant people were already beginning to decrease'. In 1210 King John sent a book of English law to Ireland: justice in his lordship was to be administered according to the rules of the Common Law. For a while it even seemed possible that the Irish themselves might become anglicised, just as the Lowland Scots had been. In

Gerald's language the Irish would be made to learn to 'conform to a better way of life and enjoy the benefits of peace'. 'Let them eat crane', as Henry II might have said. Intermarriage gave some cause for hope of assimilation. Aristocrats such as Richard de Clare and Hugh de Lacy married daughters of Irish kings. The Irish came under pressure to learn French. In the 1220s an English Cistercian abbot, after a tour of inspection of Irish Cistercian monasteries, recommended that no one should in future be received into the order in Ireland unless they had learned how to speak either French or Latin.

Unfortunately those who saw the Welsh and Irish as uncivilised were all too likely to treat them with contempt. Gerald reported that when John landed at Waterford in 1185

> he treated the Irish of those parts, though they had been loyal to the English, with disdain and derision, pulling them about by their beards which in accord with the native custom they kept long and flowing. They then went to the court of the Ua Brain king of Limerick and gave him and Ruaidri Ua Conchobair of Connacht a full account of their experiences. They reckoned that these small injustices would be followed by greater ones . . . and so they took common counsel to resist, to guard their ancient freedoms even at risk of their lives.

Because the English saw the Welsh and Irish as bloodthirsty barbarians, they were inclined to treat them far more brutally than they did their enemies on the continent. When the Irish king, Tigernan Ua Ruairc of Breifne, was killed in 1172 – treacherously assassinated by the English, according to Irish annals – his head was sent as a gift to Henry II and his body displayed, hung by the feet, in Dublin. In 1175 Seisyll ap Dyfnwal of Gwent, his wife and seven-year-old son were among the Welsh victims of a massacre at Abergavenny. In 1165 Henry II cut off the noses and ears of the daughters of Welsh princes whom he held hostage; he blinded and castrated their brothers. This atrocity signalled the end of his aggressive policy towards the Welsh. From now on he left the marcher lords to make their own way in Wales.

In the early years of his reign John continued his father's policy, content with the Crown's loose overlordship over both marcher barons and native rulers; his struggle to retain his ancestral lands in France gave him more than enough to do. But he exploited any opportunities that came his way. He supported Maelgwyn ap Rhys of Deheubarth in his feud against his own kindred and obtained Cardigan in return. He clearly favoured the English incomers. In 1200, for example, he gave William de Briouze licence to conquer all he could from his Welsh enemies. But he did not go out of his way to dethrone Welsh princes. Indeed he acknowledged the rising star of Wales, Llywelyn ap Iorwerth of Gwynedd, even recognising him as prince of North Wales by treaty in 1201 and then giving him his illegitimate daughter Joan in marriage. One consequence of John's loss of Anjou and Normandy was that from 1206 onwards he was able to give more time and energy to extending the power of the English Crown within the British Isles – a shift in emphasis that English historians have often applauded.

In 1208 John arrested Gwenwynwyn, prince of Powys, and refused to release him until he had handed over twenty high-ranking hostages. In 1209 he threatened to invade Scotland. King William of Scotland was ill, in no position

to resist, and he was forced to accept the humiliating terms
of the treaty of Norham. He had to pay John £10,000,
hand over thirteen noble hostages and send his two daughters to the English court for John to arrange their marriages.
All of this rankled still in 1215. Although by then William
was dead, his son Alexander II (1214–49) supported the
rebel barons and received his reward in Magna Carta.

> Clause 59. We will treat Alexander, King of the Scots,
> concerning the return of his sisters and hostages and his
> liberties and rights in the same manner in which we will
> act towards our other barons of England, unless it ought
> to be otherwise because of the charters which we have
> from William his father, formerly King of the Scots; and
> this shall be determined by the judgement of his peers in
> our court.

When John turned against his old friends the Briouzes,
they fled to their estates in Ireland. John ordered his justiciar there, John de Gray, bishop of Norwich, to arrest them.
But Gray was unable to carry out his orders; they were
sheltered by the most powerful English landowners in
Ireland, William Marshal, lord of Leinster, Hugh de Lacy,
earl of Ulster, and Walter de Lacy, lord of Meath. Faced by
this defiance John decided on an expedition to Ireland. A
700-ship armada was assembled. William Marshal prudently
crossed the Irish sea, met John at Pembroke and submitted, providing hostages as a guarantee of his future good
behaviour. But the Lacy brothers and the Briouzes were
still recalcitrant. John's army landed at Crook in June 1210
and in a whirlwind nine-week campaign defeated the Lacys
and captured Matilda de Briouze and her older sons.

The expedition ended with John on tense terms with the two most enterprising Irish kings, Cathal Crobderg Ua Conchobair of Connacht and Aedh Ua Neill, king of Cenel Eogain in Ulster. The latter's refusal to hand over hostages was applauded by the Irish chronicler of Inisfallen, who commented, 'The king of England came to Ireland and accomplished little'. By contrast English contemporaries were much impressed – even the king's harshest critics – by his achievement. According to Roger of Wendover, John introduced English law and currency into Ireland, while the forfeiture of the Briouze and Lacy estates, Limerick, Meath and Ulster, added greatly to royal lands in Ireland. The process of transferring English governmental and legal institutions *en bloc* into a conquered country gathered pace.

Next year John launched two invasions of Gwynedd, the first invasion of Wales by a king of England since 1165. He had become alarmed by the growing authority of Llywelyn ap Iorwerth, although it had been John's own action in humiliating Gwenwynwyn of Powys that had given Llywelyn the opportunity to annex southern Powys and Ceredigion. The Welsh retreated into Snowdonia taking their livestock with them; in consequence the English army soon ran out of supplies and John was forced to call off his first invasion. The second was much better prepared and devastatingly successful. Llywelyn was forced to surrender the whole of Gwynedd east of Conwy 'for ever', pay a tribute of twenty thousand head of cattle and agree that if he died without any children born to his wife Joan, all his lands would revert to the king of England. As a guarantee that he would abide by these terms he had to hand over 30 hostages, including an illegitimate son of his own. This, too, was reversed in Magna Carta.

Clause 58. We will restore at once the son of Llywelyn and all the hostages from Wales and the charters delivered to us as security for peace.

In 1211 one of John's mercenary captains, Fawkes de Bréauté, occupied northern Ceredigion for the Crown, and began to build a new castle at Aberystwyth. John was now in a much stronger position in both Wales and Ireland than any previous king of England. In the judgement of the Barnwell chronicler, there was 'no one in Ireland, Scotland and Wales who did not obey his nod – something which, as is well-known, none of his predecessors had ever achieved'. But his apparent mastery of the British Isles was soon shown to be illusory. The oppressive programme of castle-building with which John followed up his victorious 1211 campaign provoked nearly all of the Welsh into uniting behind Llywelyn – although previously many of them had been jealous of him. John's reaction to Welsh revolt was similar to his father's, although where Henry had mutilated hostages, his son hanged them: no less than twenty-eight met this fate on 14 August 1212.

Measures such as these inspired yet more determined resistance. Llywelyn ap Iorwerth took advantage of the baronial rebellion against John to capture even such traditional strongpoints of the English Crown in Wales as Carmarthen, making himself *de facto* prince of Wales. Soon after his death in 1240 men were calling him Llywelyn the Great. His grandson, Llywelyn ap Gruffudd, even made the English government recognise him as prince of Wales. It took a massive display of armed power and castle-building (Harlech, Conwy, Caernarfon, Beaumaris, Flint, Rhuddlan, Aberystwyth) by Edward I (1272–1307) to conquer Wales. In 1301 the first

English prince of Wales was created when Edward I bestowed that title upon his son, known from his birthplace as Edward of Caernarfon. But the policy of reducing the Welsh to the position of being second-class subjects in their own country ignited one further major revolt, that of Owain Glyn Dwr in the early fifteenth century.

In Ireland the struggle went on for much longer even than it had in Wales, partly because the English government almost always gave its claims and ambitions in France a much higher priority than it did Irish affairs. Between 1210 (John's second expedition to Ireland) and 1395 (Richard II's first expedition) no king of England troubled to go to the island of which he claimed to be lord. After the catastrophe of the Black Death, when up to a third of the English population died, no new English settlers came to Ireland; indeed, many crossed the Irish Sea in the other direction, returning to the relative security and job opportunities of England. In the event it would be more than four hundred years before the English could boast that they had completed the conquest begun by Henry II and John in the twelfth century.

CHAPTER 14

The Wider World

All merchants are to be safe and secure in leaving and entering England both by land and by water.

Magna Carta, Clause 41

In 1537 a book on the shape of the earth was printed in Lisbon. By then Columbus had crossed the Atlantic four times and Magellan's fleet had circumnavigated the world. Yet for instruction in the theory of the shape of the world, Europe's most advanced seafaring nation, the Portuguese, turned not to a work of recent Iberian or Italian scholarship but to one written in the early thirteenth century and by an Englishman. This was John Holywood's *De Sphaera Mundi*, On the Spherical Shape of the Earth. The Portuguese translated Holywood's Latin into their own language so that seamen could read it.

In *De Sphaera Mundi* John Holywood set out in scholarly fashion the arguments for the spherical shape of the earth. The concept seems to have been accepted by almost everyone who had given any thought to the subject since classical Greek times. In eighth-century Northumbria, for example, the Venerable Bede described the earth as not round like a shield but like a ball. The same line of thought led Gervase of Tilbury, the author of *Recreation for an Emperor*, a book dedicated to John's nephew, Emperor Otto IV, to compare the earth to an item of royal regalia, the orb. In a work dedicated to John's grandfather, Count Geoffrey Plantagenet, William of Conches pointed out that the earth could not be flat because if it were it would be day at the same time in both the far east and the far west. All that John Holywood did was to add some fashionable sophistication to a position that everyone took for granted. He did this by making heavy use of material from the *Encyclopaedia of Astronomy* written in Arabic by the ninth-century geographer al-Farghani, which had been translated into Latin in the mid-twelfth century. This learned gloss ensured that Holywood's book remained the standard text-book on the subject until well into the sixteenth century. It was still recommended reading in Elizabethan England.

In 1215 people knew that there were three continents, Europe, Asia and Africa, and that they were surrounded by ocean. What they did not know was how many islands also lay in the ocean. The Vikings had discovered Iceland, Greenland and, in North America, Vinland, where, wrote Adam of Bremen in his *History of the Archbishops of Hamburg*, 'vines producing excellent wine grow wild'. 'But,' Adam continued, 'beyond that island no habitable land is found in the ocean, every place beyond it is full of impenetrable ice and intense darkness.' Further south there were rumours of islands such as the isles of Brazil; when Columbus sailed he kept his eyes open for them. Neither did they know if there were any undiscovered continents. Where the greatest uncertainty reigned was over the Antipodes. Was there land, even another continent, there? Could such a land be inhabited? Some thought not, but the English scholar Alexander Nequam, the son of Richard I's wet-nurse Hodierna, in his book *On the Nature of Things*, noted that although people commonly talked about the Antipodeans being beneath our feet, 'scientifically speaking we might just as well say that *we* are beneath *their* feet.' Were the Antipodes accessible from the north? Or was there a great belt of ocean at the equator impossible to sail across because of the unbearable heat of the sun? This had been the opinion of Aristotle, and he was the great authority. It was, wrote Nequam, 'as superfluous to praise his genius as to use torches in order to add to the brightness of the sun'. But, despite their veneration for Aristotle, some thirteenth-century scholars came to believe that the equator was in fact habitable, and by the early fourteenth century European travellers to India had shown that it was.

It was not easy to make accurate calculations of size. How big were the continents? The dimensions of Europe were fairly well known, but what about Africa and Asia? How big, indeed, was the earth? In a discussion of the universe, Alexander Nequam stated that Venus, the Moon and Mercury were smaller than the earth, while the Sun, Jupiter, Saturn and Mars were all bigger, and the biggest of all was the Sun at rather more than 166 times the size of the earth. In *De Sphaera Mundi*, John Holywood gave a figure for the circumference of the earth which came, via al-Farghani, from Eratosthenes, the head of the great library at Alexandria around 200 BC. Eratosthenes had calculated the earth's circumference at 28,000 miles. Holywood had a much more accurate picture of the Earth's size than Christopher Columbus had when he set sail in 1492. Although Columbus also used al-Farghani's calculation that a degree of longitude measured 56⅔ miles, he made the mistake of assuming that al-Farghani's mile was the mile he knew, the Italian mile of 1480 metres, whereas it was in fact the Arab mile of 2165 metres. So Columbus reckoned there were only 45 nautical miles to a degree of longitude, whereas in fact there are 60. And he made another colossal error by believing – or hoping – that Asia stretched much further east than it actually does. Since he planned to start his epoch-making voyage from the Canary Islands, 9 degrees west of Cape St Vincent, he reckoned that if he sailed 2,400 nautical miles west he would reach Japan. The real distance from there to Japan is 10,600 nautical miles. Had he been right Tokyo would be in the Sargasso Sea.

It had long been known that, theoretically, it was possible to travel around the earth and arrive back at your starting point. In the 1370s a French scholar, Nicholas Oresme, calculated that it would take four years, sixteen weeks and two days. This was unduly pessimistic, but more optimistic calculations still left the mariners with an insoluble practical problem. Unless, by sheer good luck, they discovered unknown lands of which no evidence existed, it would be impossible to carry food and drink in quantities sufficient to keep the crews alive during a lengthy voyage. This is why, on 9 October 1492, having sailed west for one month, Columbus was forced to agree to turn back if land were not found within three days. As it happened they sighted land on 12 October. On all these matters the old-fashioned experts who had been sceptical of Columbus's claims had been right, and the discoverer of America hope-lessly wrong. The more influential America became in shaping the fortunes of the whole world, the more heroic seemed to be the achievement of the man who first discovered a *convenient* way of getting there from Europe (which the Vikings had not done). Heroically brave Columbus undoubtedly was, but as one of the scholars at the Spanish court was quick to point out, whatever he had discovered, it could not possibly be the eastern shore of Asia.

There was nothing original in what medieval scientists wrote about the size and shape of the earth and its continents; they were merely following where the Greeks had led. Originality came in the nineteenth century when historians decided that in the Middle Ages people had been 'flat-earthers', probably because they considered that the centuries between the fall of Rome and the Renaissance had been a time of barbarism, superstition and ignorance: the Dark Ages. Even today many people still believe that in the Middle Ages everyone thought the earth was flat; we live in our own age of faith, the faith that 'we' are superior, more rational than the superstitious people of the past.

Holywood's textbook was a typical product of the massive transfer of Greco-Arabic science into western Europe during the course of the twelfth and thirteenth centuries. The most striking outcome of this process was the spread of what we call 'Arabic numerals' – although they were devised in India and in the Middle Ages were known as 'Indian numerals'. Some names from mathematics and astronomy still reflect the fact that they came to us from Arabic, in which 'al' means 'the'. Algorithm, for instance, comes from the name of a ninth-century Baghdad mathematician, al-Khwarizmi; algebra, more poetically, from 'al-Jabar', meaning the restitution of broken bones. Before the twelfth century western Europe seems to have been a closed society in the sense that its inhabitants shut their eyes and ears to the cultures of their Greek and Muslim neighbours. The few who investigated Greco-Arabic science acquired the reputation of dabbling in the black arts. Not even the fact that one such western scholar, Gerbert of Aurillac, became pope, as Sylvester II (997–1002), prevented him from coming under suspicion of being a magician. Not until western forces won the military initiative that led to them conquering territory from Greeks and Arabs in south Italy, Sicily, Spain, Syria and Palestine did significant numbers of western scholars show a real and sustained interest in Greco-Arabic learning. Not surprisingly it was within or on the edges of these newly conquered territories that the key stages in the transmission of Greco-Arabic science to the Latin West occurred. Spain, with its population of Muslims, Jews and Arabic-speaking Christians, played an important role in this, especially after the conquest of Toledo by the Christian kings of Castile in 1085.

The late twelfth-century English astronomer Daniel of Morley spoke for many of his generation when he wrote, 'I hurried to Toledo, that celebrated centre where the world's distinguished scientists were to be found.' One of the attractions of the new astronomy was that it seemed to offer a better way of forecasting the future. In Daniel's opinion, those who dismissed the notion that the movement of the stars could have an effect on the affairs of this world were the sorts of brainless idiots who condemned things before they had taken the trouble to acquire a thorough knowledge of them.

The politician's need to peer at least a short distance into the future, in the hope of getting the timing of difficult choices right, meant that few rulers could afford to dismiss astrology. Non-astronomical methods were tried too: Henry II's chancellor, Thomas Becket, consulted a palm-reader before embarking on an expedition against the Welsh in 1157. But the transfer of Arabic science made astrology the most impressively academic of all methods for telling the future in the twelfth-century West and many rulers turned to astrologers much as politicians today turn to economists. Such useful academics were drawn to court, especially during Henry II's reign while John was a boy. In the 1180s two of the most distinguished English 'Arabists', Daniel of Morley and Roger of Hereford, acted as judges in the king's courts.

To cast horoscopes it was necessary to know which stars were overhead at any particular moment, and hence to understand latitude and longitude. Since it was well known that the earth was a sphere, it followed that the concept of co-ordinates of latitude and longitude had also been well known to scholars ever since the early Greeks. In practice ascertaining latitude is easy using either a quadrant or an astrolabe, an instrument that makes astronomical measurements, but finding longitude remained difficult without a truly accurate instrument timepiece such as a chronometer. It was known theoretically that longitude could be ascertained by observations of the times of eclipses in different places. Indeed, Roger of Hereford tells us that by observing an eclipse in 1178 he worked out the longitudes of Hereford and Marseille. However, rather than trying it for themselves, most westerners relied on the tables of latitude and longitude that had been calculated by Muslim scholars and translated into Latin during the twelfth century. The ninth-century *Khorazmian Tables*, for example, were translated by Adelard of Bath. He also translated Arabic versions of Euclid's *Elements of Geometry* and wrote a number of treatises of his own, including one on the astrolabe – all in all an achievement which has led to him being called 'the first English scientist'.

In his quest for knowledge Adelard travelled far. He dedicated one of his treatises to the bishop of Syracuse in Sicily, and describes being on the bridge at Mamistra – modern Misis – on the way to Antioch when it was shaken by an earthquake. In his treatise on the astrolabe he explained how the earth was a sphere at the centre of a spherical universe. Nearest the earth was the moon, then Mercury, Venus, the Sun, Mars, Jupiter and Saturn. Beyond the planets, the wandering stars, were the fixed stars, so called because they constantly maintained the same relative positions. Beyond the stars was a zone entirely without distinguishing features – or none that could be detected by human senses. This treatise Adelard dedicated to the young Henry II. Its close relationship to astrology made it natural for rulers to be intrigued by astronomy.

The English government clerk, Roger of Howden, copied into his chronicle the texts prophesying hurricanes and plagues after an unusual conjunction of planets predicted for September 1186:

This conjunction will take place on the sixteenth day of September, being the third day of the week, at the first hour; Mars being the lord of the hour, and the Sun in the east, Libra the house and the planets in their places as follows: the Sun in the 30th degree of Virgo, Jupiter in 2 degrees 3 minutes; Venus in 3 degrees 49 minutes; Saturn in 8 degrees 6 minutes; Mercury in 4 degrees 10 minutes;

Mars in 9 degrees 18 minutes . . . Now Saturn who is most elevated in orbit signifies the Pagans and all who are opposed to Christianity, and so the Saracen magicians are predicting a victory for their side. However from our analysis of the figure we form a very different opinion . . .

He followed this with a letter, allegedly from Faramella, son of Abdullah of Cordova, to John, bishop of Toledo, correcting 'the false astrologers of the West' and concluding, after a similarly detailed analysis of the planets, that there would be a poor grape harvest, a moderate wheat harvest, a lot of bloodshed and many shipwrecks 'unless God shall ordain otherwise'.

It was for this reason that John of Salisbury thought that astrologers were wasting their time. 'If the future can be changed, why create a science to understand it, and if it cannot, what is the point of such a science?' Others were even more dismissive. The Winchester monk Richard of Devizes noted an eclipse of the Sun on 23 June 1191: 'People marvelled greatly that in the middle of the day the sun's brightness was dimmed even though it was not all obscured by clouds. Such people do not understand the causes of things. By contrast those who study the way the universe works say that eclipses of the sun and moon tell us nothing about the future.' Evidently then, as now, different people held varying opinions about the science of forecasting.

When the Lateran Council met in 1215 Europeans knew the world better than they had in 1000 and it was becoming much more accessible. In 1000 a few English merchants

travelled as far as north Italy, and some pilgrims visited
Rome; only those who were exceptionally adventurous
made it as far as Constantinople or Jerusalem. By 1215
much had changed. The most dramatic and bloody signs
of this were the crusades. In 1096 several Christian armies
set out from the West and, in 1099, captured Jerusalem
from the Muslims. This was followed by the settlement of
many thousands of westerners in Palestine and Syria, in the
land they called 'Outremer' – the land beyond the sea –
and by the establishment of a Latin kingdom of Jerusalem
as well as two other crusader states based on Antioch and
Tripoli. This had been made possible by the opening up
of the eastern Mediterranean by the fleets of the Italian
maritime powers, Venice, Genoa and Pisa. Although the
Second Crusade (1147–8) achieved little in Syria, a fleet
containing a sizeable English contingent managed to
capture Lisbon from the Muslims of Spain. One quirky
result of this was that the first bishop of Lisbon was an
Englishman, Gilbert of Hastings.

The strategic position of the crusader states, distant
outposts of the West in the Middle East, was always vulnerable. The thousands of western settlers were few in number
when compared with the millions of Muslims there already.
For their reinforcement the crusader states depended on a
long supply line stretching back to southern Italy and Sicily.
Despite their religious differences, the Greek Orthodox
empire of Byzantium, from its capital at Constantinople,
proved a powerful ally to the Latins in the East – but
Constantinople, too, was far away from Jerusalem, when the
enemy was on the doorstep. Only the deep-seated divisions
within the Muslim Middle East had allowed both the initial
establishment and the later survival of the crusader states.

But in 1169 al-Malik al-Nasir Salah ed-Din Yusuf, known in the West as Saladin, became Sultan of Egypt. He understood the value of *jihad*, the holy war against unbelievers, as a powerful religious force capable of uniting the otherwise deeply fragmented Muslim world. In 1176 he brought Syria under his control. This meant he could now attack the kingdom of Jerusalem simultaneously on two fronts. In that same year the crusaders' greatest ally and protector, the Emperor of Constantinople, suffered defeat at the hands of the Muslims of Anatolia in the battle of Myriocephalon. From now on the crusader states were in a parlous position, faced by an opponent with the political understanding and diplomatic skill to bring together forces vastly superior to their own. The king of Jerusalem, Baldwin IV, was a courageous leader and warrior, but he was also a leper, increasingly suffering paralysis and blindness, unlikely to live much longer; his heir was his eight-year-old nephew. Without the strong rule of a fit, adult king, the outlook for the Christians of Outremer was bleak. They sent appeal after desperate appeal for help to the West. In 1185 Heraclius, patriarch of Jerusalem, came in person to plead with the rulers of western Europe.

Henry II met him at Reading. Heraclius prostrated himself at the king's feet and begged for help. An eyewitness, Roger of Howden, reported his words.

My lord king, our lord Jesus Christ cries out to you, and the clamour of the people of God summons you to the defence of the land of Jerusalem. Behold the keys of the kingdom which the king and princes of that land transmit to you, because in you alone, after God, they have trust and hope of safety. Come therefore, lord, do not delay, but

save us from the hands of our enemies. Saladin, the prince
of the enemies of the cross of Christ, and all his people
arrogantly boast that they are coming to conquer the land
of Jerusalem.

Heraclius had some grounds for hope. In penance for his
part in Becket's murder Henry had promised to mount a
crusade of his own, and he had been transferring money
to Jerusalem since 1172. The kings of Jerusalem were his
cousins, descendants of his grandfather Count Fulk of Anjou
who had become king of Jerusalem in 1127. Protecting
Jerusalem was, therefore, his responsibility not just as a
Christian king but also as head of the family. Henry said
he would consider the matter and summoned a great assembly to meet at Clerkenwell in March 1185.

Here, in the presence of the kings, barons and prelates
of both England and Scotland, Patriarch Heraclius received
his reply. Henry would send more money but he would
not go himself. To go, he said, would expose his dominions to attack from barbarians – the Irish, Scots and Welsh
– as well as from the French. Heraclius was dismayed: 'We
don't need more money, we need a leader,' he insisted.
Doubtless he knew that if a king went to Jerusalem even
more money and men would follow. But Henry would not
budge. Heraclius then asked if the king would at least send
one of his sons, so that the Jerusalem branch of the Angevin
dynasty could be revitalised by a cutting taken from the
main stock. This was John's cue. He fell at his father's feet
and begged to be allowed to go to Jerusalem. But Henry
refused permission. Bitterly disappointed, Heraclius sailed
from Dover on 16 April 1185.

What he and many others had foreseen very rapidly

came to pass. The leper-king died on 15 April, the day before Heraclius left England. The child-king, Baldwin V, died in 1186. Next year the kingdom collapsed. On 4 July 1187 the army of Jerusalem was annihilated in the battle of Hattin. Immediately afterwards Saladin executed captured Templars and Hospitallers; as the élite troops of Outremer, these monk-knights could not be allowed to live to fight another day. On 2 October 1187 Saladin's army marched into the Holy City, and the al-Aqsa mosque was restored to Islam. Ever since 1099 the Christians had treated Jerusalem as though it had belonged to them alone and it is symptomatic of the greater tolerance of the Muslims that they allowed the Jewish community to return and permitted four Christian priests to hold services in the Church of the Holy Sepulchre. When Saladin offered to spare their lives many garrisons surrendered quickly; Christians knew from experience that they could rely on him to keep his word. By the end of 1187 only a handful of castles and three coastal towns, Antioch, Tripoli and Tyre, were left in Christian hands.

The West was shocked by the fall of Jerusalem. Public pressure was such that even kings such as Henry II and Philip Augustus who had both rejected the patriarch's appeal in 1185 now had no choice but to reconsider. They met in conference in January 1188, listened to an impassioned sermon from the archbishop of Tyre and took the cross. It was agreed that the followers of the king of England should wear white crosses, of the king of France red, and of the count of Flanders green.

But one man had not waited for the kings. In the previous autumn John's elder brother Richard had become the first prince north of the Alps to take the cross, and he did so without asking his father's permission. When he heard this, Henry refused to see anyone for several days. But however disconcerted his father may have been, most contemporary commentators praised Richard's example. Whatever we, in the twenty-first century, might think of the morality of the crusading movement, in the twelfth-century West it was universally regarded as right and proper that the land they called the Holy Land, the 'patrimony of Christ', should be held by Christians. If it was lost it was the duty of every responsible ruler to assist in its recovery. In that sense, by the values of the time, the crusade was as morally justified as the war against Hitler's Germany was reckoned to be in the twentieth century. The crusade was indeed portrayed at the time as a world war, an intercontinental struggle: Europe against the combined forces of Asia and Africa. Those who went on crusade were thought to be playing their part in the great events of world history. Those who stayed at home were hard put to justify what seemed like cowardly inaction.

Although Richard was one of the first to take the cross, he was one of the last to set out. He and Philip Augustus finally left 4 July 1190, three years to the day since the battle of Hattin. By this time Henry II was dead and Richard had been crowned at Westminster in September 1189. The two kings wintered in Sicily, and Richard did not arrive in the Holy Land until the early summer of 1191. Fortunately for the Christian cause, other crusaders had moved much faster. Since 1189 a Christian army had been entrenched around the great harbour-fortress of Acre and its Muslim garrison. The besiegers were themselves besieged, hemmed in by Saladin's field army. For the last two years all eyes in both the Muslim and Christian worlds had focused on this great struggle. It was when describing Richard's first glimpse of the beleaguered city of Acre and the surrounding hills covered with the tents and pavilions of Saladin's soldiers that Ambroise, author of the *Estoire de la Guerre Sainte* and himself an eyewitness, gave him that name by which he is known: Coeur de Lion. The arrival of the two kings sealed Acre's fate. On 12 July 1191 the heroic garrison surrendered.

As soon as Acre had been captured, Philip returned to France. A contemporary historian from Marchiennes, in north-eastern France, wrote that Philip and those of his men who returned with him – many preferred to stay and fight with Richard – 'ran like frightened rabbits'. In consequence the Third Crusade became Richard's crusade. It was he who took the decision to execute some 3000 Muslim prisoners captured at Acre when Saladin failed to meet the agreed ransom terms. In the end Richard failed to recover Jerusalem, but – even though Saladin held all the logistical advantages – he regained the vital coastal strip of Palestine, and negotiated a treaty that enabled Christian pilgrims to visit the Holy City. His combination of knightly prowess, brilliant generalship and skilful diplomacy won him the admiration of even Saladin's headquarters staff. Presumably these warriors understood the cruel military logic that had led to the massacre of Acre. Moreover, by conquering Cyprus on his way to Acre, Richard had transformed the strategic situation in the eastern Mediterranean. From now on the West possessed a secure forward base that could be used both as a source of renewable supply to the remaining rump of the crusader states and as a springboard for future crusades. It was this conquest that enabled the crusader states to survive for another hundred years. A pious tourist trade developed: from Marseille or the Italian ports convoys sailed so regularly to Acre that pilgrimages to the Holy Land were organised like package tours.

While Richard's leadership of the crusade made him a legend in his own lifetime, there was not much John could do but watch from afar – unless, of course, he were to be tempted to take advantage of Richard's absence. In fact, however jealous he might have been of his elder brother's reputation as the heroic champion of Latin Christendom, while Richard was fighting Saladin, he made no move against him. It was not until after the crusade was over and Richard, captured at Vienna by Duke Leopold of Austria, was held prisoner by Emperor Henry VI of Germany that John decided to risk rebellion. Even though he himself never went on crusade, he knew perfectly well that those who did won respect and admiration. This he had demonstrated in 1185 when he begged his father for permission to go. In the crisis of 1215 he would play the crusade card once again.

Richard I's crusade caused the Eastern Mediterranean and the Muslim world to loom large in English minds. Like many westerners they were fascinated by the great champion of Islam. The contemporary Yorkshire historian, William of Newburgh, had a story to tell about Saladin. Two Cistercian monks were taken prisoner and brought before him. On hearing that they followed a profoundly Christian philo-sophy, he asked, through an interpreter, about their life and principles. They told him that they followed the Rule of St Benedict. When he learned that, among other things, they professed celibacy, he asked whether they drank wine and ate meat. They replied that they had a daily allowance of wine, but were not allowed to eat meat, unless they were ill or compelled to by necessity. He ordered them to be detained in prison and supplied them with meat and water served by two attractive women. They ate and drank what the women brought to them, but took care not to get into conversation with such dangerous creatures. When Saladin was informed of this, he ordered the meat and water to be changed for fish and wine in conformity with the rule of their order. But they forgot the apostolic injunction: 'Use a little wine for thy stomach's sake' (1 Timothy 5: 23) and, encouraged by the women, drank a little too much. Inevitably they fell into temptation. When the monks were discovered next morning in the women's arms, they were taken, sobered up and weeping, before Saladin. 'Does it not seem', he said, 'that the author of your philosophy of life, Benedict, was foolish to forbid you meat, which, after all, has no effect on the will, and allow you wine, which has the power to disturb even the strongest mind? Was not our Muhammad far more sensible? But since you have broken your own rule, what can you do now in expiation?' 'Penance according to the judgement of our abbot,' they replied. 'Then since you cannot find that here, go back home to your own people,' and with those words he set them free.

William of Newburgh defended the western custom of allowing monks to drink wine in moderation and called Saladin 'a man too quick to scoff at what he did not truly understand'. None the less he was impressed by the story – as is shown not only by the fact that he repeated it, but also by his own explanation for the enmity between Muslims and Christians: 'It was and is', he wrote, 'the luxury and greed of our Christian world, displayed in our feasting and drunkenness, that has made the Muslims hate us, for they glory in their frugality.'

As scholars, as crusaders, as pilgrims to Rome and

Compostella, as litigants at the papal curia, in all of these roles Englishmen were now travelling more frequently than ever to Spain, Italy and to the eastern Mediterranean. The growth of international commerce made a major contribution to this development. The twelfth-century Arab geographer Edrisi called the Bay of Biscay 'the sea of the English'. Spain was the chief supplier of silk and oriental spices to Henry II's court. To judge by purchases recorded in the records of the English Exchequer, the Pipe Rolls, Queen Eleanor had a highly developed taste for pepper, cumin, cinnamon and almonds. Sugar first appears in the Pipe Rolls in John's reign, as its cultivation spread from Egypt and the Middle East to Sicily and Spain. John also bought rice, cloves, ginger and saffron. As Spain was thought of as the principal source of high-class leather, members of the English guilds of shoemakers were called cordwainers, the name derived from that of the great Muslim city of Cordova. In the 1160s a Jewish traveller, Benjamin of Tudela, noted the presence of English merchants at Alexandria, where western businessmen dealt with Muslim traders bringing spices and silks from the East. By the later twelfth century there was an English business community in Genoa.

England was becoming more closely integrated into a wider European economy. Because English coins were 'fine' – that is they contained a high silver content, over 1.3 grams of silver in each penny – sterling came to be regarded as the standard of fineness for silver in the two greatest ports of the western Mediterranean, Venice and Genoa. While no coins with a face value of more than one penny were produced anywhere in the Latin West at this time, the high value sterling penny functioned as a coin worth three pence, four pence or five pence in continental currencies. Imitation sterling coins were manufactured in continental mints. The raising and spending of English money on the Third Crusade and on Richard's ransom resulted in large quantities of sterling silver being taken into the Mediterranean region. Western Europe became a sterling zone.

Commerce and the crusades took international politics to a new level. The family connections of the Plantagenets were vastly more cosmopolitan than those of all preceding kings of England. Roger of Howden's narrative of the negotiations that preceded the marriage of Joanna to William II of Sicily gives a good idea of how much travel this involved. Three high-ranking Sicilian envoys, two bishops and a count arrived in London in 1176, asking on behalf of William for Joanna's hand. With Henry's permission they moved on to Winchester to inspect her. 'When they had seen how pretty she was, they were very pleased indeed.' On their return journey to Henry's court, they travelled with another foreign visitor, Cardinal Hugo Pierleone, the papal legate. Once the two parties had reached agreement, one of William's envoys was sent back to Sicily, with four of King Henry's envoys, two clerks and two laymen, to confirm the terms. On 15 August 1176 a council at Winchester decided that Joanna's uncle, Count Hamelin, and three more of Henry II's men, the archbishop of Canterbury, the bishop of Ely and the bishop of Evreux, should escort her to the port of St Gilles on the south coast of France where galleys sent from Sicily would be waiting for her. Early in 1177 Joanna, accompanied by Bishop Giles of Evreux, was received at Palermo. The party arrived at night, and to greet them the city of Palermo was magnificently illuminated. (It was no doubt stories of occasions like this that led Gerald de Barri to state that Palermo alone generated a larger regular annual income for the king of Sicily than the whole of England for the king of England.) In June 1177 Bishop Giles returned to England, bringing with him a charter listing the estates and revenues assigned to Joanna as her dower. (Howden made a careful copy of the document.) At every stage of these negotiations the principal envoys had been accompanied by entourages of their own: their own status required this. In any case both kings sent not only envoys but also splendid treasures, which had to be carefully guarded. Not that the journeys were entirely incident-free. When Henry's first embassy sailed back from Messina to St Gilles, two galleys sank loaded with treasure.

Earlier in 1177 Henry II had received two delegations from Spain. The kings of Castile and Navarre asked him to arbitrate in their territorial dispute. As well as diplomats and clerks both kings had sent along champion knights in case he decided that it should be settled in trial by battle. Henry summoned a great council to London so that as many as possible of his English subjects should see and hear this evidence of his standing in the wider world. It was this great court occasion, when Henry posed as the arbiter of western Europe, that led Matthew Paris to write that the great days of King Arthur seemed to have returned.

When the king of Germany, Frederick Barbarossa, quarrelled with Henry the Lion, the latter was forced into exile and decided to stay at the court of his father-in-law, Henry II. From this moment on the kings of England were to be crucially involved in the internal politics of Germany. Plantagenet support for Henry the Lion's family, the Welfs, led to the Hohenstaufen, the German royal dynasty, entering into closer ties with the Capetians of France. After the

death of the Hohenstaufen Henry VI in 1197, Richard I's
wealth and standing were such that he was able to secure
the election of his nephew, Henry the Lion's son Otto, as
Otto IV of Germany. (Later Otto was crowned emperor by
Pope Innocent III at Rome.) Under John the Plantagenet-
Welf alliance faltered and in the end the consequences for
both him and Otto were disastrous. Otto's defeat in the
Battle of Bouvines in 1214 meant that he lost the German
and imperial throne and that John was confronted by the
Magna Carta rebellion. English affairs were now part of a
wider political world.

By the time Columbus sailed in 1492 people knew a great
deal more about the world than they had known in the time
of John Holywood and Alexander Nequam. Above all, they
knew much more about Asia, thanks to the accounts
composed by thirteenth-century travellers, missionaries and
businessmen who went to the Mongol court at Karakorum
in Mongolia, then on to China and India. So immense were
the distances involved that it took the first of these pioneers,
Giovanni di Piano Carpini – a Franciscan who had known
St Francis – fifteen months to reach the Mongol camp outside
Karakorum in July 1246 in time to witness the enthrone-
ment of Genghis Khan's grandson as Great Khan. Chinese
silk was first available in Genoa in 1257. A later traveller, the
Venetian Marco Polo, provided a glowing description of
Kublai Khan's palaces at Shangtu (Xanadu) and Khanbalik
(Peking). He also reported that the Great Khan was inter-
ested in Christianity. In 1305 a Franciscan friar, John of
Monte Corvino, reported that he had built a church in
Peking and baptised six thousand of the city's inhabitants.
Two years later he was appointed archbishop of Peking.

In 1215 Europe stood on the threshold of the discovery

of Asia. But by now envoys, pilgrims, litigants, businessmen and students had been criss-crossing Europe with such frequency that already a real sense of European community had developed. One sign of this was the fact that people were choosing their names from the same rather limited pool. In the eleventh century it had been easy to tell just from their names whether a person was English, or Scots, or French, or Slav or German, or Italian. But from the twelfth century onwards the same names crop up over a wider area. Slav princely families took German names. The English gradually adopted the French names of their conquerors such as Alice, Blanche, Constance, Eleanor, Geoffrey, Henry, Isabella, Joan, Katherine, Matilda, Philip, Robert and William. Biblical names such as John, Mary, Nicholas, Peter and Thomas became increasingly popular everywhere in Europe.

It was the same with saints. In the eleventh century many churches and shrines were dedicated to local saints whose cults were unknown outside a small region. But from the twelfth century onwards, new churches all over Europe tended to be dedicated to the same saints: George, Catherine, Nicholas, Lawrence, Mary, John, Thomas, Stephen. By 1215 contacts between England and the continent, including the Mediterranean region, were on a scale not seen since the days when Britain had been a province of the Roman Empire. John's England was fully integrated into a new Europe.

CHAPTER 15

The Great Charter

*We have granted all the aforesaid things for God, for the reform
of our realm and the better settling of the quarrel which has arisen
between us and our barons.*

Magna Carta, Clause 61

In January 1215 John met his baronial opponents at a
conference in London. They came armed, an unmistak-
able signal that rebellion was in the air, and he prepared for
the worst. He ordered trusted castellans to put royal castles
in a state of readiness for war. Yet at the same time he
continued to make things worse – by insisting, for example, on his right to collect scutage to meet the costs of the
recent campaign. Despite his unpopularity would-be rebels
had their problems too. The king was within his rights when
he demanded scutage and when he demanded payment of
debt. He sent agents to Rome, urging the pope to condemn
subjects who disobeyed an obedient son of the church – as
he now chose to represent himself.

In 1215 rebellion was far from easy to justify. This might seem an odd thing to say since there had been rebellions against William I, William II, Henry I, Stephen, Henry II and Richard – every king since the Norman Conquest. But in virtually all of these confrontations the rebels had been able to present themselves as men fighting not in their own private interests but for a just cause. The English rebelled against William the Conqueror on behalf of the old royal family. In William II's and Henry I's reign rebels took up arms on behalf of their elder brother Robert Curthose. The barons had fought for the Empress Matilda against Stephen, for Henry II's sons against their father. A few had even been willing to fight for John against Richard I in 1193–4.

But in 1215 there seemed to be neither an alternative royal dynasty nor a disgruntled member of the present royal family on whose behalf would-be rebels could claim to fight. John's brothers were dead and his sons were much too young either to rebel or to be convincing figureheads for revolt. If he had lived, John's nephew, Arthur of Brittany, would have been the obvious leader of opposition – as he had been in 1199 and 1202–3. But he had been removed. The accidents of birth and death, and the non-accident of Arthur's disappearance, meant that in 1215 there were no royal princes whose discontents could serve as a focus for revolt.

The only possible claimant was Prince Louis of France but as the husband of Blanche of Castile, daughter of Henry II's daughter Eleanor, he was a distant kinsman. Anyway, after the wars of the last thirty years or so, a son of Philip Augustus hardly made an attractive candidate for the throne of England. Yet if John's enemies were to win widespread support when they asked men to risk life and limb by taking up arms they needed a good cause. It was in this awkward predicament that his opponents took their step into the unknown. They invented a new kind of focus for revolt: a programme of reform. Lacking a prince they devised a document, a charter of liberties. If they could not fight for the rights of a prince since none was to hand, they would fight for the rights of the whole realm, for what they referred to in Magna Carta itself as 'the community of the whole land'.

In a way the rebels of 1215 were following a path marked out not by former rebels but by kings. More than a century earlier, on the occasion of his coronation in the year 1100, Henry I had granted a charter 'to all his barons and faithful men'. In it he promised to 'abolish all the evil customs by which the kingdom of England has been unjustly oppressed' and listed some of his predecessor's unpopular practices. Henry's coronation charter had been a sort of election manifesto issued in 1100 when the new king was anticipating a challenge from his brother and was keen to win as much support as possible. Once firmly in control of the kingdom he paid little heed to the promises he had made. None the less the Coronation Charter was never entirely forgotten and by the winter of 1214 its ghost had risen up to haunt King John. His opponents were now using it as the framework around which they formulated their own demands. They could do this all the more easily since some of the grievances uppermost in their own minds had also been dealt with in 1100 – in particular, abuses of the system of royal patronage. When the rebels, by drawing up their big charter, a detailed programme of government reform, took their revolutionary step forward, they deliberately looked to the past, to Henry I's charter and to what they believed had been a 'golden age' before the more oppressive government of recent kings. But precisely because they saw the past in this way, not as it really was, they in fact created something entirely new.

At the meeting of January 1215 John's opponents took an oath that they would 'stand fast together for the liberty of the church and realm'. They demanded that the king confirm the Coronation Charter and make further reforms; they threatened war if he did not agree to do as they wished. John played for time. He promised to reply to their demands at a meeting to take place at Northampton on 26 April. The barons now sent envoys to Rome to counter those whom John had dispatched before Christmas. In vain: although the pope asked John to listen to any legitimate requests the barons might make, he roundly condemned leagues and confederations that attempted to coerce the king with threats of force, and he ordered everyone to pay the scutage they owed. John demanded a new oath of allegiance. Men were to swear loyalty to him not only 'against all men', as was the customary formula, but also 'against the charter'. The idea of a charter of liberties for which, and against which, men might fight to the death was gaining ground. And John still had other tricks in his locker. On 4 March he took the cross as a crusader, and handed out white crosses to those of his entourage who followed his example. Now, wrote Innocent III, those who opposed John were 'worse than Saracens'. But few people thought the king's crusading vow anything other than a cynical manoeuvre.

All the while both sides carried on with their preparations for civil war. John raised loans to pay mercenaries brought over from Flanders and Poitou – and was, in consequence, represented as a king who used 'aliens' to oppress his own subjects. The northern barons mustered in arms at Stamford, then marched to Northampton to be there in time for the meeting with the king. As they marched they were joined by others led by John's old enemy Robert FitzWalter, and also by Geoffrey de Mandeville and Giles, bishop of Hereford. In January 1214 Geoffrey had, no doubt rashly, agreed to pay twenty thousand marks for the hand of John's ex-wife, Isabel of Gloucester, yet since then had been unable to establish his right to the vast Gloucester estate. As for Bishop Giles, he was a Briouze. Although not all the rebels came from the north of England, the 'Northerners' were sufficiently prominent among them for this to become a label commonly affixed to the rebels as a whole. When they got to Northampton, they waited for the king, but he stayed away. On 5 May they formally renounced their fealty. The first civil war of 1215 had begun.

The rebels, led by Robert FitzWalter, who styled himself Marshal of the Army of God and the Holy Church, won a decisive victory when the city of London opened its gates to them. This was on 17 May, just ten days after John had granted the Londoners a new charter confirming their traditional liberties and allowing them to elect a new mayor every year. Evidently his bid to win their support had come too late. As lord of Castle Baynard, Robert had some influence in London, but most likely it was John's taxation of the Londoners that had turned them against him. From then on, throughout 1215 and 1216 London was the capital of the rebellion. And the city was rewarded in Magna Carta with clauses 12 and 13. After this, although there was no actual fighting, the barons won a landslide of support. The king retained the loyalty of a few magnates such as William Marshal, but he soon realised that he would have to make – or appear to make – big concessions if he were to buy time in which to build up enough military power to have a hope of reversing the tide. Mediators went to and fro. Documents setting out peace proposals were drafted and discussed. One such document, now known as the Articles of the Barons, survives in the British Library. On 15 June terms were agreed and John went to Runnymede where he confirmed the final draft of the Charter. Over the next few days the envoys for the barons worked hard to persuade the rest of the rebels to accept the terms. Not all were satisfied, and a group of Northerners rode away, refusing to lay down their arms. It was an ominous sign. None the less most of the rebels were persuaded. On 19 June they renewed their homage to the king and peace was proclaimed.

Despite the existence of Henry I's Coronation Charter and similar charters issued by King Stephen at the beginning of his reign in 1135 and 1136, the fact remains that never before had there been anything quite like Magna Carta. As the product of rebellion it was conceived and drawn up in an atmosphere of crisis. John and his enemies were bidding against each other for political and military support. In these circumstances the barons could not afford to be identified with a programme that suited only their own sectional interests. They ended up by demanding a charter of liberties that was long, detailed and contained something for everyone. Thus Magna Carta took shape not just as a criticism of the way John had been treating his barons, but as a thoroughgoing commentary on a whole system of government. This meant that when, after some last-minute wriggling which enabled him to win a point or two, John bowed to the demands of the rebels he was in effect accepting the first written constitution in European history. Paradoxically, in more recent times English people have tended to pride themselves on their unwritten constitution.

There is much that is paradoxical in the history of Magna Carta. Despite its huge later success and mythical status as the cornerstone of English liberties, in 1215 Magna Carta was an abysmal failure. It was intended as a peace treaty, a formula to put an end to the conflict between king and barons. But civil war broke out again within three months of the meeting at Runnymede. The fact is that, as drawn up in June 1215, Magna Carta was bound to fail. Naturally no king could look kindly upon a document to which his consent had been extorted by force. No one could have expected John to implement its terms with enthusiasm. But the problem with Magna Carta went much deeper than this. The rebels had foreseen John's reluctance. They had anticipated that he would try to wriggle out of the commitments made at Runnymede and so in the charter itself they set up mechanisms designed to meet this eventuality:

52. If, without lawful judgement of his peers, we have deprived anyone of lands, castles, liberties or rights, we will restore them to him at once. And if any disagreement arises on this let it be settled by the judgement of the twenty-five barons

Who were these twenty-five?

61. The barons shall choose any twenty-five barons of the realm they wish . . . so that if we or any of our servants offend

in any way . . . then those twenty-five barons together with the community of the whole land shall distrain and distress us in every way they can, namely by seizing castles, lands and possessions . . . until in their judgement amends have been made.

After Magna Carta had been sealed and peace proclaimed, the committee of Twenty-Five set themselves up in London and went to work. But it was a committee of John's enemies. They decided, for example, that Nicholas de Stuteville, not the king, should have possession of Knaresborough and Boroughbridge castles. Clearly if everything was to depend on the judgement of a committee of twenty-five barons chosen by the king's enemies and if, further, these twenty-five were empowered to seize his castles, lands and property whenever they thought it necessary, then the king had in effect been dethroned. This was not merely to reform the realm; this was to destroy the sovereignty of the Crown. No king could have submitted to this, except as a tactical manoeuvre designed to gain time. So deep was the distrust between king and rebel barons that it is unlikely that any agreement could have preserved the peace for long. But a peace treaty that included Causes 52 and 61 made it certain that the renewal of war would come sooner rather than later. The barons had created a political monstrosity, a constitution that could not possibly survive. The Magna Carta of 1215 was the cause of its own undoing.

For the moment John pretended to comply with Magna Carta's terms. Many copies of the document were made and circulated. Arrangements were made for the text of the charter to be translated into French or English (or both) and read out at meetings of county courts throughout England. But by mid-July John had written secretly to the pope asking him to annul the charter. Throughout the rest of July and August he carried on pretending to comply. In May 1215 John had, in his preparation for war and with Archbishop Stephen's agreement, taken possession of Rochester Castle, but he now acquiesced in the Twenty-Five's decision that it should be restored to the archbishop. Then, early in September, the papal letters arrived. Innocent announced that Magna Carta was

> not only shameful and base but also illegal and unjust. We refuse to overlook such shameless presumption which dishonours the Apostolic See, injures the king's right, shames the English nation, and endangers the crusade. Since the whole crusade would be undermined if concessions of this sort were extorted from a great prince who had taken the cross, we, on behalf of Almighty God, Father, Son and Holy Ghost, and by the authority of Saints Peter and Paul His apostles, utterly reject and condemn this settlement. Under threat of excommunication we order that the king should not dare to observe and the barons and their associates should not insist on it being observed. The charter with all its undertakings and guarantees we declare to be null and void of all validity for ever.

Few if any of the rebel barons were diverted one jot from their chosen course of action by Innocent III's threats. The only real effect of the best rhetoric the papal chancery could deploy was to undermine the position of those churchmen, like the archbishop of Canterbury, who were still hoping that a spirit of compromise might avert civil war. When Archbishop Stephen refused to condemn the charter, the pope's commissioners suspended him from office – and this was the archbishop for whose appointment the pope had fought so hard and long.

John was sufficiently encouraged by Innocent's words to decide that the time had come for him to throw off the mask. He had continued to recruit foreign mercenaries during the last few weeks and from Dover, where he had been awaiting their arrival, he marched towards London. Barring the way was Rochester Castle, held for Stephen Langton by Reginald of Cornhill. Although for many years Reginald had been one of the king's most important administrators he, like many of his friends and co-workers, preferred to side with those who wanted fundamental reform. When the barons sent troops under the command of William d'Albini to reinforce Rochester, Reginald opened the castle gates to them. Their plan was that the castle should keep John at bay until they had received reinforcements from France. Both John and the rebels had sent envoys to the French court asking for aid, but the rebels had more to offer. Realising that Magna Carta was now dead in the water, they offered the crown of England to Prince Louis of France. Although at one level the selection of an anti-king marked a return to a much more traditional form of rebellion, it is a measure of just how desperate and determined John's enemies were that they were now prepared to countenance a French king. Louis was happy to accept the offer. Once again an ambitious political leader showed that he had no compunction in going against the pope's strongly expressed wishes. It was just a question of how quickly he could assemble an army and bring it to England.

The siege of Rochester Castle showed King John at his most determined. For seven weeks he remained there, taking personal charge of operations. To prevent the defenders being reinforced from London, his first action was to break down the bridge over the Medway. It made tactical sense, but if he intended a decisive march on London, it was questionable strategy. The city of Rochester fell almost immediately, allowing John's troops to stable their horses in the cathedral just below the castle walls. The castle itself was strongly garrisoned and proved a much tougher nut to crack. On 14 October he sent orders to Canterbury. All the smiths there were to work day and night making pick-axes for his miners. He brought up his siege artillery, five stone-throwing machines with which to batter the castle's walls. Day and night they kept up a bombardment. After a breach had been made in the outer walls and the bailey captured, all that remained was the great tower keep.

On 25 November John sent a writ to the justiciar: 'Send to us with all speed by day and night forty of the fattest pigs of the sort least good for eating so that we can bring fire beneath the tower'. His miners dug under the tower in the south-east corner of the keep, and bacon fat was used to fire the pit props that shored up its foundations. The tower cracked and fell outwards. (When it was rebuilt, the original rectangular turret was replaced by the cylindrical one that can still be seen today.) Despite this the defenders within the keep continued to fight, withdrawing behind an interior cross-wall. Not until their food was all gone did they surrender, on 30 November. 'No one alive', wrote the Barnwell chronicler, 'can remember a siege so fiercely pressed and so manfully resisted.' John set up a gallows and declared his intention of hanging the garrison

that had delayed him for so long. But Savari de Mauléon
told him that hanging brave knights would only mean that
the rebels would do the same to any prisoners they took,
and the result would be that no one would dare to remain
in the king's service. In the event John hanged only one
crossbowman, a man who had previously served him, and
by whom he felt personally betrayed.

While John was detained in the south-east corner of
England, his enemies enjoyed a free hand elsewhere. In
Wales Llywelyn ap Iorwerth captured no less than seven
castles in just three weeks, including Carmarthen, one of
the traditional strongholds of the English Crown in Wales.
Eleven other Welsh princes joined him in what was virtually a triumphal progress. In the north things went just as
badly for John. Alexander II of Scotland was awarded
possession of Northumberland, Cumberland and
Westmorland by judgement of the Twenty-Five; the
Northerners with estates in those counties did homage to
him. In December an advance guard of 140 French knights
and their followers, several thousand in all, arrived at last
in London. But for John the situation on England's borders
now took priority over any thoughts of an attack on the
rebel capital. He divided his forces: one army group was
to keep a check on his enemies in London; the other
followed him north.

As he advanced his routiers laid waste the lands of his
enemies, burning crops, destroying woods and orchards,
seizing livestock. Towns and villages were burned down –
or had to pay the king protection money to escape this
fate. As a demonstration of military might it was impressive and some rebels decided to submit – among them John
de Lacy, lord of Clitheroe and Pontefract, constable of

Chester. He had to take an oath: 'I will not in any way hold to the charter of liberties which the lord king has granted to the barons of England as a body and which the lord pope has annulled.' The Yorkshire rebels retreated before him, taking refuge with Alexander II. Swearing that 'by God's teeth, he would run the little sandy fox-cub to earth', John invaded Scotland. On 13 January 1216 he captured Berwick, Scotland's biggest town. He launched raids into the Scottish lowlands, then turned south again – but not until he had burned Berwick to the ground, setting fire with his own hand to the house in which he had lodged. In March he moved into East Anglia, and captured Colchester from the rebels. For the last three months he had held the military initiative. But his government had broken down; no money was forthcoming from the Treasury. His army commanders and the constables of his castles had to collect the money to pay their troops by whatever means they could.

The king's implacable enemy, the chronicler Roger of Wendover, witnessed this campaign and gave a vivid description of the methods employed by John's mercenaries.

These limbs of the devil covered the whole country like locusts. Sword in hand they ransacked towns, houses, cemeteries, churches, robbing everyone, sparing neither women nor children. They put the king's enemies in chains until they paid a heavy ransom. Even priests at the altar were seized, tortured and robbed. Knights and others were hung up by their feet and legs or by their hands, fingers and thumbs, salt and vinegar were thrown into their eyes; others were roasted over burning coals and then dropped into

cold water. None was released until they had handed over
all the money they had to their torturers.

No doubt Wendover exaggerated. None the less, the sheer
destructiveness of John's campaigning methods was no way
for a ruler to win the love of his people. A number of
rebels had submitted, but their most important leaders held
firm. Although he badly needed a decisive success before
Louis's arrival tipped the balance against him, John made
no attempt to recapture London. Meanwhile the French
advance guard did nothing to inhibit his ravaging of his
own kingdom – or so it seemed to many of the English
victims of their king's wrath. According to one contemporary, the French troops stayed safely in London throughout the winter, thoroughly enjoying themselves until their
wine ran out and they had to endure the discomfort of
drinking beer.

Louis's army of invasion disembarked at Sandwich on
22 May 1216. With commendable foresight and efficiency
John had mustered both land and naval forces in the right
place and at the right time to repel the invasion, but when
the French appeared he rapidly retired to the comfort of
his chambers at Winchester. This left Louis free to join his
friends in London. On 2 June the citizens, led by their
mayor and Robert FitzWalter, swore allegiance to him in
a ceremony in St Paul's churchyard. On 6 June Louis left
London, heading for John at Winchester, but by then the
king was already on his way westwards, to Wiltshire and
Dorset where he stayed for over three weeks at Corfe, one
of his favourite castles. After standing siege for ten days the
defenders of Winchester received John's permission to
surrender to Louis. At this point some of the earls who

had hitherto stayed loyal to John changed sides, including even his half-brother, William Longsword, earl of Salisbury. It was said that this was because the king had taken advantage of William's absence in a French prison to make an attempt on his wife. More likely, William and his peers were not impressed by the way John had abandoned Winchester to its fate.

By now two-thirds of the English baronage had abandoned John. Even more remarkably, so had a third of his own household knights, that group whose careers, lives and fortunes were most closely tied to the king. Louis now controlled the whole of the eastern counties, except for the castles of Windsor, Lincoln and Dover and these were under siege. Alexander II came south from Scotland to Canterbury to do homage to Louis. In return Louis, as king-to-be of England, confirmed the committee of Twenty-Five's grant of the three northern shires to Alexander. In September John at last mounted a challenge to Louis's control of the richer part of England. He marched north-east to reinforce his garrison at Lincoln and perhaps in the hope of intercepting Alexander on his way back to Scotland. He missed the king of Scots but made the Lincolnshire countryside pay for its allegiance to a French king. 'No one could remember that so great a conflagration had ever before been made in this part of the world in so short a space of time,' wrote a Cambridgeshire contemporary.

At Lynn John suffered an attack of dysentery during the night of 9–10 October. According to the Cistercian Ralph of Coggeshall, it was brought on by the sin of gluttony 'for he could never fill his belly full to satisfaction'. It looks as though he was badly frightened by the attack since when morning came he made a gift to Margaret, daughter of William de Briouze, for the sake of the souls of her parents and brother. Next day, 11 October, he left Lynn and by the evening of the 12 October he had reached Swineshead Abbey. Somewhere on that journey the baggage train got into difficulties. According to Ralph of Coggeshall: 'Some packhorses and several members of his household were sucked into quicksand where the Wellstream meets the sea because they had set out in too much of a hurry and careless of the fact that the tide had not yet fully receded. His household effects, his relics and other contents of his chapel were lost.' The breakdown of administration meant that no list survives of what was lost, and perhaps it was never drawn up – but the image of the mortally ill king who lost all or, far more likely, a part of his treasure in the Wash is a powerful one that has gripped the imaginations of generations of treasure hunters.

Over the next few days John's health continued to deteriorate, but he managed to struggle on as far as Newark. There, during the night of 18–19 October 1216, he died. He had wanted to be buried in Beaulieu Abbey, which he had founded, but that was in enemy hands. Worcester, however, was still held by his men and so John asked to be buried in the cathedral there close to the tomb of one of his favourite saints, St Wulfstan of Worcester. After his servants had helped themselves to his personal effects and made off with their loot, the corpse was buried as he had requested. The effigy on his tomb was probably not made until his body was moved into a new sarcophagus in 1232, so it cannot be taken as reliable evidence of his appearance.

King John's heir, who had been kept for safety during

the last few months in the castle of Devizes, was a nine-year-old boy. Henry was anointed and crowned king at a makeshift ceremony at Gloucester on 28 October. From Louis's point of view the accession of Henry III was a disaster. Even a child king represented a more formidable opponent than John, particularly when his council included several elder statesmen and a papal legate capable of turning a dynastic struggle into a holy war. Prevailing sentiment disapproved of depriving a boy of his inheritance – now that his father was dead there was no need to press on with so unpleasant a scheme. In any case the boy was English, and people were starting to grumble about French acquisitiveness and arrogance.

John's death brought Magna Carta back to life. Within a month of Henry's coronation his advisers had reissued the charter, shorn of its more objectionable clauses. In doing this the child-king's counsellors not only ignored the pope's attempt to annul Magna Carta but also, and more importantly, cut the ground from beneath the feet of the barons who had called in Prince Louis. In this sense, reissuing Magna Carta was a propaganda move in the struggle for control of the kingdom – and a highly effective one. If the new king would govern according to the rules as set out in Magna Carta, what point could there possibly be in supporting a foreign king? So English support ebbed inexorably away from Louis. He was forced to rely more and more on fellow Frenchmen and on reinforcements from abroad – which only added to his unpopularity. By 1217 he was forced to concede defeat and return to France.

No sooner had peace been restored than a start was made on a building universally acknowledged as one of the masterpieces of English architecture: Salisbury Cathedral. This was a new model church, using revolutionary techniques in building engineering, thinner walls, slimmer pillars, taller arches, more room for windows and, above all, more light flooding into the interior. This French style, still known as 'Gothic' – the name given it in a sixteenth-century sneer – had been brought to England in new work at Canterbury, Lincoln and Wells, but now for the first time it was applied systematically to a whole cathedral.

By 1218 Bishop Richard Poore of Salisbury had obtained papal permission to move his cathedral from its old, constricted site on the windy and waterless hill of Old Sarum to a new and spacious site by the river Avon. Here, on flat, open ground, there was room for one of the most ambitious projects in British and European history: the simultaneous building from scratch of an entirely new cathedral and an entirely new town. By 1219 the government had authorised the establishment of a new market on the site. In April 1220 the foundation stones of the new cathedral were laid. The bishop himself placed three, one for the pope, one for Canterbury and one for Salisbury; the earl and countess of Salisbury laid one each. The bishop and canons of Salisbury were in a hurry to build their new church, palace and houses. Donations were sought throughout England. Richard Poore was responsible for initiating the project, and was a brilliant diocesan bishop. His new set of statutes governing the clergy of his diocese was a model of its kind, and his revision of the liturgy, the Use of Sarum, traditionally ascribed to St Osmund, the first Norman bishop of Salisbury, was eventually adopted by the whole English Church. He appreciated radically minded clerics such as the Franciscans whom he invited to make a base for themselves in Salisbury. Bishop Richard's Salisbury was the intellectual powerhouse of new ideals.

There is no doubt, however, that the great building project itself was masterminded by someone else, by one of the most radical and gifted clerics of the age: Elias of Dereham. In 1220 he had only just returned to England from the exile imposed on him as punishment for the active and inspirational part he had played in the opposition to John. During the interdict Elias, from Dereham in Norfolk, had been on the staff of the exiled archbishop of Canterbury and had been sent on missions to England in the hope of ending the quarrel. By 1215 Elias had clearly sized John up. In June he was at Runnymede in his role as Stephen Langton's steward. In the days and weeks that followed the sealing of Magna Carta, he played a prominent role in the distribution of the charter and its accompanying documents. On 24 June he received four copies of the charter, and twelve copies of the royal letters announcing the peace. On 22 July he was entrusted with another six copies of the charter. It seems that some people, among them Elias, were so suspicious of the king's intentions that they were not prepared to leave to the royal chancery and its messengers the business of informing the country of the precise terms that had been agreed. They took upon themselves the responsibility for seeing that the job was done. Later that year when Pope Innocent declared Magna Carta null and void and when Stephen Langton went to Rome to appeal against his suspension from office by papal commissioners, his steward took the far more drastic step of actively promoting war as one of the keenest supporters of Louis of France.

When Innocent III excommunicated the leading rebels, Elias defied him, preaching at St Paul's Cross in London that the excommunications were invalid because the pope had not been accurately informed of the true facts.

Just how important Elias and three other like-minded clerics had been to Louis's cause became clear in 1217. In that year, when Louis saw that he would have to concede defeat, one of his main concerns in negotiating a settlement was to ensure that his supporters would not be victimised. Those representing Henry III in these talks, and the papal legate Guala was prominent among them, were willing to promise Louis that laymen who had supported him would not be, but they drew the line at clerics. In June 1217 peace negotiations broke down over this issue. But by September Louis had decided he could protect them no longer. One of the conditions of the peace was that Elias should go into exile. During the interdict he had gone into exile for the sake of his allegiance to the papacy; now he suffered the same fate as a consequence of his public opposition to papal policy.

Elias was a man of uncompromising principle and ready to put his mouth where his mind was. But his opponents evidently admired rather than hated him for that. When William Marshal died in 1219 he had appointed Elias as one of the executors of his will. Bishop Richard Poore was praised for resisting Louis and the French 'who tried to seize the kingdom', but diocesan records make plain that the bishop had great confidence in the Salisbury canon who had been one of the French prince's leading advocates. In 1237 Elias was even named as an executor of the bishop's will. Indeed, an astonishing number of prelates asked Elias to act as executor.

As the archbishop of Canterbury's steward Elias had been responsible for the maintenance of the archiepiscopal castles and palaces, and for new building works. On 7 July 1220 Becket's body was moved into a magnificent new shrine at the east end of Canterbury Cathedral. According to Matthew Paris: 'among those present were Masters Walter of Colchester, sacristan of St Albans, and Elias of Dereham, the incomparable craftsmen (*artifices*) by whose advice and skill everything necessary for the making and erection of the shrine, and for the ceremony, had been impeccably prepared.' There is no doubt that Walter of Colchester was a painter and a sculptor. Was Elias also an artist? Matthew Paris's words suggest that he was, at the very least, a man of considerable taste with a flair for supervising the creation of great works of art. Henry III evidently thought so too, for in the 1230s Elias often worked for the king, on new windows in the hall of Winchester Castle, on Clarendon Palace on a hill overlooking Salisbury, and on a tomb for his sister Joan, queen of Scotland. This was the man who was a canon of Salisbury until his death in 1245. In Salisbury tradition as recorded by John Leland in the sixteenth century he was 'the rector of the new fabric of the church of Salisbury from its foundation for twenty-five years'. The cathedral was not consecrated until 1258, but the coherence and restrained elegance of the design leaves no one in any doubt that the whole had been conceived as a unit, although the astonishing spire, which is now the cathedral's landmark, would not be started until half a century later.

A large site of eighty-three acres had been set aside for the great new cathedral close. Elias's own house, Leadenhall – named for its fine roof of shining lead – was one of the first of the canons' houses to be built, and was acclaimed at the time as a model of its kind. More than twice as much ground had been allocated for the new town. Tax returns in 1377 show that at that date it was the most successful of all the new towns founded during the twelfth and thirteenth centuries. Laid out, like many of them, on a regular grid plan, it combined roads and waterways in a way that commanded the admiration of visitors over four hundred years later.

It was almost certainly the radicalism of his commitment to Magna Carta in 1215 and 1216 that prevented Elias of Dereham being promoted to high office within the English Church. However, in partnership with Richard Poore, Elias's vision for a new church and a new town at Salisbury stands for the rebuilding of a new England after the trauma of civil war and rebellion.

CHAPTER 16

The Myth

The men in our realm shall have and hold all the aforesaid liber-
ties, rights and concessions well and peacefully, freely and quietly,
fully and completely for them and their heirs of us and our heirs
in all things and places for ever.

Magna Carta, Clause 63

When the rebels offered the throne of England to
Prince Louis, they were reverting to the old style
of rebellion. Once again barons were taking up arms on
behalf of a rival king, as barons had in the past. By offering the crown to Louis they were publicly acknowledging
that the new style had failed. Magna Carta had been
intended as a peace treaty, a formula to bring to an end
the conflict between king and barons. In fact civil war had
quickly broken out again. Denounced by the pope, rejected
by the king, discarded by the rebels, by the end of 1215
Magna Carta was surely dead.

Yet it survived. In 1770 William Pitt the Elder called it

'the Bible of the English Constitution'. It remained on the Statute Book until the Law Reform Act of 1863. In 1956 the English judge, Lord Denning, described it as 'the greatest constitutional document of all times – the foundation of the freedom of the individual against the arbitrary authority of the despot'. A Welsh historian, Natalie Fryde, explaining the importance of Magna Carta to German students, has recently described it as 'one of the holiest cows in English history'. But it was not just in England that it came to enjoy the status of a fundamental law. Taken to the American colonies, it influenced both the Constitution of the United States and the laws of individual states.

How was it that a failed peace treaty survived to become 'the corner-stone of liberty in the English-speaking world'? A failure when used by rebels as a weapon against the Crown, it succeeded when it was taken over by royalists and turned against the rebels. But the decision to reissue Magna Carta so soon after King John's death was more than just clever civil war propaganda. Minor changes in the text of some of its clauses demonstrate that the detail of the document was being studied carefully and thoughtfully. For example, the charter of 1215 conceded that an heir who had been in the wardship of the Crown should not have to pay a relief when he came of age and entered into his inheritance. The charter of 1216 made the same concession and went on to fix the age at which an heir entered his majority, 'namely when he is twenty-one years old'. Magna Carta was evidently thought of as a serious and valuable statement of the law of the land, worth modifying, worth keeping up to date, not just a political manifesto to be jettisoned as soon as the emergency was over.

After Louis had given up his fight for the English throne and had gone back to France, in the autumn of 1217, Magna Carta was reissued again, and with further modifications. These included the issue of a supplementary charter dealing with forest law. Since the Forest Charter was a much shorter document, the main charter became known as the 'big charter' – Magna Carta. In 1225 the charter was reissued yet again, this time in return for a grant of taxation to the king. The text of the 1225 version is particularly important because it is this version, and not the Runnymede charter, that entered the statute books and so became the Magna Carta of subsequent history and myth. Like the charter of 1215, these reissues were translated into French and English and read out at meetings of the shire courts throughout the realm. All this meant that Magna Carta was a highly publicised concept.

In 1265 when the government of England was in the hands of Simon de Montfort it was decreed that the charter should be proclaimed twice a year so that in future no one could claim to be ignorant of it. One demand commonly made was for copies of Magna Carta to be nailed to church doors. It rapidly became widely known as a 'Good Thing', a touchstone of good government. From now on whenever a king was thought to be governing badly, to be infringing men's liberties, the cry went up for confirmation of the charter. Edward I was forced to confirm the charter in 1297. When lawyers compiled their books of statutes it was always Magna Carta, the text of 1225 as confirmed in 1297, that had pride of place. It came to be thought of as the first statute of the realm.

Believing Magna Carta to be a 'Good Thing', men assumed that it contained what they wanted it to contain.

In this way it took on a mythical life of its own. King John's promise in Clause 39 not to take any action against the free man, 'except by the lawful judgement of his peers' came to be interpreted as a guarantee of trial by jury. In fact, in June 1215 'the lawful judgement of peers' meant that people should be tried in courts composed of their social equals. It was only after Innocent III, coincidentally later in the same year, banned priests from participating in trials by ordeal that the verdict-giving jury gradually came to be employed in criminal trials. But the myth that the right to trial by jury goes back to Magna Carta is one that remains widely believed in today. It was this myth that led Tony Hancock, playing Henry Fonda's role in Twelve Angry Men, to turn to his fellow jurors with the plea: 'Does Magna Carta mean nothing to you? Did she die in vain?'

A myth that was once widely believed by lawyers is that Magna Carta embodied the ancient laws of Anglo-Saxon England, subverted by the 'Norman Yoke' after 1066, but then recovered and set out for all time in the charter. This myth mattered greatly in the run-up to the English civil war of the seventeenth century. In opposition to the Stuart monarchy, which was making increasing use of its prerogative powers, the lawyers and gentry in the House of Commons emphasised the notion of the subordination of the Crown to the common law of England. For many lawyers of the time, in particular Sir Edward Coke, Magna Carta was 'the fountain of all the fundamental laws of the realm . . . a confirmation or restitution of the common law'. From 1610 onwards Coke cited the charter again and again, in and out of the House of Commons, always claiming that it limited the king's power to alter ancient customs. When Charles I was informed that Coke was working on a book on Magna Carta, he ordered its suppression. But after Coke's death, the Long Parliament ordered the publication of his confiscated papers and in consequence his commentary on Magna Carta was published as part of the revolution of 1642.

The radical Levellers appealed to Magna Carta to justify their resistance not only to Charles I but also to the Long Parliament which they felt had betrayed the cause, and then, in turn, to Oliver Cromwell. Once in power, even Cromwell was inclined to override the provisions of Magna Carta. On one occasion when the judges complained, he reminded them who had appointed them and told them that 'their Magna F— should not control his actions'. (Lord Chief Justice Keeling may have been remembering Cromwell's words when, in 1667, he referred dismissively to 'Magna Farta'.)

Against these seventeenth-century tyrants the Leveller John Lilburne proudly proclaimed his rights as a free-born Englishman:

'I am a freeman, yea a free-born denizen of England . . . and I conceive I have as true a right to all the privileges that do belong to a freeman as the greatest man in England, whosoever he be . . . and the ground of my freedom, I build upon the Grand Charter of England.'

In a pamphlet composed after he had been arrested in 1648, Lilburne wrote that the arresting officer 'stabbed Magna Carta . . . to the very heart and soul'. Other Levellers succeeded in turning the political debate into a piece of street theatre. The pamphleteer Richard Overton described how, after his arrest, he was dragged to Newgate gaol by his head and shoulders 'as if I had been a dead dog', yet all the while managing to hold on to his copy of Coke on Magna Carta.

> I clapped it in my arms, and I laid myself upon my belly, but by force they violently turned me upon my back, then smote me . . . to make me let go my hold, whereupon as loud as I could, I cried out, murder, murder, murder. And thus by an assault they got the great Charter of England's Liberties and Freedoms from me; which I laboured to the utmost of power in me to preserve and defend, and ever to the death shall maintain.

All this seventeenth-century fuss meant that Magna Carta was headline news at the time that the American colonies were being settled. 'Nor shall any persons be deprived of life, liberty or property, without due process of law': the resounding phrases of the Fifth Amendment are an echo of Magna Carta Clause 39. In America as in England Magna Carta became a potent symbol of men's struggle for freedom and human rights. Thus a tablet commemorating Magna Carta was set up at Runnymede by the American Bar Association, and an adjacent site was chosen as a memorial to John F. Kennedy. Fortunately these memorials were not placed on what has become known as Magna Carta Island since the notion that Magna Carta was sealed on an island at Runnymede is just another myth, in this case spun out of the name Runnymede, which means 'the meadow in council island'.

'To no one will we sell, to no one will we deny or delay right or justice.' Most people will think governments everywhere should still be reminded of the principle stated in Clause 40. The law's delays are with us still, and it is all too clear that the wealthy have so great an advantage when brought before courts of law that to talk of 'selling justice' does not seem much – if at all – wide of the mark. Similarly the much misunderstood Clause 39 encapsulates a fundamental principle: 'No free man shall be arrested or imprisoned or have their property confiscated or be outlawed or exiled or in any way ruined, nor will we take any action agaisnt him, except by the lawful judgement of his peers or by the law of the land.' Despite a few archaic terms such as 'outlawry' or 'peers', despite the fact that it says 'man', not 'person', this remains a sweeping general statement of the individual's rights in the face of government power.

It is striking that the sweeping statements of lofty general principle in Clauses 39 and 40 come so late in the charter; this hardly suggests that they were uppermost in the minds of those who negotiated the charter in 1215. The first ten clauses of Magna Carta are principally concerned with the property rights of earls and barons, and so, too, are many of the later clauses. At the beginning of the twentieth century it became fashionable to take a debunking view of Magna Carta, to see it as being all about the selfish interests of 'feudal barons'. But none of this has touched the symbolic value of Magna Carta. It was the product of a society accustomed to dealing with the problems and privileges of freedom: freedom from slavery or from serfdom, the freedom of boroughs, the freedom of the Church, the freedom of trade. The charter still retains its iconic status. Anyone with a cause against the government of the day is very likely to defend his or her right to protest by referring to Magna Carta.

There is much to be said for the protesters' view of

Magna Carta. Although there is not a word in it about the right to protest, there is a sense in which Magna Carta in its entirety represents protest. It was in origin the product of direct political action, of negotiation after rebellion. As a symbol of the struggle against tyranny it will always retain its value.

The Text of Magna Carta

John, by the grace of God, King of England, Lord of Ireland, Duke of Normandy and Aquitaine, Count of Anjou, to the archbishops, bishops, abbots, earls, barons, justiciars, foresters, sheriffs, stewards, servants and all his officials and faithful subjects greeting.

Know that we, from reverence for God and for the salvation of our soul and those of all our ancestors and heirs, for the honour of God and the exaltation of Holy Church and the reform of our realm, on the advice of our reverend fathers, Stephen, Archbishop of Canterbury, Primate of all England and Cardinal of the Holy Roman Church, Henry, archbishop of Dublin, William of London, Peter of Winchester, Jocelin of Bath and Glastonbury, Hugh of Lincoln, Walter of Worcester, William of Coventry and Bendict of Rochester, bishops, Master Pandulf, subdeacon and member of the household of the lord pope, brother Aimeric, master of the knighthood of the Temple in England, and the noble men, William Marshal, Earl of Pembroke, William, Earl of Salisbury, William, Earl of Warenne, William, Earl of Arundel, Alan of Galloway, Constable of Scotland, Warin fitz Gerold, Peter fitz Herbert, Hubert de Burgh, seneschal of Poitou, Hugh de Neville, Matthew fitz Herbert, Thomas Basset, Alan Basset, Philip d'Aubigny, Robert of Ropsley, John Marshal, John fitz Hugh and others, our faithful subjects:

1. In the first place have granted to God and by this our present Charter have confirmed, for us and our heirs in perpetuity, that the English church shall be free, and shall have its rights undiminished and its liberties unimpaired: and we wish it thus observed, which is evident from the fact that of our own free will before the quarrel between us and our barons began, we conceded and confirmed by our charter freedom of elections, which is thought to be of the greatest necessity and importance to the English church, and obtained confirmation of this from the lord pope Innocent III, which we shall observe and wish our heirs to observe in good faith in perpetuity. We have also granted to all the free men of our realm for ourselves and our heirs for ever, all the liberties written below, to have and hold, them and their heirs from us and our heirs.

2. If any of our earls or barons, or others holding of us in chief by knight service shall die, and at his death his heir be of full age and owe relief, he shall have his inheritance on payment of the ancient relief, namely the heir or heirs of an earl £100 for a whole earl's barony, the heir or heirs of a baron £100 for a whole barony, the heir or heirs of a knight 100s. at most for a whole knight's fee; and anyone who owes less shall give less according to the ancient usage of fiefs.

3. If, however, the heir of any such person has been under age and in wardship, when he comes of age he shall have his inheritance without relief or fine.

4. The guardian of the land of such an heir who is under age shall not take from the land more than the reasonable revenues, customary dues and services, and that without destruction and waste of men or goods. And if we entrust the wardship of the land of such a one to a sheriff, or to any other who is answerable to us for its revenues, and he

destroys or wastes the land in his charge, we will take amends
of him, and the land shall be entrusted to two lawful and
prudent men of that fief who will be answerable to us for
the revenues or to him to whom we have assigned them.
And if we give or sell to anyone the wardship of any such
land and he causes destruction or waste, he shall lose the
wardship and it shall be transferred to two lawful and prudent
men of the fief who shall be answerable to us as is aforesaid.

5. Moreover so long as the guardian has the wardship of the
land, he shall maintain the houses, parks, preserves, fishponds,
mills and the other things pertaining to the land from its
revenues; and he shall restore to the heir when he comes of
age all his land stocked with ploughs and wainage such as
the agricultural season demands and the revenues of the
estate can reasonably bear.

6. Heirs shall be given in marriage without disparagement, yet
so that before a marriage is contracted it shall be made
known to the heir's next of kin.

7. After her husband's death, a widow shall have her marriage
portion and her inheritance at once and without any
hindrance; nor shall she pay anything for her dower, her
marriage portion, or her inheritance which she and her
husband held on the day of her husband's death; and she
may stay in her husband's house for forty days after his
death, within which period her dower shall be assigned to
her.

8. No widow shall be compelled to marry so long as she wishes
to live without a husband, provided that she gives security
that she will not marry without our consent if she holds of
us, or without the consent of the lord of whom she holds,
if she holds of another.

9. Neither we nor our bailiffs will seize any land or rent in payment of a debt so long as the chattels of the debtor are sufficient to repay the debt; nor shall the sureties of the debtor be distrained so long as the debtor himself is capable of paying the debt; and if the principal debtor defaults in the payment of the debt, having nothing wherewith to pay it, the sureties shall be answerable for the debt; and, if they wish, they may have the lands and revenues of the debtor until they have received satisfaction for the debt they paid on his behalf, unless the principal debtor shows that he has discharged his obligations to the sureties.

10. If anyone who has borrowed from the Jews any amount, great or small, dies before the debt is repaid, it shall not carry interest as long as the heir is under age, of whom-soever he holds; and if that debt fall into our hands, we will take nothing except the principal sum specified in the bond.

11. And if a man dies owing a debt to the Jews, his wife may have her dower and pay nothing of that debt; and if he leaves children under age, their needs shall be met in a manner in keeping with the holding of the deceased; and the debt shall be paid out of the residue, saving the service due to the lords. Debts owing to others than Jews shall be dealt with likewise.

12. No scutage or aid is to be levied in our realm except by the common counsel of our realm, unless it is for the ransom of our person, the knighting of our eldest son or the first marriage of our eldest daughter; and for these only a reasonable aid is to be levied. Aids from the city of London are to be treated likewise.

13. And the city of London is to have all its ancient liberties and free customs both by land and water. Furthermore, we

will and grant that all other cities, boroughs, towns and ports shall have all their liberties and free customs.

14. And to obtain the common counsel of the realm for the assessment of an aid (except in the three cases aforesaid) or a scutage, we will have archbishops, bishops, abbots, earls and greater barons summoned individually by our letters, and we shall also have summoned generally through our sheriffs and bailiffs all those who hold of us in chief, for a fixed date, with at least forty days' notice, and at a fixed place; and in all letters of summons we will state the reason for the summons. And when the summons has thus been made, the business shall go forward on the day arranged according to the counsel of those present, even if not all those summoned have come.

15. Henceforth we will not grant anyone that he may take an aid from his free men except to ransom his person, to make his eldest son a knight and to marry his eldest daughter once; and for these purposes only a reasonable aid is to be levied.

16. No man shall be compelled to perform more service for a knight's fee or for any other free tenement than is due therefrom.

17. Common pleas shall not follow our court but shall be held in some fixed place.

18. Recognizances of novel disseisin, mort d'ancestor, and darrein presentment shall not be held elsewhere than in the court of the county in which they occur, and in this manner: we, or if we are out of the realm our chief justiciar, shall send two justices through each county four times a year who, with four knights of each county chosen by the county, shall hold the said assizes in the county court on the day and in the place of meeting of the county court.

19. And if the said assizes cannot all be held on the day of the county court, so many knights and all freeholders of those present in the county court on that day shall remain behind as will suffice to make judgements, according to the amount of business to be done.

20. A free man shall not be amerced for a trivial offence, except in accordance with the degree of the offence; and for a serious offence he shall be amerced according to its gravity, saving his livelihood; and a merchant likewise, saving his merchandise; in the same way a villein shall be amerced saving his wainage; if they fall into our mercy. And none of the aforesaid amercements shall be imposed except by the testimony of reputable men of the neighbourhood.

21. Earls and barons shall not be amerced except by their peers and only in accordance with the nature of their offence.

22. No clerk shall be amerced on his lay tenement except in the manner of the others aforesaid and without reference to the size of his ecclesiastical benefice.

23. No vill or man shall be forced to build bridges at river banks, except those who ought to do so by custom and law.

24. No sheriff, constable, coroners or other of our bailiffs may hold pleas of our Crown.

25. All shires, hundreds, wapentakes and ridings shall be at the ancient farm without any increment, except our demesne manors.

26. If anyone holding a lay fief of us dies and our sheriff or bailiff shows our letters patent of summons for a debt which the deceased owed us, it shall be lawful for the sheriff or our bailiff to attach and list the chattels of the deceased found in lay fee to the value of that debt, by the view of

lawful men, so that nothing is removed until the evident debt is paid to us, and the residue shall be relinquished to the executors to carry out the will of the deceased. And if he owes us nothing, all the chattels shall be accounted as the deceased's saving their reasonable shares to his wife and children.

27. If any free man dies intestate, his chattels are to be distributed by his nearest relations and friends, under the supervision of the Church, saving to everyone the debts which the deceased owed him.

28. No constable or any other of our bailiffs shall take any man's corn or other chattels unless he pays cash for them at once or can delay payment with the agreement of the seller.

29. No constable is to compel any knight to give money for castle guard, if he is willing to perform that guard in his own person or by another reliable man, if for some good reason he is unable to do it himself; and if we take or send him on military service, he shall be excused the guard in proportion to the period of his service.

30. No sheriff or bailiff of ours or anyone else is to take horses or carts of any free man for carting without his agreement.

31. Neither we nor our bailiffs shall take other men's timber for castles or other work of ours, without the agreement of the owner.

32. We will not hold the lands of convicted felons for more than a year and a day, when the lands shall be returned to the lords of the fiefs.

33. Henceforth all fish-weirs shall be completely removed from the Thames and the Medway and throughout all England, except on the sea coast.

34. The writ called praecipe shall not, in future, be issued to

anyone in respect of any holding whereby a free man may lose his court.

35. Let there be one measure of wine throughout our kingdom and one measure of ale and one measure of corn, namely the London quarter, and one width of cloth whether dyed, russet or halberjet, namely two ells within the selvedges. Let it be the same with weights as with measures.

36. Henceforth nothing shall be given or taken for the writ of inquisition of life or limb, but it shall be given freely and not refused.

37. If anyone holds of us by fee-farm, by socage or by burgage, and holds land of someone else by knight service, we will not, by virtue of that fee-farm, socage or burgage, have wardship of his heir or of land of his that belongs to the fief of another; nor will we have custody of that fee-farm or socage or burgage unless such fee-farm owes knight service. We will not have custody of the heir or land of anyone who holds of another by knight service, by virtue of any petty sergeanty which he holds of us by the service of rendering to us knives or arrows or the like.

38. Henceforth no bailiff shall put anyone on trial by his own unsupported allegation, without bringing credible witnesses to the charge.

39. No free man shall be taken or imprisoned or disseised or outlawed or exiled or in any way ruined, nor will we go or send against him, except by the lawful judgement of his peers or by the law of the land.

40. To no one will we sell, to no one will we deny or delay right or justice.

41. All merchants are to be safe and secure in leaving and entering England, and in staying and travelling in England, both

by land and by water, to buy and sell free from all male-totes by the ancient and rightful customs, except, in time of war, such as come from an enemy country. And if such are found in our land at the outbreak of war they shall be detained without damage to their persons or goods, until we or our chief justiciar know how the merchants of our land are treated in the enemy country; and if ours are safe there, the others shall be safe in our land.

42. Henceforth anyone, saving his allegiance due to us, may leave our realm and return safe and secure by land and water, save for a short period in time of war on account of the general interest of the realm and excepting those imprisoned and outlawed according to the law of the land, and natives of an enemy country, and merchants, who shall be treated as aforesaid.

43. If anyone dies who holds of some escheat such as the honours of Wallingford, Nottingham, Boulogne or Lancaster, or of other escheats which are in our hands and are baronies, his heir shall not give any relief or do any service to us other than what he would have done to the baron if that barony had been in a baron's hands; and we shall hold it in the same manner as the baron held it.

44. Henceforth men who live outside the forest shall not come before our justices of the forest upon a general summons, unless they are impleaded or are sureties for any person or persons who are attached for forest offences.

45. We will not make justices, constables, sheriffs or bailiffs who do not know the law of the land and mean to observe it well.

46. All barons who have founded abbeys of which they have charters of the kings of England, or ancient tenure, shall have custody thereof during vacancies, as they ought to have.

47. All forests which have been afforested in our time shall be disafforested at once; and river banks which we have enclosed in our time shall be treated similarly.

48. All evil customs of forests and warrens, foresters and war-reners, sheriffs and their servants, river banks and their wardens are to be investigated at once in every county by twelve sworn knights of the same county who are to be chosen by worthy men of the county, and within forty days of the inquiry they are to be abolished by them beyond recall, provided that we, or our justiciar, if we are not in England, first know of it.

49. We will restore at once all hostages and charters delivered to us by Englishmen as securities for peace or faithful service.

50. We will dismiss completely from their offices the relations of Gerard d'Athée that henceforth they shall have no office in England, Engelard de Cigogné, Peter and Guy and Andrew de Chanceaux, Guy de Cigogné, Geoffrey de Martigny with his brothers, Philip Mark with his brothers and his nephew Geoffrey, and all their followers.

51. Immediately after concluding peace, we will remove from the kingdom all alien knights, crossbowmen, sergeants and mercenary soldiers who have come with horses and arms to the hurt of the realm.

52. If anyone has been disseised or deprived by us without lawful judgement of his peers of lands, castles, liberties or his rights we will restore them to him at once; and if any disagreement arises on this, then let it be settled by the judgement of the Twenty-Five barons referred to below in the security clause. But for all those things of which anyone was disseised or deprived without lawful judgement of his peers by King Henry our father, or by King Richard our brother, which we hold in our hand or which are held by

others under our warranty, we shall have respite for the usual crusader's term; excepting those cases in which a plea was begun or inquest made on our order before we took the cross; when, however, we return from our pilgrimage, or if perhaps we do not undertake it, we will at once do full justice in these matters.

53. We shall have the same respite, and in the same manner, in doing justice or disafforesting or retaining those forests which Henry our father or Richard our brother afforested, and concerning custody of lands which are of the fee of another, the which wardships we have had hitherto by virtue of a fee held of us by knight's service, and concerning abbeys founded on fees other than our own, in which the lord of the fee claims to have a right. And as soon as we return, or if we do not undertake our pilgrimage, we will at once do full justice to complainants in these matters.

54. No one shall be taken or imprisoned upon the appeal of a woman for the death of anyone except her husband.

55. All fines which were made with us unjustly and contrary to the law of the land, and all amercements imposed unjustly and contrary to the law of the land, shall be completely remitted or else they shall be settled by the judgement of the Twenty-Five barons mentioned below in the security clause, or by the judgement of the majority of the same, along with the aforesaid, Stephen, Archbishop of Canterbury, if he can be present, and others whom he wishes to summon with him for this purpose. And if he cannot be present the business shall nevertheless proceed without him, provided that if any one or more of the aforesaid Twenty-Five barons are in such a suit they shall stand down in this particular judgement, and shall be replaced by others chosen and sworn in by the rest of the same Twenty-Five, for this case only.

56. If we have disseised or deprived Welshmen of lands, liberties or other things without lawful judgement of their peers, in England or in Wales, they are to be returned to them at once; and if a dispute arises over this it shall be settled in the March by judgement of their peers; for tenements in England according to the law of England, for tenements in Wales according to the law of Wales, for tenements in the March according to the law of the March. The Welsh are to do the same to us and ours.

57. For all those things, however, of which any Welshman has been disseised or deprived without lawful judgement of his peers by King Henry our father, or King Richard our brother, which we have in our possession or which others hold under our legal warranty, we shall have respite for the usual crusader's term; excepting those cases in which a plea was begun or inquest made on our order before we took the cross. However, when we return, or if perhaps we do not go on our pilgrimage, we will at once give them full justice in accordance with the laws of the Welsh and the aforesaid regions.

58. We will restore at once the son of Llywelyn and all the hostages from Wales and the charters delivered to us as security for peace.

59. We will treat Alexander, King of the Scots, concerning the return of his sisters and hostages and his liberties and rights in the same manner in which we will act towards our other barons of England, unless it ought to be otherwise because of the charters which we have from William his father, formerly King of the Scots; and this shall be determined by the judgement of his peers in our court.

60. All these aforesaid customs and liberties which we have granted to be held in our realm as far as it pertains to us

towards our men, shall be observed by all men of our realm, both clerk and lay, as far as it pertains to them, towards their own men.

61. Since, moreover, we have granted all the aforesaid things for God, for the reform of our realm and the better settling of the quarrel which has arisen between us and our barons, wishing these things to be enjoyed fully and undisturbed in perpetuity, we give and grant them the following security: namely, that the barons shall choose any twenty-five barons of the realm they wish, who with all their might are to observe, maintain and cause to be observed the peace and liberties which we have granted and confirmed to them by this our present charter; so that if we or our justiciar or our bailiffs or any of our servants offend against anyone in any way, or transgress any of the articles of peace or security, and the offence is indicated to four of the aforesaid twenty-five barons, these four barons shall come to us or our justiciar, if we are out of the kingdom, and shall bring it to our notice and ask that we have it redressed without delay. And if we, or our justiciar, should we be out of the kingdom, do not redress the offence within forty days from the time when it was brought to the notice of us or our justiciar, should we be out of the kingdom, the aforesaid four barons shall refer the case to the rest of the twenty-five barons and those twenty-five barons with the commune of all the land shall distrain and distress us in every way they can, namely by seizing castles, lands and possessions, and in such other ways as they can, saving our person and those of our queen and of our children, until, in their judgement, amends have been made; and when it has been redressed they are to obey us as they did before. And anyone in the land who wishes may take an oath to obey the orders of the said twenty-five

barons in the execution of all the aforesaid matters, and to join with them in distressing us to the best of his ability, and we publicly and freely permit anyone who wishes to take the oath, and we will never forbid anyone to take it. Moreover we shall compel and order all those in the land who of themselves and of their own free will are unwilling to take an oath to the twenty-five barons to distrain and distress us with them, to take the oath as aforesaid. And if any of the twenty-five barons dies or leaves the country or is otherwise prevented from discharging these aforesaid duties, the rest of the aforesaid barons shall on their own decision choose another in his place, who shall take the oath in the same way as the others. In all matters the execution of which is committed to those twenty-five barons, if it should happen that the twenty-five are present and disagree among themselves on anything, or if any of them who has been summoned will not or cannot come, whatever the majority of those present shall provide or order is to be taken as fixed and settled as if the whole twenty-five had agreed to it; and the aforesaid twenty-five are to swear that they will faithfully observe all the aforesaid and will do all they can to secure its observance. And we will procure nothing from anyone, either personally or through another, by which any of these concessions and liberties shall be revoked or diminished; and if any such thing is procured, it shall be null and void, and we will never use it either ourselves or through another.

62. And we have completely remitted and pardoned to all any ill will, grudge and rancour that have arisen between us and our subjects, clerk and lay, from the time of the quarrel. Moreover we have fully forgiven and completely condoned to all, clerk and lay, as far as pertains to us, all offences occasioned by the

said quarrel from Easter in the sixteenth year of our reign to the conclusion of peace. And moreover we have caused letters patent of the Lord Stephen, Archbishop of Canterbury, the Lord Henry, Archbishop of Dublin, the aforesaid bishops and Master Pandulf to be made for them on this security and the aforesaid concessions.

63. Wherefore we wish and firmly command that the English church shall be free, and the men in our realm shall have and hold all the aforesaid liberties, rights and concessions well and peacefully, freely and quietly, fully and completely for them and their heirs of us and our heirs in all things and places for ever, as is aforesaid. Moreover an oath has been sworn, both on our part and on the part of the barons, that all these things aforesaid shall be observed in good faith and without evil intent. Witness the above-mentioned and many others. Given under our hand in the meadow which is called Runnymede between Windsor and Staines on the fifteenth day of June in the seventeenth year of our reign.

Acknowledgements

We are extremely grateful to the following distinguished historians, archaeologists and curators who very generously gave of their time and knowledge:

Prof Robert Bartlett, University of St Andrews
Dr Matthew Bennett, Royal Military College, Sandhurst
Dr Ian Betts, Museum of London
Dr Paul Brand, All Souls, Oxford
Dr Claire Breay, Department of Manuscripts, British
   Library
Dr Michelle Brown, Department of Manuscripts, British
   Library
Prof David Carpenter, King's College London
Dr Justin Champion, Royal Holloway College
Prof Christopher Dyer, Birmingham University
Dr Anne Davies, Museum of London
Dr Geoff Egan, Museum of London
Dr Charles French, Department of Archaeology,
   Cambridge
Dr Ian Friel, Chichester Museum
Dr Damian Goodburn, Museum of London
Dr A.C. Grayling, Birkbeck College
Dr Christopher de Hamel, Corpus Christi College,
   Cambridge

Prof John Hatcher, Corpus Christi College, Cambridge
Dr Catherine Hills, Newnham College, Cambridge
Dr John Hudson, University of St Andrews
Prof Tony Hunt, St Peter's College, Oxford
Dr Edward Impey, English Heritage
Prof Martin Jones, Department of Archaeology,
    Cambridge
Dr Maurice Keen, Oxford
Dr Nick Mayhew, Ashmolean Museum
Dr Beverly Nenk, British Museum
Dr Peter Neumann, Queen's College, Oxford
Dr Christopher Page, Sidney Sussex College, Cambridge
Dr Jackie Pearce, Museum of London
Prof Jane Renfrew, Lucy Cavendish College, Cambridge
Dr James Robinson, British Museum
Prof Nigel Saul, Royal Holloway College
Dr John Schofield, Museum of London
Dr Emma Smith, Hertford College, Oxford
Dr Terry Smith, Museum of London
Dr Jacqueline Steadall, St Peter's College, Oxford
Dr John Steane
Dr David Stone, Corpus Christi College, Cambridge
Dr Christopher Tyerman, Hertford College, Oxford
Dr Liesbeth van Houts, Emmanuel College, Cambridge
Dr Charles Webster, All Souls, Oxford
Dr Bill White, Museum of London

Illustrations

Map on p. viii from *The History Today Companion to British History* eds. Juliet Gardiner and Neil Wenborn, Collins & Brown, London 1995

Illustrations for chapter openers from C.C.C.C. Ms 16 and Ms 26, reproduced by permission of the Master and Fellows of Corpus Christi College Cambridge/ photographs Conway Library, Courtauld Institute of Art, University of London.

Bibliography

Astill, Grenville and Grant, Annie, eds. *The Countryside of Medieval England* Oxford: Blackwell 1988

Baldwin, John W., *The Language of Sex. Five Voices from Northern France around 1200* Chicago: University of Chicago Press 2000

Barber, Richard, *Henry Plantagenet* Woodbridge: Boydell & Brewer 2001

Barber, Richard and Barker, Juliet *Tournaments. Jousts, Chivalry and Pageants in the Middle Ages* Woodbridge: Boydell & Brewer 1989

Barlow, Frank *Thomas Becket* London: Weidenfeld and Nicolson 1986.

Bartlett, Robert *England under the Norman and Angevin Kings 1075–1225* Oxford: OUP 2000

Bartlett, Robert *Gerald of Wales 1146–1225* Oxford: OUP 1982

Bartlett, Robert *Trial by Fire and Water. The Medieval Judicial Ordeal* Oxford: OUP 1986

Bartlett, Robert *The Making of Europe: Conquest, Colonization and Cultural Change, 950–1350* Harmondsworth: Allen Lane 1993

Beresford, Maurice *New Towns of the Middle Ages* London: Lutterworth Press 1967

Bolton, J. L. *The Medieval English Economy 1150–1500* London: Dent & Sons 1980

Bradbury, Jim *Philip Augustus, King of France, 1180–1223*
London: Longman 1998

Breay, Claire *Magna Carta. Manuscripts and Myths*
London: British Library 2002

Britnell, Richard H. *The Commercialisation of English
Society* 2nd edn., Manchester: Manchester UP 1996

Brooke, Christopher and Keir, Gillian *London 800–1216:
The Shaping of a City* London: Secker and Warburg
1975

Burton, J. *Monastic and Religious Orders in Britain
1000–1300* Cambridge: CUP 1994

Carpenter, D. A. *The Minority of Henry III* London:
Methuen 1990

Cheney, C. R. *Hubert Walter* London: Thomas Nelson
1967

Church, S. D., ed. *King John: New Interpretations*
Woodbridge: Boydell & Brewer 1999

Clanchy, Michael *From Memory to Written Record. England
1066–1307* 2nd edn. Oxford: Blackwell 1993

Clanchy M. T. *England and its Rulers 1066–1272* 2nd edn.
Oxford: Blackwell 1998

Crouch, David *William Marshal* 2nd edn. London:
Longman 2002

Davies, R. R. *The First English Empire. Power and
Identities in the British Isles 1093–1343* Oxford: OUP
2000

Dobson, R. B. & Taylor, J. *Rymes of Robyn Hood* London:
Heinemann 1976

Duby, Georges *The Legend of Bouvines* Berkeley and Los
Angeles: University of California Press 1990

France, John *Western Warfare in the Age of the Crusades
1000–1300* London: UCL Press 1999

Dyer, Christopher *Making a Living in the Middle Ages. The People of Britain 850–1520* New Haven and London: Yale UP 2002

Gillingham, John *Richard I* New Haven and London: Yale UP 1999

Gillingham, John *The Angevin Empire* 2nd edn. London: Hodder Arnold 2001

Harvey, Barbara, ed. *Living and Dying in England 1100–1540. The Monastic Experience* Oxford: OUP 1993

Harvey, Barbara, ed. *The Twelfth and Thirteenth Centuries* (volume 4 in the *Short Oxford History of the British Isles*) Oxford: OUP 2001

Hastings, Adrian *Elias of Dereham, Architect of Salisbury Cathedral* Much Wenlock: R. J. L. Smith 1997

Hindle, Brian Paul *Medieval Roads* Princes Risborough: Shire 1982

Holmes, Urban T. *Daily Living in the Twelfth Century* Madison USA: University of Wisconsin Press 1952

Holt, J. C. *Magna Carta* 2nd edn. Cambridge: Cambridge UP 1992

Holt, J. C. *The Northerners: A Study in the Reign of King John* Oxford: OUP 1961

Hunt, Tony *The Medieval Surgery* Woodbridge: Boydell & Brewer 1992

Harper-Bill, Christopher and Van Houts, Elisabeth *A Companion to the Anglo-Norman World* Woodbridge: Boydell & Brewer 2002

Keen, Maurice, ed. *Medieval Warfare. A History* Oxford: OUP 1999

Knowles, David *The Monastic Order in England* 2nd edn. Cambridge: CUP 1963

Labarge, Margaret Wade *A Baronial Household of the Thirteenth Century* London: Eyre and Spottiswoode 1965

Leyser, Henrietta *Medieval Women: A Social History of Women in England 450–1500* London: Weidenfeld & Nicolson 1995

Liddiard, Robert, ed. *Anglo-Norman Castles* Woodbridge: Boydell & Brewer 2003

Miller, Edward and Hatcher, John *Medieval England. Trade, Commerce and Crafts 1086–1348* London: Longman 1995

Mortimer, Richard *Angevin England 1154–1258* Oxford: Blackwell 1994

Nightingale, Pamela *A Medieval Mercantile Community. The Grocers' Company and the Politics and Trade of London 1000–1465* New Haven and London: Yale UP 1995

Norgate, Kate *John Lackland* London: Macmillan 1902

Orme, Nicholas *English Schools in the Middle Ages.* London: Methuen 1973

Orme, Nicholas *Medieval Children* New Haven and London: Yale UP 2001

Owen, D. D. R. Eleanor of Aquitaine: Queen and Legend Oxford: Blackwell 1993

Pallister, Anne *Magna Carta. The Heritage of Liberty* Oxford: OUP 1971

Phillips, J. R. S. *The Medieval Expansion of Europe* Oxford: OUP 1988

Rackham, Oliver *Trees and Woodland in the British Landscape* London: J. M. Dent 1996

Shahar, Shulamith *Childhood in the Middle Ages* London: Routledge 1992

Spufford, Peter *Money and its Use in Medieval Europe*
Cambridge: CUP 1988

Steane, John *The Archaeology of the Medieval English Monarchy* London: Batsford 1993

Strickland, Matthew *War and Chivalry. The Conduct and Perception of War in England and Normandy, 1066–1217* Cambridge: Cambridge UP 1996

Tatton-Brown, Tim *Great Cathedrals of Britain* London: BBC 1989

Thomas, Christopher *The Archaeology of Medieval London* Stroud: Sutton 2002

Turner, Ralph V. *King John* London: Longman 1994

Tyerman, Christopher *England and the Crusades 1095–1588* Chicago: University of Chicago Press 1988

Warren, W. L. *King John* London: Eyre and Spottiswoode 1961

Warren, W. L. *Henry II* London: Eyre Methuen 1973

Woolgar, C. M. *The Great Household in Late Medieval England* New Haven and London: Yale UP 1999

Young, Charles R. *The Royal Forests of Medieval England* University of Pennsylvania Press 1979

Some prose and poetry written during John's lifetime is readily available in paperback in modern translation.

Weiss, Judith, trans. *The Birth of Romance. An Anthology* London: J. M. Dent & Sons 1992

Greenway, Diana and Sayers, Jane trans. *Jocelin of Brakelond Chronicle of the Abbey of Bury St Edmunds* Oxford: OUP 1989

Gerald of Wales, *The History and Topography of Ireland* trans. J. J. O'Meara, Harmondsworth: Penguin 1982

Gerald of Wales, *The Journey through Wales / The Description of Wales* trans. L. Thorpe, Harmondsworth:
Penguin 1978

The Lais of Marie de France trans. Glyn S. Burgess and
Keith Busby, Harmondsworth: Penguin 1986

Chrétien de Troyes, *Arthurian Romances* trans W. W.
Kibler, Harmondsworth: Penguin 1991

Index